AMERICAN IMPERIALISM
Viewpoints of United States
Foreign Policy, 1898-1941

THE ISTHMIAN HIGHWAY

A Review of the Problems of the Caribbean

Hugh Gordon Miller

ARNO PRESS & THE NEW YORK TIMES
New York ★ 1970

Collection Created and Selected
by
CHARLES GREGG OF GREGG PRESS

Reprinted from a copy in The Hoover Institution Library

Library of Congress Catalog Card Number: 76-111725
ISBN 0-405-02039-2

ISBN for complete set: 0-405-02000-7

Reprint Edition 1970 by Arno Press Inc.
Manufactured in the United States of America

THE ISTHMIAN HIGHWAY

JAMES MONROE

THE ISTHMIAN HIGHWAY

A Review of the Problems of the Caribbean

BY

HUGH GORDON MILLER, LL.D.

Former Assistant United States Attorney and Special Assistant to the Attorney General of the United States, and of the Bar of the Supreme Court of the United States, and of the State of New York

WITH ILLUSTRATIONS AND APPENDICES

FOREWORD

BY

DON MIGUEL CRUCHAGA

Formerly Chilean Ambassador to the United States. Member of the Hague Permanent Court of Arbitration. Professor of International Law at the Universities of Chile and of La Plata, Argentina.

AND INTRODUCTION BY

JAMES M. BECK

Member of the United States House of Representatives and formerly Solicitor-General of the United States.

NEW YORK
THE MACMILLAN COMPANY
1929

DEDICATED

TO

President James Monroe

The responsible Author of the Monroe Doctrine.

President William McKinley

Who insisted that the Hay-Pauncefote Treaty should be a world-view compact.

President Theodore Roosevelt

Who acquired a lease to the Canal Zone and a "right of way" through the Isthmian Highway on the basis of treaties and the right of what may be termed international Eminent Domain; initiated the construction of the Panama Canal, and evoked, in defense of the franchise, the use of the international physician and policeman.

President Woodrow Wilson

Who, with courage, brought about the Repeal of the Tolls-Exemption Clause in the Panama Canal Act.

President Calvin Coolidge

Who, following in the footsteps of his predecessors, has upheld the traditional policy of the United States, embodied in the Freedom of the Seas, the Monroe Doctrine, the Right of Eminent Domain on the Isthmian Highway and the Obligation on the United States to exercise this Right with that due sense of Responsibility which is incumbent on an International Trustee.

We base our title upon the right of mankind in the Isthmus, treaty or no treaty. We have long asserted, beginning with Secretary Cass, that the nations of Central America had no right to debar the world from its right of passage across the Isthmus. Upon that view we base the justice of our entire action upon the Isthmus which resulted in our having the Canal Zone. We could not have taken it for our selfish interest; we could not have taken it for the purpose of securing an advantage to the people of the United States over the other peoples of the world; it was only because civilization had its rights to passage across the Isthmus and because we made ourselves the mandatory of civilization to assert those rights that we are entitled to be there at all.

ELIHU ROOT.

If ever a Government could be said to have received a mandate from civilization to effect an object the accomplishment of which was demanded in the interest of mankind, the United States holds that position with regard to the interoceanic canal. Since our purpose to build the canal was definitely announced, there have come from all quarters assurances of approval and encouragement, in which even Colombia herself at one time participated; and to general assurances were added specific acts and declarations. In order that no obstacle might stand in our way, Great Britain renounced important rights under the Clayton-Bulwer Treaty and agreed to its abrogation, receiving in return nothing but our honourable pledge to build the canal and protect it as an open highway.

THEODORE ROOSEVELT.

FOREWORD

I HAVE read with a great deal of interest and profit the book discussing "The Isthmian Highway" which Mr. Hugh Gordon Miller has prepared as an additional contribution on his part to the understanding of the evolution in the policy followed by the United States in regard to the Panama Canal, viewed as an international public utility, and concerning its relations to the Monroe Doctrine.

With an enthusiasm and an industry which it is impossible to appreciate too highly, Mr. Miller has applied his legal gifts to analyzing, and stating, often for the first time in a connected and comprehensive fashion, the underlying equities of the position in Panama and the Caribbean. In this treatment of the problem, he has included a review of the policy of the United States—known as the Monroe Doctrine and the Freedom of the Seas, which will be of great service to the Pan-American Continents and indeed to the world as a whole, where misunderstandings so easily arise and are so difficult to eradicate. Mr. Miller is an American of Americans, an admirer and friend of the late President Theodore Roosevelt, but he is able to bring to bear on his subject a detached and impartial judgment, at times indulging in constructive criticisms of the institutions of his country and invariably endeavouring to recognize the just interests of other countries than his own.

The nature of the matters under consideration in the book, the deft method in the exposition, the valuable documentation accompanying the work, and especially the considerations of a lofty international policy therein contained, are merits enough to place this volume as a document worthy of frequent consultation, which is bound to give the scholar as well as public opinion throughout the world, an exact valuation of a matter of permanent import.

The juridical and political problems encountered in facing what has been called the Panama Canal question, have often been looked into from several angles, affording thereby an ample range of subjects for the gauging of the international policies of the United States. At all events, any objection that might be adduced against the Great Commonwealth of the Northern Hemisphere, should be dropped as soon as one comes to the noble words of the eminent citizen, Elihu Root, uttered in the United States Senate in 1913, which the author, with commendable fitness, has put for a motto at the head of the book. The world could not be deprived of its right to cross the Isthmian land, and the latter was cut by the United States for the benefit of the whole of mankind. On taking this step, and insuring it with the adjoining zone, the United States served the interests of civilization, and appointed itself the mandatory power of this civilization.

Accepting these appreciations of Mr. Root, Mr. Miller offers here an amendment which I consider a happy one. In his estimation, the United States is not only a mandatory power in charge of a certain enterprise, but he goes one step further, and calls it a trustee, the faithful agent for an important and delicate mission. We are all convinced of the perfect fairness inspiring the United States' every act, and are certain that it will carry out its noble mission with invariable highmindedness and justice.

The chapter dealing with the origin of the Monroe Doctrine includes both observations and data of the highest interest. This work will bring more light to a subject that has given material for so many passionate controversies.

Sometimes the Monroe Doctrine has been considered the cause of certain political moves on the part of the United States in reference to various international problems, with which it has been confronted in the course of its career as an independent nation; and so it has been charged with intentions which are alien to it, and which were never in the mind of its founders. The clarifying statements made from time to time by the most eminent public officials and statesmen of the United States, have been effective in fixing the true meaning and correct scope of the Doctrine; nevertheless, there are still left some fears and mistrusts which, even if unfounded, should be definitely dispelled in the interest of a more close understanding among all the peoples of this continental community of nations.

In this respect, this work will furnish a most needed help to the great movement for coöperation and solidarity which the countries of America are called to serve with moral unity of purpose within the great international community of peoples.

MIGUEL CRUCHAGA.

INTRODUCTION

IF "good wine needs no bush and a good play needs no epilogue," then a good book similarly needs no introduction. A good book is its own justification and if this book had needed any introduction, it has already had a graceful foreword from the pen of the distinguished Ambassador from Chile to the United States, himself a deep student of international affairs.

The author is peculiarly qualified to write this book, not only because of his interest in public affairs but because the subject has been with him a study of many years. His book has the two qualities of a good book, in that it is at once interesting and educational. While the book is a sympathetic statement of the American attitude toward the Caribbean problem and the broader issues inherent in the Monroe Doctrine and the larger doctrine of the Freedom of the Seas, yet his discussion of these controversial questions takes into consideration the principles of international equity.

It is not necessary to agree with all the author's conclusions in order to characterize this book as a very useful contribution to a subject that always has been of importance, is today of vital importance, and may be tomorrow of still greater importance. The book will be of great use in informing public opinion in America as to the facts which underlie these problems, but, if it has the world-wide circulation that it deserves, it will be of still greater use in giving to thoughtful people of other nations a sympathetic idea of the American standpoint, as well as a knowledge of facts which are known to few, as they are generally buried in the archives of Governments.

Throughout the English-speaking world, and, indeed, the world as a whole, there is today in progress an adjustment of traditional maritime authority. It cannot be solved by the rigid formulas of jurists. It is one of practical politics and, in solving it, regard must be had to the peculiar situation of different nations in the economy of civilization. The author has, therefore, rendered a public service in bringing into one perspective the varied factors which are involved in the problems. It seems to me that great good will come if thoughtful men of all nations shall be acquainted with the facts which are herein developed and explained by the author's industrious search into the past. He happily emphasizes the moral responsibility of the United States and Great Britain for a wise and just solution of these questions, and those who read this book are likely to have a deepened sense of such common responsibility.

JAMES M. BECK.

Washington, D. C.,
February 12, 1929.

CONTENTS

ILLUSTRATIONS

THE ISTHMIAN HIGHWAY

THE ISTHMIAN HIGHWAY

I

BIOGRAPHY OF THIS BOOK

IN presenting these pages, I hope that I may be permitted to explain how it came about that as a lawyer, I plunged into the unaccustomed field of authorship. During the whole of an active life in my profession, I have been fascinated by a problem which largely determines the foreign policy of the United States. It is the problem of the Panama and Nicaraguan Isthmus and of the Monroe Doctrine as it applies to the Caribbean; and it has occurred to me that a statement of this problem and a review of the equities associated with it by one whose mind has been trained to pursue the legal method, might be of value at this time when great developments in Central America are under consideration.

While the book was in a later stage of preparation, the entire situation was rendered more urgent by the discussions of naval disarmament at Geneva, and in Washington, London and Paris. To appreciate those discussions, there must be a knowledge of the diplomatic and strategic background which lies behind the mentality of the governments and departments concerned. I am of opinion that the great maritime nations ought to come to an arrangement for the control of the ocean and the maintenance of freedom for all peoples on the high seas. The analysis of the Caribbean Problem is thus an introduction to a world-wide situation which must now be faced.

The Panama Canal was the first Isthmian Highway, but it is not to be the only link between the oceans. A canal across Nicaragua is projected. The nation that controls these canals must dominate the Western World, for the canals are, as it were, the jugular vein, not only of the United States but of North and South America. Only through the canals can these continents keep in maritime touch with themselves. Hence, we are bound to conclude that political control over the canals is and will always be of vital concern to the United States as a link between her Atlantic and Pacific seaboard. But, for this very reason, the rest of the world, which shares the use of the canals with the United States, will wish to know whether they are to be operated and controlled according to the basic principles of international equality which were laid down and crystallized in the Hay-Pauncefote Treaty.

The problem includes our relations with Mexico and Nicaragua—indeed with Latin-America as a whole. Meeting at Havana in 1928, the Sixth Pan-American Conference revealed how acute are the susceptibilities involved in the problem and how far-reaching the issues, affecting the very basis of international law, that may be raised. We use the term, international law. But how are we to apply international law to conditions, so complicated, so human, as those which arise in parts of Latin-America? Is there to be a new appraisal of the Monroe Doctrine? What is the importance and scope of the so-called British Monroe Doctrine, recently promulgated as a condition of the Kellogg Treaty renouncing war? Clearly, there never was a moment when lucid thinking was more urgently demanded.

I should not have been so bold as to embark on this somewhat ambitious enterprise, had it not been that, on a former occasion, fourteen years ago, I issued a smaller volume entitled "The Panama Tolls Controversy." That book elicited the emphatic approval of statesmen, so varied in their views as President Wilson, Secretary William Jennings Bryan, as he then was; former Secretary Elihu Root, former Ambassador Choate, Mr. Lloyd George, and Lord Bryce. I have been encouraged by Viscount Grey, among others, to proceed further with a task of explanation and, I hope, conciliation. I should add that, for the treatment of the subjects as they arise, I am myself solely responsible.

It is my desire that this volume also shall be "a source book," that is, a treatise in which there will be found, not only opinion but historical data. To its preparation, I have devoted the same genuine research that a lawyer must expend upon the preparation of a complicated case, for submission to the Courts.

In preparing my earlier volume, I was assisted by Dr. J. C. Freehoff, the well-known statistician and authority on public utilities, who has aided me with his counsel on this later occasion. Dr. Freehoff has had the benefit of twenty-one years' experience on the Public Service Commission of the State of New York, and is one of the best authorities available on the subject. When I have entered special fields, I have, therefore, based my conclusions on the best expert advice.

I acknowledge also the contribution of Philip C. Jessup, Professor of International Law at Columbia University, who upon reading the manuscript wrote that, as a result of his examination, he agreed with "its general scope and plan," and further that "it presented ideas which the people of this country should be familiar with and ponder."

The problem of the Caribbean is inherent in the problem of seapower. My approach to this whole situation is based on two propositions. First, it is essential that, as Americans, we should be familiar with the actual record of what, in our treaties and other declarations, we promised to do and not to do. I have to confess that when I began my study, I was most imperfectly aware of what these commitments really had been.

My second proposition has been stated by Professor James T. Shotwell in an address which he delivered at the Berlin Institute of Political Science. He insisted that, as long ago as 1776, Adam Smith had liberated economic thought from the doctrine that one nation's gain is another nation's loss; and, argued Professor Shotwell, the same principle applies to politics.

It has taken the statesman of the world a long time to catch up with the economist, but he is arriving at that point at last. President Hoover has put the proposition in an even more definite form, and has applied the principle to modern affairs. In a speech delivered at Boston on October 15th, 1928, he said:

Trade in its true sense is not commercial war; it is vital mutual service. The volume of world trade depends upon prosperity. In fact, it grows from prosperity. *Every nation loses by the poverty of another. Every nation gains by the prosperity of another.*

In other words, the national security of one nation contributes to the national security of every nation. If the policy of the United States in the Caribbean is wisely directed, it will be no challenge but an actual assistance to the rest of the world.

When my former book was published, the country was resounding with controversy over the Panama Tolls. Believing in repeal of those exemptions, I indulged in argument. That phase of the problem was brought to an end by President Wilson's courageous action and it is possible now to adopt what I hope may prove to be a judicial tone. At the same time, it is undoubtedly within the power of the United States again to enact the exemptions. There are still proposals in certain quarters that such a step should be taken. Indeed, the very statute which reveals the exemptions in the Panama Canal Act, contains a provision which suggests that there is still an open question:

That the passage of this act shall not be construed or held as a waiver or relinquishment of any right the United States may have under the treaty with Great Britain, ratified the twenty-first of February, nineteen hundred and two, or the treaty with the Republic of Panama, ratified February twenty-sixth, nineteen hundred and four, or otherwise to discriminate in favor of its vessels by exempting the vessels of the United States or its citizens from the payment of tolls for passage through said canal, or as in any way waiving, impairing or affecting any right of the United States under said treaty or otherwise, with respect to the sovereignty over or the ownership, control and management of said canal and the regulation of the conditions of charges of traffic through the same.

It will be apparent, therefore, that here is no closed controversy. The price of correct diplomacy, like the price of liberty, is continual vigilance.

These pages thus embody two complementary theses—first, that the United States has rights in the Caribbean which she must not hesitate to assert, and secondly, that by virtue of those very rights, she has to remember obligations to mankind as a whole. In his speech, delivered at Arlington on Memorial Day, May 30th, 1927, President Coolidge put the point in his usual clear terms.

We want our relationship with other nations to be based not on a meeting of bayonets but on a meeting of minds. We want our intercourse with them to rest on justice and fair dealing and the mutual observance of all rightful obligations in accordance with international customs and law.

It is a definition, then, of such international custom and law that we must seek and apply not only to the case of the Caribbean but to the entire range of maritime activity. We use the word, international, as President Coolidge uses it, not as an epithet wrongly appropriated by political parties and social groups which are opposed to private property. The term, as it is here employed, has no relation to Communism or any cult. The right to own, accumulate, give, and bequeath private property has, in our judgment, always been and always will be, the foundation stone of civilization. It is thus in its strict legal sense that we discuss "international" law. By it, we mean the rights and duties, which are international, and relate to a world highway as distinguished from rights that are merely national when such a highway is within a sovereign state.

It was Carl Schurz who said:

> My country, right or wrong;
> If right, to be kept right;
> If wrong, to be set right.

The United States has grown greatly, in power, in wealth, in prestige. That she will discharge her immense responsibilities with a due regard to the interests of mankind, is the firm faith of the writer; and it is in pursuance of this faith that he has devoted himself to the task of setting out certain equitable interests involved.

II

CUTTING THE ISTHMUS

LET us dismiss from our minds, first of all, any idea that the Panama Canal has been a project recently developed by the ambitions of the United States. For centuries, men have dreamed that, one day, it would be possible to proceed across the Isthmus along a waterway connecting the Atlantic and Pacific oceans. Columbus supposed that such a waterway might be natural and he searched for the straits that did not exist. Other explorers continued the search, and it was only when it was found to be fruitless that projects for artificial transit began to be developed.

The first highway across the Isthmus was constructed from Panama on the Pacific to Nombre de Dios on the shores of the Caribbean Sea. This overland route was completed in 1519. In 1533 the Chagres River was made navigable from the Atlantic side to Venta Cruz, which reduced the overland route to a distance of only 20 miles and added a land and water route to the previous all-land route across the Isthmus. The all-land or overland route was shortened 15 miles in 1597 by the substitution of Puerto Bello for Nombre de Dios as the terminus. These routes are forerunners of the Panama Railroad opened in 1855, and of the Panama Canal, opened in 1914.

Other overland routes were constructed at Tehuantepec and Nicaragua. But the difficulty of such transit led to the consideration of plans for a canal. The first recorded suggestion of an artificial waterway connecting the two oceans bears the date of 1529. Panama, Darien, Nicaragua and

7

Tehuantepec were mentioned as places that might be available for the purpose. Each of these routes had advocates until consideration was narrowed down to that at Panama and the other at Nicaragua. In 1534 a survey of the land from the point where the Chagres River ceases to be navigable to the Pacific was begun by Charles V of Spain with the view of extending water transit across the Isthmus. This is the first official act looking to the construction of an Isthmian canal. The report of the commissioner, who made the survey, declared that the obstacles to be overcome were so great that even the resources of the most powerful monarch were not adequate for the purpose.

In 1567 a survey for a route by way of Nicaragua was ordered. The report was as unfavorable as the previous report on the Panama route. After this report, further consideration of an all-water route across the Isthmus was abandoned. Spain had, by this time, acquired a monopoly of the land routes across the Isthmus, and through them completed its monopoly of South American commerce including the rich output of precious metals on the west coast. This monopoly was so profitable and the maintenance of it was considered so vital that the opening of new routes including an all-water route was forbidden. An all-water-way came to be considered as strategically unwise because of its temptation to other powers from whose interference the overland trails were free. Spain continued this policy until the beginning of the 19th century.

Interest in a possible canal was then revived as a result of explorations by Humboldt. The Spanish Cortes thereupon passed a decree for the construction of an Isthmian canal and provided the legal basis for the formation of a company to undertake the enterprise. Soon thereafter the Spanish provinces of Central and South America declared and established their independence, and so the undertaking

CULEBRA CUT, PANAMA CANAL, JUNE 1913

passed out of the control of the Old World. It was this passing of control to the New World that became permanent when the United States adopted the Monroe Doctrine.

From and after this time American capitalists interested themselves more or less in the construction of an all-water route across the Isthmus. This prompted the federal republic of the united provinces of Central America to seek the coöperation of the American people through overtures to the State Department. In the year 1825 Secretary of State, Henry Clay, responded favourably. He assured the representative of the new republic to the south of the keen interest of the government of the United States in the undertaking, as an Isthmian canal would exert a profound influence on the affairs of mankind.

The need of improved transit across the Isthmus became increasingly apparent to those who had to use the overland trails. The treaty of 1846 with New Granada (now Colombia) was the concrete expression of this need. New Granada granted a charter to the Panama Railroad Company in 1848 which company was incorporated by a special act of the New York Legislature in 1849. The railroad was completed in January, 1855, and in August, 1881, it became the property of the French Canal Company which purchased the property for $25,000,000.

It is here that we encounter that other waterway which will ever be the counterpart of the Panama. In the year 1869, De Lesseps completed his great achievement at Suez, and it was to the Isthmus that he next turned his attention.

Concessions had been secured from Colombia by French interests in 1876 for the construction of such a canal between Panama and Colon, and a company was immediately organized for the purpose of carrying out the undertaking. An amended charter was secured from Colombia in 1878. In 1879 the concession was transferred to De Lesseps to be by him transferred to a new company to be organized under his control.

The new company prosecuted the work amid vicissitudes, financial and sanitary, until February, 1889, when it became insolvent and a receiver was appointed to take charge of its property. Up to this date some $260,000,000 had been raised and disbursed. Some $40,000,000, according to American engineers, were expended for concessions, organization and in excavation, the balance being the loot of financial buccaneers. The receiver continued until May 15, 1889, when he was compelled to suspend further operations for lack of funds.

A new company known as the Panama Canal Company was incorporated on October 28, 1894, to take over the concessions and other property of the old company and to secure the completion of the canal. It was organized solely for the purpose of becoming the vendor of the aforementioned assets, and of interesting either France or the United States in the undertaking.

It will be seen, then, that the history of the Isthmian Canal began with Spain, was continued under France, and when the United States was drawn in had been littered with failure, with blighted hopes and—especially under de Lesseps—with wasted treasure.

In 1898, the Spanish American War changed the entire situation. The United States became an active power in the Caribbean, and the cruise of the *Oregon* around South America from the Pacific to the Atlantic in 1898 focused American opinion. Therefore, on March 3, 1899, President McKinley appointed a commission to investigate all possible routes for a canal across the Isthmus and to determine which would be the most available. This commission reported in favour of a canal by way of Panama and Colon, provided the rights and property of the Panama Canal Company could be purchased for $40,000,000. The Panama Canal Company immediately sent word to the commission offering all of its assets to the United States for that amount. Thereupon the Spooner Act was passed, authorizing the President to acquire all "rights, privileges, concessions and property" of the Panama Canal Company, and to acquire from Colombia on such terms as he might deem reasonable, the land needed in the construction and management of a canal by the Panama-Colon route. The same Act authorized the President, after securing sufficient title to the land now known as the Canal Zone, to proceed to construct a canal of sufficient capacity and depth to afford transit to vessels of the largest tonnage then in use and of such larger tonnage as may be reasonably anticipated.

The work of the French company had been mainly in the Culebra Cut and it had been organized on the assumption that ultimately the Canal might embody locks or, alternately, might be designed for continuous sea level. This was the work which by the year 1914 the United States carried to completion.

American inter-coastal trade was relieved from the toils and perils of nine thousand miles of navigation around Cape Horn through stormy seas, with the attendant burden of wasted effort, shipwreck and loss of life. The geography of the Western Hemisphere was transformed and the trade routes of the world had everywhere to be adjusted.

To achieve what George W. Platt writing in the *New York Herald* has called "the consummation of the mightiest and longest dream for the benefit of mankind in the history of the world," no fewer than 40,000 men labored for ten years. Says Mr. Platt:

On the gripping historical canvas of Panama appear the heroic figures of Columbus, Vespucci, Balboa, Cortez, Pizarro, De Soto, Paterson (founder of the Bank of England, who vainly sought control with his Scottish settlement), Drake and Morgan, the buc-caneers; Grand, De Lesseps, Amador, Bunaw-Varilla, Goethals, Roosevelt and Gorgas, to mention a few among the great of all time.

The Panama Canal, and any other canal that may be built across the Isthmus of Panama, must be regarded, then, as essential international highways of commerce, of which the United States makes use, for which the United States is trustee. The development of such canals has been and will be inevitable. It is an element in that human progress which includes the railway, the automobile, the airplane and the use of electricity by wire and over the air.

III

THE INTERNATIONAL PHYSICIAN

CRITICS who accuse the United States of expansionist tendencies in the Caribbean usually forget one dominating circumstance. For centuries the Caribbean had been a hotbed of disease, and for centuries this disease had spread northwards and taken toll of tens of thousands of American citizens. If aggression is to be alleged, it was wholly on the side of the Caribbean, and its weapons were malaria and yellow fever, the deadliest invaders imaginable, which respect neither treaty nor any sovereignty save death.

In any study of the Isthmian Highway, there must be included, then, the conquest of disease. The story of this triumph, as here told, is based upon a number of records, notably *Walter Reed and Yellow Fever* by Dr. Howard A. Kelly and descriptive articles in the *New York Times* of various dates, and other journals. I have to acknowledge, moreover, my indebtedness to Dr. M. Benmosche, an eminent surgeon of international experience and member of the Surgical Staff of Mount Sinai Hospital who prepared a memorandum on which I have relied for many scientific details. Dr. Benmosche writes:

It is not difficult to understand that the world's sanity and happiness are directly proportionate to the state of its health. The emergence from the Dark Ages was marked by the last of the really great plagues that have ravaged mankind from time immemorial. This was the "Black Death," which convulsed and devastated Europe by a great series of epidemics in the 14th century. Plagues, apparently less grave in their severity and seriousness, followed

13

through the 15th, 16th, 17th, 18th and 19th centuries. It was in the 17th century that the Great Plague of London appeared and wiped out over 68,000 people in a population estimated at 460,000 in a year's time while the disease was at its height.

The various plagues were not alone responsible for the enormous depletion of the human race from time to time. There were and there still are a number of diseases, peculiarly confined within certain geographical boundaries, that continue to take their toll of human lives. Then again we have to recognize that, apart from the deep and irreparable rents made in the prevalent social fabrics by these pathological processes of depopulation, we have the inestimable losses in terms of economic values. And so, when we consider the great strides made by those intrepid pioneers of preventive medicine, through the agencies of hygiene, sanitation, and scientific research in making this world safe for humanity in their warfare against disease, we become impressed with the tremendous benefactions they bestowed and poignantly cognizant of the everlasting debt due them for countless generations to come.

Of the plagues that have afflicted mankind, there are two that affected the Caribbean area. The first was Yellow Fever and the second was Malaria.

Among the diseases to which human beings are subject, yellow fever has been the most deadly. The origin is obscure. It has been traced to the Aztecs in Mexico. It has been attributed to slaves brought from Africa. According to a report by the American Association for Medical Progress, the pestilence "is peculiar to the American Continent and tropical America was its great stronghold." A force sent by Napoleon in 1800 to Haiti was destroyed by yellow fever. Here a village and there a boat's crew—so we read —were decimated.

In Havana, the disease was chronic and frequently it spread northwards. Before the United States became a nation, the Colonies had lost 100,000 citizens by what Longfellow called "the pestilence" and, as "death flooded life," one victim was Evangeline's lover. In 1793, one tenth

MAJOR GENERAL GEORGE W. GOETHALS

of the entire population of Philadelphia was swept away, and according to the *Outlook* of April 6th, 1927, the United States was visited seventy-seven times by yellow fever during the nineteenth century. In 1855, New Orleans was a sufferer from an epidemic; in 1878, no fewer than 25,000 persons fled from the yellow fever which was raging in Memphis, Tennessee. In the southern cities, as recently as fifty years ago, there was thus a loss of 16,000 lives and an economic loss of $100,000,000. An instance is recorded in which yellow fever killed 1411 soldiers out of a force of 1500.

In 1898, the Spanish American War was brought to a conclusion and the Army of the United States occupied the regions most seriously infected. A year later yellow fever broke out among the Manila soldiers. The rate of sickness was 600 per 1000 of the troops. General Leonard Wood, who supervised sanitation for the army, had to see one-third of his staff succumb to disease; the other losses were described as frightful, and the army as a fighting machine was incapacitated. Its plight was pitiful.

To examine into the causes of yellow fever and the method of its transmission, a Commission was appointed, consisting of Major Walter Reed, Dr. James Carroll, Dr. J. W. Lazear and Aristide Agramonte. The work began in the heat of June, 1900.

Born in 1851, Walter Reed, a Virginian and the son of a Methodist minister, had grown up amid the horrors of the Civil War. At the University of Virginia, the Bellevue Hospital in New York and at Johns Hopkins, under the famous Professor William Welch, he had been a master of medical research. He had also practiced as an assistant surgeon in certain isolated garrisons in the Far West where settlers expected a doctor to face any and every emergency. On proceeding to Cuba, he was thus known as a brilliant and a resourceful bacteriologist. Two years before, he had been appointed to study the causes of typhoid among the troops in active service. He held, moreover, the office of Curator of the Army Museum and its laboratory in Washington where he published reports on malarial fevers at Washington Barracks and Fort Meyer.

The Chief Sanitary Officer in Havana was Surgeon General William Crawford Gorgas. Himself laid low at one period by malaria, he had been zealously cleansing the city of age-long filth and his staff produced elaborate reports upon the prevalence of yellow fever. But there was no discovery of the causes of the epidemic. To quote Mr. Poore, "the yellow dragon went on his lethal way," and "the ghastly riddle of the fever defied the world." In the words of Dr. Benmosche:

In the light of our present knowledge and all that went to establish it, we can be forgiven our amazement at the report issued by the officers of the United States Marine Hospital Service, as to their accepted mode of the transmission of yellow fever. Among many things it states that the disease was spread by articles of bedding, clothing and furniture. To quote, "the present opinion is that one has not to contend with an organism or germ which may be taken into the body with food or drink, but with an almost inexplicable poison so insidious in its approach and entrance that no trace is left behind."

This was the confused situation which Walter Reed was to clear up.

As early as 1848, Dr. Josiah Clark Nott of South Carolina had suggested that yellow fever might be communicated by mosquitoes. It was, apparently, no more than a guess at truth, but in 1881, Dr. Carlos H. Finley, a Cuban physician, pursued the idea further. But although he tried for years to demonstrate his "hallucination," he could never show a case of such actual transmission.

In the meantime, Sir Ronald Ross had been developing the methods of sanitation for the control of malaria for which in 1902 he received the Nobel prize. His work covered the years 1895-1899, and, as Dr. Benmosche puts it:

consisted in the use of screens to keep mosquitoes out, the clearing away of all rubbish, killing mosquitoes by fumigations, oiling all stagnant waters, the drainage of swamps and filling in of all pools and puddles. Ross's investigations were based on the epoch-making discovery, by Sir Patrick Manson, that the mosquito was the intermediate host of *Filaria sanguinis hominis*. One year after, Alphonse Laveran, a French army surgeon, discovered the cause of malaria to be a parasite which passed through certain life-cycles in the blood of the patient suffering with this disease. Thus we observe how the establishment of one scientific fact leads to another, and how the universality and interrelationship of all science leads to its own progress.

To the final investigation, there was a significant prelude. In 1897, Reed and James Carroll

were appointed by Surgeon General Sternberg to investigate the claim of Professor Sanarelli of Bologna that the *Bacillus Icteroides,* which he found, was the cause of yellow fever. It was Sternberg's belief that Sanarelli's bacillus was identical with his own Bacillus X, which he had observed some ten years previously. The uncertainty was finally and definitely settled by Reed, who proved that neither bacillus entered into the causation of yellow fever, but that both of them were identical organisms, responsible for a variety of hog-cholera, which Reed had frequently observed while working at the Johns Hopkins Hospital.

Walter Reed asked himself whether the discoveries relating to malaria might not apply also to yellow fever. It was considered significant that, according to Henry R. Carter, an army surgeon, working along the Mississippi, people who went to an infected house immediately after a case of yellow fever had been reported, did not catch the disease.

It was a providential coincidence that, at this juncture, men so far-seeing as General Wood and Major-General Gorgas were in control of sanitation, respectively, throughout Cuba and in Havana. Still Gorgas at first took little notice of the mosquito theory of the transmission of yellow fever, but believed that filth was mainly responsible for the apparent contagiousness of the disease, so that, by the middle of 1900 Gorgas had made Havana, in his opinion, the cleanest city in the world, and yet he was chagrined to see more cases of yellow fever than had been seen for many years previously.

There was much academic discussion of the whole matter, which continued until July 1900 when Reed went to the Pinar del Rio Barracks where yellow fever was prevalent. There he made his first important observation that an individual could not contract the disease unless he had been bitten by a mosquito.

The theory of transmission by mosquitoes could only be proved, however, by experiment on living subjects, a matter of serious difficulty. At that time, animals were supposed to be immune from yellow fever, and if the experiments were to be of value, therefore, human beings must be selected and at a serious risk to human life.

In the simple scientific terms of the report by the American Association for Medical Progress, we have the narrative of heroism that was now displayed:

Volunteers were called for and the Commissioners insisted that they themselves should be included. Every man knew that he was likely to die, but he also knew that in so dying he might save thousands of his fellow men from death. The volunteers permitted themselves to be bitten by mosquitoes which had previously bitten yellow fever patients. Lazear was one of the first, and he soon became ill with yellow fever and died in convulsions. Carroll almost died; for three days his life hung in the balance. The experiment was continued on eleven other men, and as nine of them

SURGEON GENERAL WILLIAM CRAWFORD GORGAS

contracted yellow fever, Reed felt justified in saying that the disease was carried by mosquitoes.

Still there were many men who were not convinced, and Reed and his associates decided to repeat the experiments under conditions which would leave no doubt that the results were conclusive. In a lonely place, a mile from the nearest habitations, they established an experimental station, and placed an armed guard around it. It was named Camp Lazear. An immune hospital steward brought supplies from Camp Columbia, but no other intercourse with the town was permitted. A small frame building was put up and screened to prevent mosquitoes from getting in or out. The interior was divided into two apartments, separated by wire mosquito netting. Two susceptible men were put into this building, one in each compartment, and there they remained for several days, subjected in every way to the same conditions. When they had lived there in good health long enough to prove that there could be no infection, Reed put fifteen infected mosquitoes into one of the compartments, and presently declared that compartment to be infected. When the man in the infected compartment had been bitten by mosquitoes, Reed took him out, but returned him for a short time later in the day, and again on the following day, until altogether he had been bitten fifteen times. Meanwhile two men were left in the compartment which contained no mosquitoes. These men remained perfectly well, but in four days the man who had been bitten went down with yellow fever.

Reed, after simply removing the fifteen mosquitoes, declared the infected compartment disinfected. A non-immune soldier was then placed in each compartment and the two remained perfectly well for several days.

Even the skeptics now admitted that yellow fever could be transmitted by mosquitoes, but they still maintained that this was not the only means of transmission. The volunteers then submitted to a further series of most unpleasant experiments, and finally proved conclusively that yellow fever is not contagious and that it is transmitted only by mosquitoes.

To the memory of Lazear, who died to save hundreds of thousands of lives, there is a modest tablet in Johns Hopkins University. The names of the "two susceptible men" are known also throughout the world. When Reed called for volunteers, Private John R. Kissinger and a civilian clerk, John T. Moran, both from Ohio, came forward. Dr. Reed told them plainly of the risks. Disease, he explained, would be most probable. Of the diseased, said he, bluntly, 85 out of a hundred died. As for the financial reward, it could not be more than a small government pension.

The two volunteers stipulated here that there should be no reward of this kind, and Reed rose from his chair, saying, "Gentlemen, I salute you." Such moral courage had, as he testified, "never been surpassed in the annals of the army."

In December 1900, Reed wrote to his wife:

It is with a great deal of pleasure that I hasten to tell you that we have succeeded in producing a case of unmistakable yellow fever by the bite of a mosquito. . . . Rejoice with me, sweetheart, as, aside from the antitoxin of diphtheria, and Koch's discovery of the tubercle bacillus, it will be regarded as the most important piece of work, scientifically, during the nineteenth century. . . . Major Kean says that the discovery is worth more than the cost of the Spanish War.

On February 27th, 1927, Dr. Henry Emerson Fosdick offered this moving comment:

Do you recognize the names of James Carroll and Walter Reed and Jesse Lazear and Private Kissinger? Yet they were saviors, too, in this world. They saved mankind from yellow fever. For many a long century it had taken its toll of millions. It never will again. They stopped it; and the principle of the Cross holds true: you cannot get such salvation on this earth without sacrifice. To allow yourself deliberately in Cuba to be bitten by mosquitoes in order to see if, perhaps, that is what causes yellow fever, to do it when you have a wife and children and love life as well as any man—is not that worthy of the Master's enconium: "Greater love hath no man than this?"

James Carroll did that and he went down into the dark valley of a dreadful death and barely came back again. Then Jesse Lazear, wanting to be scientifically sure that they were on the right track, did that. He went down into the valley of the shadow of the dreadful death and he never came back again. Then Walter Reed wanted to try it with extra precautions to make assurance doubly sure, but he was too old and they would not let him, so he posted a notice in the American camp that he wanted volunteers to face death in the fight against yellow fever. Before the ink was dry, Kissinger, who was a private, and Moran, who was a civilian clerk, had volunteered. Well, they won their fight. They are all dead now except these last two, and Kissinger is paralyzed from the effects. They never had any glory and reward. Their widows today are living on government pensions of $1,500 and, more shame to us, out in the Middle West Kissinger's wife has taken in washing to support him. But they won their fight. They stopped one of the most devastating scourges that ever cursed mankind.

[Let us add that the nation, by public subscription, bought and presented to Kissinger his home.]

In 1902, Walter Reed died of appendicitis. "I leave so little," said he with unconscious irony, as he lay awaiting the end. But over his tomb at Arlington, there is an inscription stating that "He gave to man control over that dreadful plague, yellow fever"—after all, a commendable legacy. A great hospital in Washington bears his honoured name and his modest home at Belroi, Gloucester County, Virginia, built originally for the overseer of a plantation, is now a national monument. The service rendered by Reed and his comrades was indeed, as it has been written, "beyond estimate and beyond reward."

> Self-sacrificing gods were they in soul—
> Scientist and Volunteer—
>
> Emblazoned names through time on glory's scroll.

It was owing to these dramatic investigations that, in the words of Dr. Benmosche:

yellow fever is known to be a specific, infective tropical disease, caused by a parasite, which resembles in its life-history the parasite of malaria, and is transmitted by the domestic mosquito, the *stegomyia fasciata*. It has been definitely and scientifically proven that without this mosquito, which acts as a host to carry the germ from a yellow fever patient which it has bitten to a prospective victim, there would be no yellow fever. The immense value of this apparently simple truth, and the vast scientific researches which established it, make the one thrilling chapter in this historical treatise.

By actual enforcement, it had been shown that individuals kept in contact with blankets, sheets and pyjamas, polluted beyond description by yellow fever patients, failed to develop yellow fever, as long as mosquitoes were rigorously excluded. On the other hand, when blood was drawn from a yellow fever patient and injected into a non-immune subject like Private Jernigan, he was brought down with yellow fever in four days.

Against the mosquitoes of Havana, as carriers of yellow fever, war had thus to be declared. It was a war that for seven months was pressed with the utmost vigour. The mosquitoes were killed wholesale by fumigation and their breeding places were sought out and destroyed. The result was an overwhelming success. For the first time in 140 years, Havana was set free from a terrible scourge.

The narrative, of which Walter Reed is the hero, leads us to a conclusion which, though simple, is fundamental to our argument. To yellow fever and malaria there are not and there never will be frontiers. Disease and health are, by their very essence, inter-national. It followed that a Sanitary Battalion, responsible for the health of the Isthmian Highway, might have to operate at any time beyond the strict limits of the Canal Zone itself.

It was a contingency for which the Treaty with Panama itself, concluded in 1903, had to make provision by Article II:

. . . The Republic of Panama further grants to the United States in perpetuity the use, occupation and control of any other lands and waters outside of the Zone above described which may be necessary and convenient for the construction, maintenance, operation, sanitation and protection of said enterprise.

On December 3rd, 1904, this provision was defined more precisely by an executive order of the United States which contains the following:

The United States will construct, maintain, and conduct a hospital or hospitals, either in the Canal Zone *or in the territory of the Republic* at its option for the treatment of persons insane or afflicted with the disease of leprosy and the indigent sick, and the United States will accept for treatment herein such persons of such classes as the Republic may request. . . .

Of this extension of the responsibilities of the United States, the Republic of Panama approved. We submit, moreover, that the other Central American Republics, interested in the Caribbean, with the world in general, not only acquiesced in the acts of the International Trustee, but applauded the achievements of the Sanitary Battalion. Indeed, we present this acceptance of the position as an international precedent, in which there is admitted the right of the United States to extend her protection of health and property to whatever area may be necessary to the security of the Canal itself.

Major Gorgas, in command of sanitation, became in fact, a co-builder of the Panama Canal with Colonel Goethals himself; and it was Major Gorgas who applied to Panama the methods which Walter Reed had applied in Cuba.

At first sight, the problem seemed now to be simple. The city of Panama was no more than one-twelfth the size of Havana and the only thing needed was to go straight ahead. A fumigating squad used 120 tons of pyrethrum, the entire supply in the United States, in smoking out mosquitoes from the houses and, three times over, the city was subjected to sulphur, of which in all, no less than 300 tons were consumed. Yet the yellow fever continued! During the years 1904 and 1905, the fever increased and unacclimatized whites were decimated.

According to Dr. Howard A. Kelly, "the Canal Construction Commission, ignorant and unsympathetic, became highly critical, excepting only General George W. Davis, the governor, who allowed for initial difficulties and continued his hearty support." A succeeding Canal Commission "looked askance at the Sanitary Corps as a horde of impractical, wild, and visionary theorists, and that too with the background of the splendid history of Havana." In April, 1905, several higher officials died of yellow fever, which was the last straw. There was even a demand "that the Chief Sanitary Officer—Gorgas—and Dr. Henry K. Carter and those who believed with them in the mosquito theory, should be relieved, and men with more practical views appointed in their stead."

Happily, the President was Roosevelt, who, during the fight with yellow fever in Havana, had been in office and therefore knew the subject. He stood firmly for the mosquito theory against the old idea of propagation by filth, and ordered that the utmost assistance be rendered to the sanitary officials. A little later the Sanitary Department was made an independent bureau and reported direct to the Chairman of the Commission. The importance of this change in status was soon apparent.

It was found that, by an unintentional defiance of sanitary laws, the French, during their previous occupation, had been devoting their efficiency to the actual propagation of yellow fever. The very hospitals, consecrated to the relief of such maladies, were transformed into ideal places for the breeding of mosquitos by the inclusion in their design of gutters under their roofs, barrels for rain water, to say nothing of discarded cans and bottles. The grounds were laid out with all the taste in which the French excel and were enriched with a profusion of tropical plants. But as a safeguard against the umbrella ant, which pest will in a single night sever every leaf from a good sized orange tree, the grounds were surrounded with a hollow ring of pottery, kept full of water and precisely suited for the multiplication of mosquitoes.

By orders of Dr. Gorgas, the shrubbery was removed a distance of 200 yards from the Ancon Hospital. What had been the botanical grounds were carefully drained and all pools were eliminated. The umbrella ants were traced to their holes and were destroyed by pouring in bisulphid of carbon which vaporized and was exploded, so drawing the gas into all parts of the nest.

As a result of these efficient measures and of the scientific skill, revealed in them, there was only one case of yellow fever developed within the Ancon Hospital during the American management of that institution, this despite the large number of cases introduced for treatment during the years 1904 and 1905. The single exception was a nurse who frequently visited an infected part of the town. Her escort was a doctor and, after her recovery, he married her!

With equal vigour the sanitary authorities undertook the eradication of malaria. In this case, it was the anopheles mosquito that had to be slaughtered and the problem was rural rather than urban. The areas bordering the canal, fifty miles in length and ten miles in breadth, were divided into 24 sanitary zones with sub hospitals, tributary to the main institutions, at the end of each territorial corridor. Every such district was served by a staff of 20 to 100 men. It was found that the anopheles is not a mosquito of strong flight and by means of clearance of 200 yards breadth, and the use of screened houses with only one door, the danger was reduced to a minimum. For any mosquitoes that effected an entrance, a test tube, with chloroform held by cotton wool, was found to be a deadly weapon. Near swamps, screened box cars were used for sleeping and persons exposed to infection were dosed with prophylactic quinine.

Major Gorgas tells us that, in his opinion, the years 1905 and 1906 were the halcyon period of the sanitary department. After May, 1905, one case only of yellow fever originated in the Isthmian Zone. In November of that year, the scourge was at an end.

An example of scientific efficiency, dated January, 1905, may illustrate this achievement. On the warship *Boston,* there developed seven cases of yellow fever. It was clear that the ship itself must be infected and all cases occurred near the ward room. There had been a ball on New Year's Day, and it was surmised that some guest had been suffering from the initial stages of a mild case of fever and had been bitten by a stegomyia which, becoming infectious at the end of a fortnight, had spread the disease. Enough to add that the guess was confirmed by Dr. G. A. Perry of the Public Health Service who going down to the ward room discovered a small flat tub under the steps in which mosquitoes of this type were breeding.

It is not too much to say that if yellow fever—and, we may add, malaria—had not been overcome in Panama, the Canal might never have been built. In nine years, yellow fever, malaria and dysentery had cost the French no fewer than 22,189 lives of labourers. Records show that, in the case of certain groups of operatives, at least three out of four of the recent arrivals perished within two or three months of their arrival. It was the chief reason why the

Walter Reed.

French abandoned their project. At least one third of their force was on the sick list, and one-fifth of the force died every year.

To have provided victims for the mortality involved would have been, to say the least, an expensive task for the United States. During ten years of construction an average of 13,000 men would have been incapacitated. In fact, 12,000 of these cases, on the average, were saved, an annual saving over ten years of 39,420,000 days of sickness and of 39,420,000 in dollars. Considering what wages would have had to be paid to keep the men at work under less favourable conditions, the real saving was much greater.

On the French scale of mortality, 200 per 1,000 per annum, the American labour force of 39,000 would have lost 78,000 lives in ten years. In fact, it lost 6,630 lives. The Sanitary Department was thus directly responsible for saving 71,370 lives, with the accompanying invalidism added.

This battle against yellow fever, fought and won in the Caribbean, was fought and won for the entire human race. In Africa, the warfare is proceeding. Along the Gold Coast, at Lagos and in Nigeria, stegomyia, with her ornamental wings, and deadly thrust, is resisted by the fever field station. The records of an organization like the Rockefeller Foundation are eloquent of the principle that a victory for life and health gained anywhere is a victory of which the fruits are everywhere distributed for the benefit of mankind.

IV

THE INTERNATIONAL POLICEMAN

As trustee for the Panama Canal, the United States assumed a threefold responsibility. First, she had to keep order in the regions affected. Secondly, she had to secure health. Thirdly, she had to complete the construction of the canal. The policeman, the physican and the labourer formed three allied battalions of peace and progress.

The laborer worked strictly within the Canal Zone. But the policeman, wearing as it were the blue uniform of the law, and the physician wearing the white uniform of the hospital, could not operate except on a wider territory. The evils of disorder, revolt and bloodshed, were not local, and for centuries, yellow fever and malaria have cast a pall over Central America as a whole and the Caribbean Islands.

But the fact that the policeman and the physician are in evidence does not mean that the United States claims a sovereignty over these regions or ownership in fee simple and absolute. Such arrangements presuppose no more than a duty on the part of the United States to maintain the Panama Canal as an international utility.

It is important that the relations between the United States and Central America, insofar as they affect the Isthmian Highway, should be neither misrepresented nor confused.

The evidence is overwhelming that, according to her explicit declarations, the United States entered Panama, not as an aggressor but as a trustee.

In a letter, dated October 19, 1904, President Roosevelt thus addressed his Secretary of War, Mr. Taft:

There is ground for believing that in the execution of the rights conferred by the treaty the people of Panama have been unduly alarmed at the effect of the establishment of a government in the Canal Strip by the Commission. Apparently they fear lest the effect be to create out of part of their territory a competing and independent community which shall injuriously affect their revenues, and diminish their prestige as a nation.

. . . *We have not the slightest intention of establishing an independent colony in the middle of the state of Panama,* or of exercising any greater governmental functions than are necessary to enable us conveniently and safely to construct, maintain and operate the canal under the rights given us by the treaty. Least of all do we desire to interfere with the business and prosperity of the people of Panama.

At a hearing on November 28, 1904, at President Amador's Palace in Panama, Secretary of War, William Howard Taft, made the following statement which is further confirmatory:

I want to be as frank as possible in this matter and I reiterate what I said before—that the Government of the United States has no desire to *exercise any power which shall not be necessary for that purpose,* the purpose that influenced you to give us the rights that we now have, and which induced us to make promises of payment and actually to pay the money which we did pay. I concur, and the Government of the United States concurs, in the construction that all these rights were given us *solely* for the purpose of enabling us to *construct, maintain* and *operate the Canal.* It is not the motive that governed the conferring of those rights, but the extent of the rights necessary to enable us to secure this common object, that has been in controversy.

Secretary of War, William Howard Taft, made a speech in the presence of the President of the Republic of Panama, in the month of December, 1904, in which he said:

It gives me great pleasure to . . . say to you that the Government of the United States has no intention in being in this Isthmus to do other than to build a canal which shall connect the two Oceans and thus bring great benefits not only to your country but to the United States and mankind. It has no desire to exercise any power except that which it deems necessary under the Treaty to insure the building, maintenance and protection of the Canal.

In the speech delivered in the City of Panama on November 16, 1910, President Taft, reassuring Panama as to the real intentions of the United States, said:

We are here to construct, maintain, operate and protect a world canal that cuts through the heart of your country, and you have conceded to us the necessary sovereignty and jurisdiction over the part of your country occupied by the Canal in order to enable us to accomplish such purposes. *We do not desire any other responsibility on the part of your Government than that necessary to carry on our purpose of constructing and maintaining that Canal.*

Major General George W. Davis, U. S. Army (Retired), a member of the Isthmian Canal Commission, and the first governor of the Canal Zone, made a statement before the Committee on Inter-oceanic Canals of the United States Senate on March 30, 1906, in which the following colloquy took place:

Senator Morgan: You consider the flag of the United States as being entirely at home in the Zone?

General Davis: Yes; I consider it is entirely at home there, but whether or not technically we have a right to fly the flag of the United States in the Zone—I say technically—it seems to me might be questionable.

Senator Morgan: Have you ever raised one?

General Davis: No; and it never will be raised, I think; but since titular sovereignty resides in Panama, I think that proposition has been stated many times.

Senator Morgan: Unless you can define the word "titular," I do not think I could accept the fact.

General Davis: Well, the Hay-Varilla Treaty recognizes some shadow of what is called sovereignty as still remaining in the Panama Zone.

General Davis thus regarded the Canal Zone as an instance of what we may call assigned sovereignty. He gave instances which may be regarded as precedents:

"In 1878 the Sultan of Turkey granted to the Emperor of Austria the entire control of all governmental functions in the Turkish provinces of Bosnia and Herzegovina, and all the rights, powers, and privileges that a sovereign could exercise, yet the nominal sovereignty of these two provinces still remained in Turkey."

"In 1878 the Sultan of Turkey granted to Great Britain all the rights, powers, and privileges that a sovereign could exercise in and over the island of Cyprus."

"In 1898 the Emperor of China granted to Great Britain, by lease for so long as Russia should remain in possession of Port Arthur peninsula, the town and district of Weihaiwei. Under this lease Great Britain exercises all the rights, powers, and privileges that a sovereign could exercise in the said town and district of Weihaiwei."

"In 1898 China granted to Russia for the period of twenty-five years with right of extension, all rights, powers, and privileges that a sovereign could exercise, of and to, the Port Arthur promontory and adjacent territory."

"In 1898 China granted to Germany, by lease for ninety-nine years, all the rights, powers and privileges which a sovereign could exercise, in and to the port of Kai-Chau and adjacent territory."

"There are probably other instances of like delegation of power equivalent to sovereignty, yet, in every one of the cases cited, the actual nominal sovereignty is still in the Sultan of Turkey in the one case and in the Emperor of China in the other, just as the nominal sovereignty of the Canal Zone is still in the Republic of Panama."

We have here, in effect, the theory of mandate which, in due course, has been developed under and recognized by the League of Nations.

In his book entitled "Government of the Canal Zone," General George W. Goethals says:

"The Zone was granted to the United States for specific purposes—'*the construction, maintenance, operation, sanitation and protection of a canal,*' and while everything has been subordinated to the first of these, with the end of the construction work in sight, and the protection of the canal omitted to be dealt with separately, the maintenance and operation became of paramount importance"; p. 55.

"No one came forward to take advantage of the opportunity which the law gave for leasing lands. The framers of the bill did not consider that the United States could give title in fee to any of the lands of the Zone, because should the strip fail at any time to be used for the specific purposes mentioned in the grant the land must revert to the Republic of Panama"; p. 61.

"It must be remembered that we have, after all is said and done, *only a right of way for a canal*"; p. 85.

President Ricardo Jimenez of Costa Rica on May 27th, 1927, in refusing the use of the National Theatre for a public demonstration for Segasson, the Nicaraguan Revolutionary Leader, made a fair and just statement when he said:

If I write in my communications to the President of the United States the words "great and good friend" I must be a great and good friend so long as there are no motives between his Government and mine for changing such an attitude, but I do not care that that attitude should be only on paper, *I want it also in practice.*

In the exercise of such an international authority by an individual nation, thus acting for mankind as a whole, there is nothing to be described as either new or unusual. It was by using such powers that the United States and Great Britain cleared the ocean of slave ships, and the Caribbean Sea of pirates; and at the hour of this writing, France, Italy, Great Britain, Japan, and the United States are proceeding under such self-assumed mandates, to police Shanghai, and are patrolling their warships over internal Chinese waters far from the regions of their national defense or special adjacent national interests.

MIRAFLORES: LOOKING SOUTH

The United States' record in China is well stated in the
following editorial in the *New York Times* of June 6th,
1927, which, with its references to "international trains," is
very pertinent to the parallel case of an international
waterway:

Concentration of foreign troops (including 2,000 additional
American marines) at Tientsin, in North China, has as its purpose
the protection of foreign lives and interests in the event of violence.
These troops serve as reinforcements for the various foreign garrisons
in Peking and Tientsin, some of which have been stationed there
for thirty years or more. Their use will depend on the nature of
the emergency.

The situation at Peking and Tientsin with respect to the foreign
garrisons is somewhat different from that at Shanghai. The Treaty
Powers established guards over their respective legations in Peking
prior to the Boxer outbreak. Experience proved that the numbers
stationed there were insufficient to afford adequate protection. As a
result, when the Legation Quarter was besieged by the Chinese, it
was found necessary to send in a relief expedition, which had to fight
its way from the seaport of Tientsin to the capital at Peking, a
distance of about eighty miles.

When the settlement with China was made after the Boxer outbreak, the Treaty Powers continued to maintain their guards at the
Legation Quarter, and, in addition, obtained the right to establish
military posts at various points between Peking and Tientsin, so as
to be able to keep open the communications between the Chinese
capital and the sea. This right was made use of in 1912, when the
garrisons in Tientsin were augmented and troops actually used to
prevent the railroad between Peking and Tientsin from being cut
by the Chinese revolutionists. During the last few years in times
of emergency so-called *"international trains"* have been run between
Peking and Tientsin, flying the flags of the Treaty Powers and
protected by their armed soldiers. This has been the only method
of keeping the line open—and sometimes even this has failed when
the foreign Powers, unwilling to take action which might prejudice
one or other Chinese faction, have permitted the road to remain
inoperative for several weeks without exercising their right of opening
it by force.

America's share in this work has been to maintain a guard of several hundred marines in Peking, where there are barracks in the American Legation compound to house them. We have also had at Tientsin since 1912 two battalions of the Fifteenth Infantry, which have taken their share in preserving communications between Peking and the sea and have helped to guard the *"international trains."* Incidentally, these troops have done patrol work about Tientsin during civil warfare, and have, sometimes unwittingly, helped to check outrages by the Chinese troops against the Chinese civilian population. On the drill ground of the Fifteenth Infantry in Tientsin is a placard recently erected with Chinese money to express the gratitude of the Chinese villagers in the neighborhood for help extended to them in times of trouble by the American soldiers.

Aside from the diplomatic and political aspects of moving marines from Shanghai to Tientsin there are technical advantages in that the American Government possesses extensive barracks and drill grounds at the latter place, and so can keep the men ashore all the time instead of, as at Shanghai, holding them part of the time cooped up in transports. This is better for their health and morale, and is also better for American prestige.

If, then, the Great Powers welcome the United States as a fellow-policeman in China, and even complain that this country does not go further than she is willing to go in her Far Eastern intervention, there is no reason why they should criticize the United States for acting on precisely the same principles in a region where she has acquired a definite franchise after long years of negotiation—a franchise which, unless fulfilled in good faith, will be subject ultimately to a movement, tending towards forfeiture. Central American republics did not complain of the scope of the operations of the United States, or the size of the area in Central America cleared by it of disease and pestilence. Nor did the nations of the Western hemisphere criticize the scope of beneficent operations, on the success of which depended the safe use of the Canal. So far as the commercial aspect of the enterprise was concerned, the United States has had no other object except healthy transportation.

Much is written of the United States as "the big brother" of the smaller Latin American Republics. It must be remembered that, if the United States were to remain quiescent on all occasions, other foreign governments might insist, despite the Monroe Doctrine, on taking action of a more extreme character in the interests of order.

In the first chapter of his book, *The United States and Peace*, which deals with "The Monroe Doctrine: Its Limitations and Implications," Chief Justice Taft thus refers to Latin American countries:

> We are concerned that their governments shall not be interfered with by European governments; we are concerned that this hemisphere shall not be a field for land aggrandizement and the chase for increased political power by European governments, such as we have witnessed in Africa and in China and Manchuria, and we believe that such a condition would be inimical to our safety and interests. More than this, where a controversy between an European government and a Latin-American republic is of such a character that it is likely to lead to war, we feel that our earnest desire to escape the possible result against which the Monroe Doctrine is aimed is sufficient to justify our mediating between the European power and the Latin-American republic, and bringing about by negotiation, if possible, a peaceable settlement of the difference. This is what Mr. Roosevelt did in Venezuela and in Santo Domingo. It was not that the use of force or threatened force to collect their debts by the European powers constituted a violation of the Monroe Doctrine that induced Mr. Roosevelt to act, but only a general desire to promote peace and also a wish to avoid circumstances in which an invasion of the Monroe Doctrine might easily follow.

The obligations of the United States, thus defined by a former President are indistinguishable from the obligations assumed by Great Britain, in her trusteeship of the Suez Canal—obligations clarified by treaties with nations in the neighbourhood of that waterway. Thus, in April, 1927, at the first hint of possible danger to the Suez Canal, Great Britain sent warships as a precaution, nor did any nation complain. Indeed, it is to the interest of other nations that, on general principles affecting an international public utility, such precautions should be peacefully taken in defence of a common carrier. Great Britain and the United States, as trustees of collective civilization, having the necessary potential power, are but guarding humanity's highways, at the inter-oceanic crossroads of the Old and the New World, under a "traditional policy" to which they are eternally bound, and bound together.

One or two illustrations of these general principles may be given. Prior to the Treaty of 1915, I was in Haiti endeavouring to protect a railroad franchise in which American clients were interested. The Government was a farce. To property and life, the Republic offered no protection. Presidents came and went by slaughter. The country was full of bandits. We did not dare venture back into the interior. Officials robbed and starved the inhabitants and confiscated the property of foreigners. There were no roads. The back country inhabitants dared not come to town to trade for fear of being compelled to fight under conscription for the so-called government. Foreign powers pressed for settlement of Haitian obligations to their nationals.

It was under these conditions that the Wilson Administration arranged voluntarily a coöperative treaty under which the United States, with the aid of marines, has supervised the customs, organized the public works, the sanitation of the island and the gendarmerie.

With what result?

The annual report of General John H. Russell of the U. S. Marines, the American High Commissioner at Port-au-Prince for 1926 shows revenues of more than $8,000,000 and a reduction within the year of $1,225,000 in Haiti's public debt, leaving no more than a third of her fiduciary currency uncovered.

Since the signing of the Treaty of 1915, more than one thousand miles of roads have been constructed, with 15 big span bridges and more than 1,000 culverts; motor vehicles which in 1915 were three, are now 2,500; 10 major hospitals have been constructed; 21 rural dispensaries are in operation and 9 more are under construction; 100 free clinics are held monthly.

An efficient native gendarmerie, with 2,433 enlisted men, officered both by United States Marines and commissioned Haitian officers, has been built up with stations in each of the 551 "sections" of the country.

Sixty permanent modern school buildings have been constructed and are in operation.

Despite the fact that all these improvements are being currently paid for out of Haitian revenue, the public national debt has been decreased during the occupation from $30,772,000 to $21,603,000 and series A Haitian bonds recently have sold above par on the New York market.

The intervention of the United States in Haiti and Cuba and the intervention suggested in 1908 to the President of Panama, were in accordance with voluntary treaties of those republics with the United States authorizing such intervention in case of trouble. When disorder arose in Cuba in 1906 the United States occupied the island, just as it had done at the time of its independence, but it withdrew again after a new government had been constituted and tranquillity had been reëstablished.

In the case of Panama, it must be remembered that the Republic directly adjoins the Canal littoral where the responsibility, special interest and national defense of the United States are concentrated.

When rumors spread in 1908 that election frauds would take place during the presidential elections, the Secretary of War, Mr. Taft, who had gone to Panama to inspect the work on the Canal, wrote to the President of Panama in a letter of May 12 that it was of direct interest to the United States, in case of threats of fraud in an election, to intervene in order to prevent them, and in case such frauds should occur, to hinder officials, for the election of whom the free choice of the people was not assured, from taking office. Thanks to this letter of the Secretary of War the elections took place without pressure on the part of the government.

Another instance is Santo Domingo. As far back as 1869 Santo Domingo indicated its wish to become a part of the United States, but the United States Senate by a tie vote blocked the arrangement. Since that date, Santo Domingo has been included among the approaches to the Isthmian Highway; yet the Republic had degenerated into chaos. When I was on the island, the conditions were similar to the conditions in Haiti. Chaos, bloodshed and disorder obliterated one of the world's fairest gardens.

Under the Monroe Doctrine, we were responsible to other nations for finding a remedy and, by friendly arrangement with the Republic, we took over the customs in 1905. We were compelled, moreover, to intervene to quell disorder in 1913. Again, and more forcibly we invoked the international police power in that Republic in 1914; and finally in 1915, under the Wilson Administration, the United States established, with the consent of that government, a relationship similar to that in Haiti, with a similar result.

Like Haiti, the Republic of Santo Domingo now enjoys order and tranquillity. Conditions indicate prosperity. In fact, the exercise of the police power has restored the two sister Republics of Haiti and Santo Domingo to the family of nations.

It may be added that, in 1911, we intervened in Honduras; and again in 1913. It was the same international police power that, in both cases, was invoked.

By all means let us hope that the world has made a final end of the Nietzscheian philosophy of the superman that "might makes right." Let us assume that this negation of justice died on the fields of Flanders. But it is really not arguable that the undoubted right of the Central American republics to govern themselves should be interpreted as meaning that, situated as they are on one of the world's highways of commerce, an international highway, they are to be entitled at any time to have a violent revolution and to settle their elections by a resort to civil war. This is a claim to indulgence in disorder which is nowhere else recognized by the governments of mankind.

When, owing to negligence, Great Britain permitted the *Alabama* to be equipped as a southern privateer, in which capacity she committed depredations on the United States, the case was referred to a special court of arbitration and damages were awarded and paid. For similar damages, we hold that Mexico is liable; and China too, after the Boxer Rebellion, paid an indemnity which was none the less sound in international law because, as an act of grace, the United States applied her share to Chinese education. To damages incurred by foreigners in China during the present trouble, a similar principle of restitution must be held, in strict international law, to apply.

So with the Suez Canal. If Great Britain failed to maintain orderly transit through that waterway, the world, including the United States, would have undoubtedly a cause of complaint, nor do we doubt that, in any armed occupation of that region by the Powers, the United States

Marines, as elsewhere, would play their part.   Indeed, we
go so far as to suggest that, if a ship canal be completed
on the St. Lawrence, bringing the Middle West into direct
oceanic contact with Europe, this highway also, though situated in part within Canadian sovereignty, would be subject to the general understanding, applicable to such routes,
that order must be guaranteed by the Government which
acts as trustee.

The Panama Canal must be similarly regarded.   If it
had been completed by M. de Lesseps, and managed under
French auspices, even so, the United States would have
insisted on safe and regular transmission of traffic.   The
world has the same right to make this demand of the
United States.   We cannot treat these obligations as "a
scrap of paper," and if in fulfilling them, we use force,
we are not to be accused for that reason of descending
to the imperialism of military autocracies in Europe, when
these menaced the peace of the human race.   The very
fact that we ask other nations to refrain from dealing
with disorders in Central America lays upon us an obligation
ourselves to keep them within bounds.

This is no merely academic contention.   A case in point,
and a recent case, may be cited.   Early in 1927, Great
Britain was disturbed by the troubles in Nicaragua.   There
is evidence that, before proceeding to a formal correspondence, she consulted the United States by friendly conversation.   We need not suppose, then, that, in what followed,
there was any challenge to the Monroe Doctrine.   Indeed,
until we have more satisfactory arrangements by treaty with
Nicaragua and Panama which arrangements are under
negotiation, we must expect that incidents with other
powers—perhaps, delicate incidents—will arise.

The British Ambassador wrote to the Secretary of State
on February 19, 1927, as follows:

U. S. TRANSPORT "NORTHERN PACIFIC" PASSING CUCARACHA
SLIDE, DECEMBER 4, 1913

They can manage their own affairs. The
only really decent people among among them are
the landowners and the businessmen,
but they're only a small part of the
population, and they can't control all
these little brown folk.

His Britannic Majesty's Ambassador presents his compliments to the Secretary of State, and has the honor to state that he has been instructed by His Majesty's principal Secretary of State for Foreign Affairs to draw the attention of the United States Government to the menace to British lives and property arising from the present disturbances in Nicaragua. In particular, His Majesty's Government has been advised by His Majesty's Chargé d'Affaires at Managua that the hostilities between the rebels and Government troops have now resulted in a situation which threatens the safety of British lives and property in Corinto, Leon, Managua, Granada and Matagalpa.

In view, therefore, of the grave risks to which British residents in Nicaragua are now exposed, His Majesty's Ambassador has been instructed to remind the United States Government that *His Majesty's Government looks to them to extend to British subjects, and especially to those in the places above mentioned, the same measure of protection as they afford to United States citizens* in the districts now threatened by revolutionary disturbances.

The Secretary of State replied to the British Ambassador as follows:

The Secretary of State presents his compliments to His Excellency, the British Ambassador, and in reply to the latter's note No. 130, of Feb. 19, 1927, concerning the protection of British lives and property in Nicaragua, has the honor to inform the British Ambassador that the American armed forces which have been landed in Nicaragua for the protection of American and foreign lives and property *will be pleased to extend to British subjects such protection as may be possible and proper under the circumstances.*

The British Ambassador's next note to the Secretary of State was as follows:

I have the honor to inform you, on instructions from His Majesty's principal Secretary of State for Foreign Affairs, that His Majesty's Government has reluctantly decided to send a man-of-war to the West Coast of Nicaragua and that H.M.S. *Colombo* is being dispatched to Corinto. She should arrive at Colon on Feb. 24 and at Corinto on Feb. 25.

His Majesty's Government feels that the presence of a war vessel may have a moral effect and would be a base of refuge for British subjects.

It is of course not intended to land forces and the commanding officer will be instructed accordingly.

In informing you of the above, I am instructed to express once more to the United States Government the thanks of His Majesty's Government for their assistance, and to add that His Majesty's Government will continue to rely on it.

The despatch of a British cruiser was also announced in a telegram, dated February 22nd, 1927, and addressed to the Department of State by Mr. Charles C. Eberhardt, the United States Minister at Managua.

I have the honor to inform your Excellency that in the absence of Guarantees from the Nicaraguan and United States Governments for the protection of the lives and properties of British subjects in the event of further street fighting, incendiarism and pillage, in the threatened districts of this Republic, His Britannic Majesty's Government are reluctantly contemplating the despatch of a man-of-war to the western coast of Nicaragua.

It is with pleasure that I am instructed to inform your Excellency that His Majesty's Government thanks the Government of the United States once more for its assistance and still continues to rely thereon.

At the Pan-American Conference of 1928, held at Havana, Mr. Hughes, representing the United States, was confronted by a difficult situation. As he said later at Princeton, "the people of the Latin American Republics resent intervention of any sort, of any possible description, anywhere. They are not disposed to draw distinctions or to admit justifications."

In his Princeton Lectures, entitled *Our Relations to the Nations of the Western Hemisphere,* Mr. Hughes emphasised the distinction drawn by Judge Bassett Moore between "political and nonpolitical intervention"—the latter being, in the words of Professor E. M. Borchard, "non-belligerent interposition," based on the duty of protecting citizens abroad.

In a statement issued subsequent to the Conference, Judge Morgan J. O'Brien, formerly President of the Supreme Court of New York, and a Democrat member of the American delegation to Havana, endorsed the attitude of Mr. Hughes in emphatic terms, so indicating that it is representative of opinion in the United States, irrespective of party.

On April 26th, 1927, President Coolidge defined the situation thus:

It is all right to say that when our citizens enter a foreign country they should do so with the understanding that they are to abide by the laws of that country. They should and they do, and our Government would be the last to interfere in the just application of the law of his domicile to our citizens. But this is only a partial statement of the case. The admission of our citizens within their territory is a voluntary act of foreign governments. It is a tacit invitation. When we permit foreigners to come here, and when other countries admit our citizens, we know and they know that such aliens come and go not only under the rights and duties imposed by domestic law, but also under the rights and duties imposed by international law. There is nothing unfair, nothing imperialistic, in this principle. It has been universally adopted and recognized as right and just, and is the only reasonable method by which enlightened humanity can safeguard friendly intercourse among the citizens of different nations. This policy has been adopted in furtherance of the humanitarian desire for a universal reign of law.

Finally, we have President Roosevelt who, in 1904, spoke as follows:

Chronic wrongdoing, or an impotence which results in a general loosening of the ties of civilized society, may in America, as elsewhere, ultimately require intervention by some civilized nation, and in the Western Hemisphere the adherence of the United States to the Monroe Doctrine may force the United States, however reluctantly, in flagrant cases of such wrongdoing or impotence, to the exercise of an international police power.

The term Latin-America is often used in senses not wholly accurate. As the dispute over Tacna-Arica has shown, to say nothing of similar disputes in Central America, we have here a civilization, by no means homogeneous whether in politics or race. Speaking in New York on Feb. 28th, 1928, Señor Carlos Silva Vildesela, the Chilean delegate at Havana, paid the highest tribute to the pronouncement on intervention made by Mr. Hughes, and added the significant remark:

You don't realize that there are fundamental differences among the Latin-American nations.

[The sudden development in December, 1928, of the trouble between Bolivia and Paraguay adds point to the remark.]

The entire situation has to be viewed in the light of rapidly developing financial and commercial relations by which Latin-America is linked not only with the United States but with the rest of the world.

V

THE ARITHMETIC OF IT

IT was thus by the associated efforts of Colonel Goethals as an engineer, and of Major Gorgas as a sanitary officer, that, in 1914, the Panama Canal was completed and opened for traffic.

The true character of the great undertaking has been obscured somewhat by two considerations. In the first place, the Isthmian Highway is managed, not by a private corporation, but directly by the government of the United States. In the second place, the Highway is an important element in the protection of the United States against attack. These factors have suggested, and rightly, that the Panama Canal is a national undertaking. But we need also to remember that not less is it also a commercial undertaking. Indeed, it is as a commercial and not as a military undertaking that its use is international and therefore a matter of interest to countries other than the suzerain Power herself. In an address before the San Francisco Commercial Club, Colonel Goethals put the point thus:

Personally I could never see why the Canal should not be made a business proposition. I do not think anyone should benefit by it at the expense of others.

Let us concentrate our attention, then, on the Panama Canal as "a business proposition," of general benefit to mankind.

It happens that, parallel to the Canal, there has been

laid a railroad. This railroad, like the Canal itself, belongs to the United States. But the railroad is organized as the Panama Canal Railroad Company, that is, as a corporation, and it is the stock in this corporation that the United States owns. Presumably it shapes its conduct in the management of this enterprise by the laws it has enacted for the regulation of corporations owning interstate railroads. If it does, the rates charged will yield no more and no less than a reasonable return on the investment. This is the basis upon which the railway corporations are permitted to charge rates under the Interstate Commerce Act.

Before a corporation can build a street railway, a steam railroad or any other public utility in the State of New York, it must obtain from the proper authority a certificate of public convenience and necessity, including permission to exercise it. The avowed purpose of this procedure is to protect the public against the investment of an excessive amount of capital in such enterprises and then charge it an exorbitant rate to secure a fair return on the capital invested. In New York State, the law limits capital to the amount needed to render a safe and adequate service and then limits the rate or charge to the amount required to give a reasonable return on the investment.

I submit that there is no material difference in principle between the Panama Canal Railroad Company, as a public utility, and the Panama Canal itself. The ownership of stock in one case corresponds to the perpetual leasehold granted in the other case; and it is only in name that the investments differ. The essential function, that is, traffic, is the same. After all, transportation, whether by rail or by water, is equally transportation, be it of persons or of goods. Indeed, the construction of the Panama Canal by the United States was continued in succession to the ownership of the New Panama Canal Company, and I venture the opinion that the financial administration of the Canal would have been greatly simplified if, from the outset, there had been organized a separate corporation to handle the business end of the enterprise.

Indeed, I am satisfied that the United States will eventually be compelled, in justice to its taxpayers, as well as the interests of the world in general, to put the commercial phase of the Panama Canal into the hands of a Public Utility Common Carrier Corporation modelled after that of the Emergency Fleet Corporation, now operating ships and acting as common carrier on the high seas, thereby completely separating its commercial accounts from those which pertain to defense. There is no other practicable way to protect the taxpayers and to fix tolls that are "just and equitable" to all in its commercial use.

It seems to me, if I may be so bold as to say it, that the great work accomplished by Colonel Goethals and Major Gorgas is still awaiting the master hand of a trained financier. During the period of construction, there was no attempt, apparently, to adopt a comprehensive financial policy; and not yet is the balance sheet of the Canal presented in a form which would be satisfactory to the accountants of a properly managed business. Happily, it is not too late to reduce the accounts to order.

In insisting on this friendly criticism, I desire to avoid all possibility of a misunderstanding. I do not suggest that, during the construction of the Canal, there was either waste or dishonesty. That is not at all the point that I desire to press home. Assuming as we are entitled to do, that such irregularities were wholly avoided, we may still appreciate the vital importance of having the finances of the Canal arranged in a scientific form. Only by such a clarity can the United States safeguard the rights of her citizens and perform her duty to mankind.

The trouble is not administration. It is not the officials responsible for the conduct of the Canal who are to blame. On the contrary, these officials are conscious of the difficulties under which they have to fulfil their task on its financial side—a conclusion which we may draw from the "Annual Report of the Governor of the Panama Canal for the Fiscal Year Ended June 30th, 1922." We read:

> The treatment of interest in connection with the amortization and depreciation reserve caused some complication in canal accounting. The interest accrual will be entirely theoretical, since the canal does not have control of the funds which would ordinarily be set aside by business concerns for accomplishing the purpose for which the charges are made. The United States, through the repayment of amounts covering such charges, is in a position to save the accrual of interest of the funds so repaid; therefore, it seems entirely proper for the canal to take credit for interest on funds theoretically set aside, which funds it could and would set aside if it had control of the same.
>
> I believe that all those who have examined into the financial transactions of the canal will now agree that it is necessary to keep the appropriations of The Panama Canal on a continuing basis and that the reserves which have been built up should be continued as a working fund.

This passage is sufficient indication that the blame—if blame there be—for the present unsatisfactory situation does not rest with representatives of the United States on the Isthmian Highway. The root of the trouble is to be traced to the system which legislation has imposed upon the officials. If an adequate system of accounts is to be adopted, there will have to be new legislation correcting the faults of the old. The changes, here to be outlined, could not be effected without statutory authority, granted by Congress.

At first sight, it might seem as if the strict and commercial accountancy to be applied to the Panama Canal, which I am about to advocate, were of no more than an academic importance. I shall now submit that this accountancy is fundamental to the trusteeship of the United States over a great international public utility. All the facts concerning the enterprise should be assembled and set out in their proper relation to the politics and the material interests of the world at large. The administration of the Canal is not correct unless it secures to the United States the last penny to which she is entitled and determines accurately what is the share of revenue which the commerce of the world should provide. It is the larger issues involved in finance that will justify, I hope, a discussion which must be technical, though I trust that I have made it as simple as the nature of the case permits.

The revenues earned by the Canal are paid into the Treasury at Washington as Miscellaneous Receipts. Expenditure on the Canal is paid out of the Treasury at Washington in much the same manner. Up to this point, there may not be any specific reason for complaint. In the management of the post offices, whether of the United States or of Great Britain, it is a principle of public finance that the Treasury shall receive and shall disburse all items. It is, however, in the subsequent accounting that we discover serious omissions.

To begin with, it is evident that the accounts of the Canal and the accounts of the Government should be presented in two statements, as separate from each other as if the Canal had been a distinct corporation, only connected with the Government, if at all, owing to the financial backing of the Treasury. For the Canal, as for a distinct corporation, there should be a balance sheet, showing at any particular moment precisely what has been the investment in the enterprise and what is its financial condition.

The General Balance Sheet for the Canal, presented on June 30th, 1926, was as follows:

DEBITS—ASSETS

Canal fixed property	$236,115,089.01
Canal equipment	4,140,923.88
Cash due treasury	193,296.68
Cash working	2,346,898.87
Accounts receivable	795,926.04
Business property	30,341,290.56
Stores	4,045,530.67
United States Treasury	71,815,510.79
Theoretical interest accruals	614,276.05
National defense expenditures	112,662,732.60
Undistributed business capital	1,813,000.00
Total	$461,258,475.15

CREDITS—LIABILITIES

Canal transit and business capital	$273,673,818.51
National defense capital	112,662,732.60
Accounts payable	1,522,114.10
Unclassified canal credits	20,561.02
Amortization	1,903,435.69
Depreciation	5,667,204.16
Repair reserves	1,803,731.42
Gratuity reserves	538,632.72
Canal surplus	58,393,182.47
Business surplus	5,073,062.46
Total	* $461,258,475.15

It will be seen at once that this balance sheet offers no sufficient information as to the profit actually earned or the

* The failure of these figures to total accurately is, perhaps, significant. They are printed as officially presented.

GATUN SPILLWAY AND DAM

loss actually incurred during the year in question. I will suggest, then, the steps which, as I submit, should be taken to put the accounts into a proper shape.

To begin with, there should be a careful ascertainment of what capital has been invested in the Canal. In the term, capital, there should be included the early deficits incurred by the Government during the period when the Canal was not yet a going concern. All such annual deficits—as in the case of a railroad running through new territory—should be treated as an interest-bearing liability due to the United States; and, in that liability, there should be included whatever interest has accrued at a reasonable rate on the whole capital invested. In popular terms, the United States should be credited with whatever has been spent on the construction and the inauguration of the Canal, with interest up to date. This total investment, thus definitely ascertained, should be expressed in Panama Canal Bonds, the charges on which, whether for interest or for amortization, should be borne by the Canal as a commercial undertaking.

As matters stand at present, the United States has been unfair in some ways to herself. We have seen the Treasury footing bills, the burden of which clearly should be borne by the traffic through the Isthmian Highway. In some cases, these charges fell directly upon the taxpayer—an injustice which, for the future, Congress should prevent by Statute. With regard to such illogical contributions to a common carrier, made up to date, I suggest that they be accurately computed and charged to a suspense debit, carrying interest. The money, thus accounted for, should be repaid into the United States Treasury out of surpluses earned by the Canal and so allotted to the relief of the taxpayer who, in the first instance, ought never to have been asked to submit to the burden.

It should be realized that the United States rejected a

collective management of the Canal by the Powers and insisted on her own individual political control. The cost of the Canal as a waterway should be distinguished therefore, from the cost of the fortifications and other undertakings by which the Canal is defended. The commercial costs fall naturally and properly on all nations using the Canal. But the military and naval costs ought to be borne by the suzerain trustee; and for a simple reason. The Canal was constructed by the United States, not only as a commercial undertaking but as an element in natural security. If the Canal had not been constructed, the defense of the two widely separated seaboards would have been more expensive than, in fact, it has become. As a result of the strategic link supplied by the Canal, therefore, the military burden, borne by the United States, is reduced. All that the United States has a right here to claim is that her public vessels engaged in the maintenance of the Canal, in the training needed for its protection, and in the guarantee of its neutrality, shall be allowed freedom of transit.

On June 30th, 1926, this item, "national defense expenditures," stood at $112,662,732.60—a figure which I venture to call grotesque. Many items chargeable properly to the Canal have been put down to defense. I have suggested that all expenditure on the Canal as a commercial undertaking, should be regarded as a liability to the United States, the burden of which ought to be borne by the traffic passing through the Canal.

On these principles, it should be possible to exhume from the records an accurate statement of what capital has been, in fact, invested in the Canal. Clearly, this should be done. It is a first step in the direction of effective financial management of the Canal as a commercial undertaking. The information could be incorporated in simple statistical tables, published in the annual reports.

In the report on the Panama Canal for the year ending June 30th, 1926, there is no complete statement of income and expenditure. By assembling all the available items, I have arrived, however, at the following result:

GENERAL INCOME STATEMENT

Revenues:
Canal transit revenues:

Tolls	$22,927,456.03	
Taxes, etc., Canal Zone.....	64,128.48	
Postal receipts	143,037.90	
Interest on bank balance....	10,000.00	
Miscellaneous revenues	514.12	
		$23,145,136.53
Canal transit expenses: (A)..	11,038,613.93	
Less incidental earnings.....	3,045,145.46	
		7,993,468.47
Net canal transit earnings...........		$15,151,668.06
Canal business revenues ...$15,874,478.07		
Canal business expenses (A) 15,033,167.78		
Net canal business earnings.........		841,310.29
Net canal earnings.................		$15,992,978.35

I would draw attention, first of all, to the two items, marked (A), and entitled respectively, "Canal Transit Expenses" and "Canal Business Expenses." From those items, the expenditure on defense, whatever it may have been, should be excluded. This would mean that the net revenue of the Canal, namely, $15,992,978.35, would be increased by the total of those amounts and would be greater, therefore, than the sum named.

It is by these steps that we arrive at the final question whether the Canal is really making a profit or a loss; and this is a question to which, as the accounts now stand, no

one can give an answer. For against the net earnings of the
Canal, there are to be debited certain "fixed charges."
These are:

(1) Interest on Bonds and other Capital invested in the
Canal, including initial losses on development.

(2) The Amortization of this Capital.

(3) Depreciation.

Since the investment in the Canal has never been ascertained, the first item is, to this day, indeterminate. It follows that the second item must be indeterminate also.

Depreciation is also indeterminate. Yet, as every business man knows, there could be no more important item in
a balance sheet. Clearly, the operating revenues of the
Canal should be so adjusted as to provide for a reserve, adequate to cover the actuarial estimate of whatever physical
deterioration has been suffered by the Canal as a going
concern. All such obsolescence of plant, inadequacy and
other contingencies should be covered in successive balance
sheets. For by no other method of accounting is it possible to equalize the real burden of the Canal over a suitable period of years, and ensure that this burden falls on the
traffic and not on the taxpayers of the United States.

So far as we are able to gather from the figures, no
account has yet been taken of the payments of $25,000,000
and $10,000,000 made on behalf of the Canal to the Repub-
lics of Colombia and Panama respectively that is, of a
capital expenditure amounting in all to $35,000,000, nor of
the $250,000 of annual rental paid to Panama.

In this chapter, I am content to limit my appeal to one
simple objective, namely, financial lucidity. The appeal may
be summed up and visualized in a draft of the Balance Sheet
for the year ending June 30th, 1926, as it ought to have been
presented. The items entitled "not available" or "incomplete" will emphasize the preceding argument:

GENERAL BALANCE SHEET

Assets

Fixed Capital:

Canal fixed capital..........	Incomplete	
Canal equipment	$4,140,923.88	
Undistributed business capital..	1,813,000.00	
Unamortized operating losses...	Not available	

Total fixed capital.................   Not available

Current Assets:

Cash on hand..............	$2,346,898.87
Cash due treasury...........	193,296.68
Accounts receivable	795,926.04
Stores	4,045,530.67

Total current assets.................	$7,381,652.26
Sinking Fund—Cash and Investments.......	None
Suspense items	(?)
Total assets	Not available

Liabilities

Accounts payable	$1,522,114.00

Reserves as reported:

Unclassified canal credits......$	20,561.02
Depreciation reserve	5,667,204.00
Amortization and sinking fund	
reserve	Insufficient
Repair reserves	1,803,731.42
Gratuity reserves	538,632.72

Total reserves ....   Incomplete

Capital:

Bonds outstanding	Not available
Surplus	" "
Total	Not available

Total liabilities ....   Not available

It is thus a fact, for the years 1914 onwards, that we have no information of the true profit and loss on the Canal. These figures are simply not available, and have to be included in any statement of accounts, merely as a reiterated mark of interrogation. We cannot tell what is the excess of loss over profit during this period of development—an adverse balance which, of course, should be carried into the balance sheet and subjected to amortization. It is this series of omitted statistics which represent the case for financial exactitude in all the departments which are included in the Panama Canal as a commercial enterprise.

An American newspaper has thus referred to the commercial policy of Great Britain:

While Great Britain has maintained freedom of commerce, the Germans have surrounded their territory with tariff barriers and have extended to special interests all sorts of favors in the way of Government-controlled transportation rates and the like. Their aim has been not open competition such as the English have offered, but exclusive trade so far as they have been able to obtain or enforce it. And they are so obsessed by their own ideal that they seem unable to understand that another nation, particularly a rival nation, can have a different one.

We are far from contending that British foreign policy has always been unselfish or free from mean motives. History contradicts any such assumption. But we are persuaded that in the matter of commerce it has more and more nearly approached the highest level of fairness, self-dependence, and faith in the final efficacy of freedom and quality. It will be a great blessing to the world, it will immensely strengthen the chances of general and lasting peace if, at the close of this war, the spirit that has animated the English policy of commerce can be made to prevail.

On the whole, we believe that this tribute represents the facts.

Yet we doubt whether any nation can be trusted to hold

an unrestricted monopoly without temptation to abuse it. The fleecing of the world's commerce by the Suez Canal Company was at one time so grave an injustice that British ship owners themselves talked of financing an alternative waterway. On the Panama Canal, as traffic develops and as debt is amortized, there is a prospect of large surpluses which would enable the suzerain authority to adjust rates. There might arise a danger, indeed, of laying on shipping a burden equal to several times the actual cost of management.

On March 27th, 1928, Senator McKellar proposed a resolution providing for the construction of a canal across Nicaragua at an early date. In his speech to the Senate he said that "it will not take long for the Panama Canal to pay for itself and furnish a very substantial income." These are words which, we think, deserve careful interpretation. We have suggested that the revenues derived from the Canal should provide amply for the amortization of the capital invested in the enterprise, for depreciation of those assets which do depreciate and for the payment of a just interest on the capital outstanding. But we cannot agree that in addition to these charges the United States is entitled to levy tolls calculated to yield a margin in relief of her own taxation. We are sufficiently wealthy as a nation to ignore such opportunities of deriving a profit which is contrary to the true and accurate definition of a public international trusteeship.

It is a principle of public utilities that such rates should be subject to revision by superior authority. In 1915, we read:

The Public Service Commission of the Second District, which has jurisdiction over telephone companies, rendered a decision in the pending New York City telephone rate case yesterday in which it ordered important reductions other than those agreed to by the New York Telephone Company in its statement of March 4, 1915.

The New York Telephone Company accepted this order for a reduction in telephone rates. It was estimated that it would save the customers of the company about $2,700,-000 a year.

Of the same import is the following from a decision rendered by the Public Service Commission for the First District on March 16, 1915:

On and after May 1, 1915, and for a period of three years thereafter, the maximum price to be charged by said The New York Edison Company for electric service furnished by it in the city of New York, exclusive of the installation and renewals of electric lamps, shall be eight cents per kilowatt hour.

The following excerpt from a news item of a metropolitan daily is to the point:

In a statement given out last night by the New York Edison Company it is announced that the cut in the maximum rate will be accompanied by a general revision of all its rates, and so practically all its consumers will get their light and power cheaper. It is reckoned that this will cost the company about $1,750,000.

To collective civilization, it is thus of the utmost importance that Great Britain shall not waive the rights guaranteed to her in the Hay-Pauncefote Treaty. Indeed, we go further.

The United States has a great opportunity at once of disarming suspicion, promoting good will and of setting an example in the keeping of solemn engagements. She would be well advised to ask the Hague Court to appoint an auditing (advisory) committee to represent the interests of collective civilization in this international waterway. Such a committee would safeguard the reputation of the United States and assist the President in fixing rates, within the discretionary limit fixed by the Panama Canal Act, that would be just and equitable to all concerned, nor can we see any reason why there should not be a similar international supervision over the accounts of the Suez Canal.

Such a victory over a misguided pride would go far to release the world from national prejudices and contribute to a broader appreciation of the general interest.

We ought never to lose sight of the fact that, in the nature of things, the Panama Canal must be a monopoly. In the words of Commissioner Roemer of Wisconsin:

That public utilities are virtual monopolies is the principle upon which the Public Utilities Law of Wisconsin is based. The theory that free competition is essential to the public welfare was abandoned and that of regulated monopoly substituted. It cannot be successfully controverted that potential competition has ever been a feeble and inefficient means of enforcing either the common law or the contractual obligations which public service corporations owe the public in respect to charges and service, and that actual competition has almost universally been short-lived and inevitably resulted in economic waste and entailed an unnecessary burden upon the public, as well as financial loss on the investors in the securities of the competing corporations. It would therefore seem that any system of public supervision that may be devised, in order to be just and effective in its operation, should recognize the economic fact that public utilities are natural monopolies, and should protect them from ill-advised and ill-designed competition.

A canal alternative to the Panama Canal is doubtless in prospect. But, even so, it would be a canal owned and managed by the United States. It would be built, not to deprive the Panama Canal of traffic, but to accommodate traffic which exceeded the capacity of the Panama Canal.

An excellent illustration of the principle involved is to be derived once more, from railways. The Public Service Commission of the Second New York District refused a certificate to the Buffalo, Rochester and Eastern Railroad Company to construct a railroad from Buffalo to Troy on the ground that existing facilities were adequate and that duplication of lines where existing facilities were adequate meant either insolvency or excessive rates to pay returns on excess capital. The State of New York has embodied in statute law the unassailable economic principle that the unnecessary duplication of public utilities with ruinous competition as the result, is to be prevented.

If then the Isthmian Highway as a whole must be a monopoly, it is all the more advisable that its financial policy be placed upon the broadest basis of obvious equity.

The arithmetic of the enterprise must include, if only as an academic detail, a valuation of the Canal which would represent a fair purchase. In the case of Suez, Great Britain bought the actual shares owned by the Khedive of Egypt. If the United States failed over the Panama Canal, presumably she would sacrifice the good will, included in the enterprise and the franchise itself. She would be reimbursed her capital expenditure, whatever it had been, whether amortized or not, less whatever had fairly to be deducted for depreciation.

It may be said that the idea of ousting the United States from the Canal is ridiculous. But here again we need to apply analogy. The United States Supreme Court has no power to enforce a judgment against any Sovereign State in the Union. Public opinion in the United States has to attend to that. World opinion might also cause the United States to settle such claims for damages to commerce, for failure to ensure such peace and order in the Canal littoral, as international law and civilization require, and keep the Canal open for use.

VI

RIGHTS AND DUTIES

THE Panama Canal was clearly an achievement that redounded to the glory of the United States, and the nation would not have been human if it had not been proud of so signal a triumph over the obstacles of nature. The fact that American enterprise had succeeded where the projects of Spain and France in turn had failed, only added to the justifiable enthusiasm of our citizens.

Viscount Bryce's tribute was as follows:

There is something in the magnitude and the methods of this enterprise which a poet might take as his theme. Never before on our planet have so much labor, so much scientific knowledge, and so much executive skill been concentrated on a work designed to bring the nations nearer to one another and serve the interests of all mankind.

In no previous age could an enterprise so vast as this have been carried through; that is to say, it would have required a time so long and an expenditure so prodigious that no rational government would have attempted it.

It is no matter for surprise, therefore, that public opinion, thus exuberant, should have regarded the Panama Canal as our own private property and should have assumed that the United States had a right to do with her "ditch" precisely what she pleased. The case of a hotel-keeper was cited as an illustration. Can he not charge what he likes for the use of his rooms and even allow such use, if he wishes, free of charge to his friends? Why should not the same principle apply to a great possession like the Panama Canal?

I confess that there was a time when I myself accepted as axiomatic this claim by the United States to an absolute title to the Isthmian Highway—a claim by its very nature unrestricted, as I supposed, by obligations and conditions. The assumption was plausible, for, after all, if it had not been for the United States, there would have been no canal at all. The assumption was also supposed to be patriotic, and, therefore, it was popular.

But when I began to enquire into the matter and to analyze the claim, as stated here, I came to realize that a possession, supposed to be absolute, may be subject to the terms of treaties, still in force, and to the analogies of history. The ownership of the Canal did not need to be emphasized. It was and it is obvious. But for this very reason the reservations to this as to all ownership should be carefully examined.

To begin with, we are faced by the circumstance, familiar to all lawyers and easily demonstrable by numerous examples, that the conception of an absolute right in property is fast disappearing. Within a sovereign state, the social right that is the claim of collective welfare is coming to be recognized as supreme. We may mention the well-known limitations imposed on the right of property through the police power of the state,—for instance, health and fire regulations wherever there is density of population. Restrictions on the rights of public utilities are to-day almost as thoroughly established as constitutional law.

Even the case of a hotel, just quoted, is subject to qualifications. Every manager of such a hotel knows that he must submit to a code of rules which have been imposed on him in the interests of the community as a whole. If then the Panama Canal be, as in fact it is, a common carrier, it

MIRAFLORES: LOCK-GATES: JULY 5, 1913

must be subject as an enterprise to similar regulations, devised in the common interest.

That is not a complete statement of the problem, and again we may argue from analogy. Let us suppose, for the sake of illustration, that a realty company is developing an interurban property. It gives title to lots with restrictions as to use. In a limited section stores are allowed. In other sections, it allows only private dwellings of a prescribed character. Although owners are given a title in fee, they cannot do with their own lots as they please. Their titles have covenanted restrictions. These must be complied with or damages can be collected in a court of equity.

Limitations, similar in principle to these, have been incorporated in the instruments which define the rights of the United States in the Canal Zone. We have thus to consider, first, the general obligations which must be fulfilled by the Canal as a common carrier and secondly, the special undertakings which may have been included in treatises and agreements.

A railroad is obliged by domestic law to furnish an efficient and a safe service to the public. In return for this service, it is permitted to charge rates which will cover the cost of maintaining the railroad, and, in addition, a reasonable return on the capital invested in the enterprise.

It is such a rate on shipping that, as manager of the Isthmian Highway, the United States is entitled to impose. The yield of the rate should be sufficient to defray the costs of maintenance, the interest on capital invested in the enterprise, the depreciation of assets which do depreciate, and a contribution to other reasonable reserve funds.

To quote Representative Stevens:

The terms of the Hay-Pauncefote Treaty and the existing situation would seem practically and legally to make the United States a corporation sole, for the purpose of constructing, operating, and managing the Canal, with exactly the same rights, obligations and responsibilities which would pertain to any other corporation provided for by the Treaty, doing exactly the same thing under the Treaty.

With entire clarity, ex-President Taft has stated the policy that the United States should pursue:

I believe that the cost of such a government work as the Panama Canal ought to be imposed gradually but certainly upon the trade which it creates and makes possible. So far as we can, consistent with the development of the world's trade through the canal and the benefit which it is intended to secure to the east and west coastwise trade, we ought to labor to secure from the canal tolls a sufficient amount ultimately to meet the debt which we have assumed, and to pay the interest.

In the fixing of tolls, the President is vested with a certain discretion. A maximum and a minimum rate are determined in the Panama Canal Act. The amount imposed on the traffic must cover carrying charges, as that is understood in modern business, as soon as it can be done without exceeding the maximum rate fixed by the Panama Canal Act. The Panama Canal Act is thus in harmony with the view expressed by ex-President Taft.

In the early stages of the Canal as an enterprise, there arose the question whether it was likely to be self-supporting. At first, there were bound to be deficits. A waterway which changes the trade routes of the world must be allowed a period within which to develop its maximum traffic. Owing to the European war, only the coastwise traffic between our eastern and western seaboards was normal during the first ten years of the operation of the Panama Canal. This was appreciably heavier than was estimated, which indicates that when international trade becomes completely normal again, the estimates will be found to have been too low.

Moreover, the Panama Canal does not represent an

absolute monopoly in the worldwide field of transportation. For a certain volume of traffic, there are alternative routes—for instance, the Suez Canal, Cape Horn and the Cape of Good Hope. That such competitive traffic, as we may call it, can only be secured by the Panama Canal if rates are attractive, is probable enough.

But the evidence appears to be overwhelming that, whatever happens to the alternative routes, the Government can control a sufficient minimum traffic to make the Canal profitable. Huebner, in his article on the *Economic Aspects of the Panama Canal,* says:

Canal tolls constitute an important routing consideration only at those distant marginal points which are commercially so located as to bring the canal into direct competition with other routes. Much the larger share of its regular traffic is naturally so tributary to the canal that it would seek the canal route quite regardless of any tolls which might reasonably be charged. In fixing tolls in the future the government will constantly be confronted with the question whether or not it is more desirable to reduce the tolls on all traffic so as to reach out for a somewhat larger share of that small minority of additional vessels which might use the canal if the tolls were lower, than to conserve the revenues by maintaining reasonable tolls and fixing them primarily to that much larger portion of the traffic which the canal now benefits in many ways.

That the Canal, as now capitalized, is self-supporting, goes without saying. With a traffic of 30,000,000 tons annually, I cannot doubt that, if it were capitalized as I suggest it should be, it would still be a financial success. It is true that the Canal would have to meet fixed charges on the whole of the money, genuinely invested in it, including the "military" items which belong properly to its commercial aspect. But the income should be sufficient for this.

In any event, the capacity of the Canal to accommodate traffic is not yet fully utilized. It includes an unused margin of accommodation which is either available or might be made available at a relatively slight cost. The revenue on that additional tonnage, accommodated at current rates may be expected easily to cover the items that would be charged to such revenue, including interest and sinking funds on the capital account, as defined in the last chapter.

Of course, it is not essential that the owner of such a permanent undertaking amortize the investment therein. This is desirable yet optional. An amortized investment is merely a later interest charge avoided. It simply means that larger payments will be made by the earlier traffic and a resulting smaller burden will remain to be borne by later traffic. If the United States decides to amortize its investment in the Canal, it will transmit the Canal to posterity as an unencumbered asset, that is, an asset without any offsetting liability or debt burden.

To sum up the foregoing argument, then, in one general conclusion, I submit that the collection of an adequate revenue to make the Canal self-supporting should be the unbroken policy of the government and that lowering of rates should only be resorted to when revenue yields more than the reasonable return to which the owner is entitled on his investment. Therefore, in fixing tolls, the Government will be wise to disregard the marginal and speculative traffic. Tolls should be fixed solely with reference to adequate revenue as that expression is used in the finance of a public utility.

Again to quote from Huebner:

The rate of toll on merchant vessels is now practically the same at Panama and Suez and the average tolls collected are slightly lower at the former because the measurement rules upon which they are based are somewhat more liberal. While the Suez Canal Company charges a special toll of 10 francs for each passenger on board a vessel in addition to the main tolls based on its net tonnage, no special passenger tolls are collected at Panama. The two great waterways, however, are competitors for but a small portion of the traffic which they handle.

VII

WE have now to envisage the Isthmian Highway as a factor in international relations.

The foreign policy of the United States in so far as it affects the Caribbean has been determined by five landmarks. First, there is the Farewell Address, delivered by George Washington in 1795, and this famous pronouncement may be dealt with, perhaps, by direct quotation. He said:

Observe good faith and justice toward all Nations. Cultivate peace and harmony with all. . . . The great rule of conduct for us, in regard to foreign Nations, is, in extending our commercial relations, and have with them as little *political* connexion as possible. . . . Europe has a set of primary interests which to us have none, or a very remote relation. Hence, she must be engaged in frequent controversies, the causes of which are essentially foreign to our concern. Hence, therefore, it must be unwise in us to implicate ourselves by artificial ties in the ordinary vicissitudes of her politics or the ordinary combinations and collisions of her friendships, or enmities. . . . Why, by interweaving our destiny with that of any part of Europe, entangle our peace and prosperity in the toils of European ambition, rivalship, interest, humour, or caprice?

So was established the policy of disentanglement which, for a quarter of a century, served the purposes of our national diplomacy.

Obviously it was unilateral. The fact that the United States threw off European entanglements did not mean of necessity that Europe, on her side, severed her American entanglements.

Indeed, it rapidly became obvious that, in matters which inherently and of necessity affect the rights and vital interests of other nations, the United States could not expect to play a lone hand. Neither by history, nor by the facts of our situation, nor by our ambitions, were we destined for the rôle of a solitary Colossus, sitting astride the western hemisphere. From the first, we have had to consider the legitimate interests of the rest of the world.

Hence, we have to examine in turn, four further diplomatic instruments, each the logical sequel of the other. They are the Monroe Doctrine, declared in 1823, the Clayton-Bulwer Treaty concluded in 1850, the Hay-Pauncefote Treaty of 1901 and the settlement of the Panama Tolls by President Wilson in 1914. It is to the Monroe Doctrine that we will first devote our attention.

In the nature of things, the Declaration of Independence from England, announced in 1776, could not stand alone. It was followed by a series of similar declarations, covering almost the whole of Latin-America. In the birth of these sister Republics, Spain and Portugal were directly concerned. Indeed, the Old World in its entirety was conscious of a grave challenge to its imperial privileges.

After the defeat of Napoleon in 1815, Europe organized the Holy Alliance in which France was included. Its aim was to "put an end to the system of representative government" and its authors were statesmen of the school of Talleyrand and Metternich. Indeed, it was known as the "Metternich Alliance" and Metternich, a graduate of the school of Macchiavelli, was the canniest and most unscrupulous diplomat of his time.

To this Holy Alliance, Great Britain was opposed. But, none the less, she belonged to the European system and the question arises what part she played in the momentous drama which was so soon to determine the fate of the new world.

We shall examine this question with what we hope will prove to be a detached mind. We shall set out the record as we find it. But on the facts of the case as distinct from whatever may have been the motives of statesmen at any particular moment, we are bound in bare justice to Great Britain to suggest that she played a friendly part. It should be a matter of satisfaction to us that, in matters affecting the western hemisphere, Great Britain suggested in the first instance and has supported, definitely and effectively, the policy of the United States.

Into this outline we have no wish to introduce mere sentiment. Still it is, we think, not inappropriate to insist that American statesmanship of a responsible authority does not encourage a merely small-minded attitude towards the British people. "We lose nothing," said Mr. Hughes, in October, 1927, "in acknowledging when due, our common heritage to the culture of the Old World, especially our indebtedness to the unequalled contribution of England and the Great Bard of Avon."

Similarly, James M. Beck, a representative American of his time who has served as Congressman and *ad interim* Attorney General, has, in his work on the Constitution, told us that this peaceful instrument "has its roots imbedded deep down in the great and heroic past of the English-speaking race."

In the words of Bishop Stires (November 14th, 1927) we hold that "the Declaration of Independence is the child of Magna Carta" and that mere prejudice against England should be dismissed from the mind.

In the year 1822, Castlereagh committed suicide and George Canning was appointed his successor in London as Secretary of State for Foreign Affairs. Of the Holy Alliance, Canning was an avowed enemy and, this being his attitude, he was confronted by an intervention of France into the affairs of Spain. Richard Rush was the United States Minister in London.

On March 31st, 1823, Canning wrote to the British Ambassador in Paris a note in which—as reported by Rush to Washington—he suggested to France that "as His Britannic Majesty disclaimed all intention of appropriating to himself the smallest portion of the late Spanish possessions in America, he was also satisfied that no attempt would be made by France to bring any of them under his dominion, either by conquest, or by cession from Spain." This warning to France that she must keep her hands off Latin-America is, we take it, the beginning of what we now describe as the Monroe Doctrine.

In a report to the Secretary of State at Washington which was despatched on August 19th and received on October 9th, so taking seven weeks in transmission, Mr. Rush tells of an interview with Mr. Canning in which he reminded the British statesman of this intimation to France, "in terms sufficiently distinct" that she "would not be passive" if France tried to seize the Spanish colonies. Mr. Canning, so continues Mr. Rush,

asked me what I thought my government would say to going hand in hand with this, in the same sentiment; not as he added that any concert in action under it, could become necessary between the two countries, but that the simple fact of our being known to hold the same sentiment would, he had no doubt, by its moral effect, put down the intention on the part of France, admitting that she should ever entertain it. This belief was founded he said upon the large share of the maritime power of the world which Great Britain and the United States shared between them, and the consequent influence which the knowledge that they held a common opinion upon a question on which such large maritime interests, present and future, hung, could not fail to produce upon the rest of the world.

Geo Canning

I replied that in what manner my government would look upon such a suggestion, I was unable to say, but that I would communicate it in the same informal manner in which he threw it out.

In diplomatic manner, Mr. Rush then pressed Canning to say—if we may put the point bluntly—whether Great Britain would acknowledge the independence of the new republics.

For Canning, it was a difficult question. He was himself personally in favour of recognition. But he had to deal with a hostile Court, a divided Cabinet, and an unreformed Parliament. It must be remembered that Great Britain was still living under a Hanoverian oligarchy. She had still to advance towards the constitutional liberty which in our own day has included not only a Liberal but a Labour administration. It is the political system to which Britain submitted in 1823 that has to be criticized. Today, as we frankly admit, Great Britain has achieved what is, in many respects, the most democratic government in the world, not even excepting the United States. Responding directly to the electorate, which is practically universal, its executive can be overthrown by the representatives of the people in a day and so subjected to an immediate general election.

To Mr. Rush, asking for recognition of the Latin-American Republics, Canning replied, therefore, that while objecting to their transference to France, he "would not interfere to prevent" their reunion with Spain. He hastened to add, however, that he did not "controvert" the opinion of Mr. Rush that "all idea of Spain ever recovering her authority over the colonies had long since gone by." In saying what he had said, he was not "predicting results" but rather "indicating the feeling which this Cabinet still had towards Spain in relation to this controversy." If the quarrel between Spain and the revolting states should be settled, Britain would ask "to stand upon as favoured a footing as any other country after Spain." The fact was, of course, that Canning well knew that the severance between the Republics and Spain was final. But he was not allowed by others to act on this obvious assumption.

It was under these circumstances that Canning wrote to the United States Minister in London the letter which here follows:

GEORGE CANNING TO RICHARD RUSH

Foreign Office, Aug. 20, 1823

Private and confidential

My dear Sir:—Before leaving Town I am desirous of bringing before you in a more distinct, but still in an unofficial and confidential shape, the question which we shortly discussed the last time that I had the pleasure of seeing you.

Is not the moment come when our Governments might understand each other as to the Spanish American Colonies? And if we can arrive at such an understanding, would it not be expedient for ourselves, and beneficial for all the world, that the principles of it should be clearly settled and plainly avowed?

For ourselves we have no disguise.

1. We conceive the recovery of the Colonies by Spain to be hopeless.

2. We conceive the question of the recognition of them, as Independent States, to be one of time and circumstances.

3. We are, however, by no means disposed to throw any impediment in the way of an arrangement between them and the mother country by amicable negotiations.

4. We aim not at the possession of any portion of them ourselves.

5. We could not see any portion of them transferred to any other Power, with indifference.

If these opinions and feelings are as I firmly believe them to be, common to your Government with ours, why should we hesitate mutually to confide them to each other; and to declare them in the face of the world?

If there be any European Power which cherishes other projects, which looks to a forcible enterprise for reducing the colonies to subjugation, on the behalf or in the name of Spain; or which meditates the acquisition of any part of them to itself, by cession or by conquest; such a declaration on the part of your government and ours would be at once the most effectual and the least offensive mode of intimating our joint misapprobation of such projects.

It would at the same time put an end to all the jealousies of Spain with respect to her remaining Colonies, and to agitation which prevails in those Colonies, an agitation which it would be but humane to allay; being determined (as we are) not to profit by encouraging it.

Do you conceive that under the power which you have recently received, you are authorized to enter into negotiation and to sign any Convention upon this subject? Do you conceive, if that be not within your competence, you could exchange with me ministerial notes upon it?

Nothing could be more gratifying to me than to join with you in such a work, and, I am persuaded, there has seldom, in the history of the world, occurred an opportunity when so small an effort of two friendly Governments might produce so unequivocal a good and prevent such extensive calamities.

I shall be absent from London but three weeks at the utmost; but never so far distant but that I can receive and reply to any communication within three or four days.

I have the honor to be

My Dear Sir, with great respect and esteem

Your obedient and faithful servant

(Signed)   GEORGE CANNING.

R. Rush, Esqr.

The importance of this communication was emphasized by a further letter:

(Enclosure with Mr. Rush's No. 326, August 28, 1823.)
GEORGE CANNING TO RICHARD RUSH

Liverpool, August 23, 1823

Private and confidential

My Dear Sir:—Since I wrote to you on the 20th, an additional motive has occurred for wishing that we might be able to come to some understanding on the part of our respective Governments on the subject of my letter; to come to it soon and to be at liberty to announce it to the world.

It is this. I have received notice, but not such a notice as imposes upon me the necessity of any immediate answer or proceeding—that so soon as the military objects in Spain are achieved (of which the French expect, how justly I know not, a very speedy achievement) a proposal will be made for a Congress, or some less formal concert and consultation, especially upon the affairs of Spanish America.

I need not point out to you all the complications to which this proposal, however dealt with by us, may lead.

Pray receive this communication in the same confidence with the former; and believe me with great truth

  My Dear Sir, and esteem,

   Your obedient and faithful servant,

     (Signed) GEO. CANNING.

R. Rush, Esqr.

It meant that Europe was actually organizing an endeavour to renew her hold over Latin-America.

We take it that these various communications by Canning are a decisive proof that he was the original author of the ideas, embodied subsequently in the Monroe Doctrine. The date of the vital letter, August 20th, 1823, was nearly four months before the doctrine was promulgated.

The negotiations which followed were greatly impeded by the difficulty of communications between London and Washington. On the one hand, Mr. Rush urged Canning to recognize the Spanish Republics. On the other hand, Canning, in a letter to Mr. Rush, dated August 31st, deplored "your want of specific powers" and "the delay which may intervene before you can procure them; during which events may get before us."

Under these circumstances, Mr. Rush, in a letter dated September 15th, and addressed to President Monroe, did not hesitate to speak his mind about Great Britain:

I shall continue to receive in a conciliatory manner his further overtures, should he meditate any; but I am bound to own, that I shall not be able to avoid, at bottom, some distrust of the motives of all such advances to me, whether directly or indirectly, by this government, at this particular juncture of the world.

As regards the principles of traffick and especially as regards the whole range of her foreign trade, we have, it is true, witnessed of late on the part of this nation an approach to more liberality than has governed her heretofore. It is possible that she may go farther in this policy; a policy irresistibly recommended, and, as she will not scruple herself to admit, forced upon her, by the changing circumstances of the commercial world. But, as regards the principles of political freedom, whether in relation to herself or other states, we shall not find it easy to perceive as yet any such favorable alteration in her conduct. Even if there be indications of a coming change in this latter line too, the motives of it are perhaps not all of a nature to challenge our ready confidence and cooperation. We have seen her wage a war of 20 years at a cost of treasure and blood incalculable, in support of independence of other states (as she said) when that independence was threatened by a movement proceeding from the People of France. We have seen her at the close of that contest abandoning the great interests of the people of other states, anxious apparently only about monarchs and thrones. We have seen her at the same epoch become in effect a member of the Holy Alliance; though she could not in form, and continue to abet its principles up to the attack on Naples. Even then the separation was but partial, and, true to her sympathy with the monarchical principle, we find her faith pledged and her fleets ready to interpose not on any new extremity of wrong or oppression to the people of Naples, but on any molestation to the royal family. Since the present year set in, she has proclaimed and until now cautiously maintained her neutrality under an attack by France upon the independence of Spain, as unjust, as nefarious, and as cruel, as the annals of mankind can recount, this attack having been made upon the people of a country, by a legitimate king, urged on by legitimate nobles. It is thus that Britain has been from the very beginning, positively or negatively, auxiliary to the evils with which this Alliance under the mark of Christianity has already affected the old, and is now menacing the new world. It is under this last stretch of ambition that she seems about to be roused, not, as we seem forced to infer after all we have seen, from any objections to the arbitrary principles of the Combination, for the same men are still substantially at the head of her affairs; but rather from the apprehensions which are now probably coming upon her, touching her own influence and standing through the formidable and encroaching career of these continental potentates. She at last perceives a crisis likely to come on, bringing with it peril to her own commercial prospects on the other side of the Atlantic, and to her political sway in both hemispheres. Hence probably some of her recent and remarkable solicitudes. The former war of 20 years more than once shook her prosperity and brought hazards to her existence though for the most part she was surrounded by allies. A second war of like duration with no ally for her in Europe might not have a second field of Waterloo for its termination. Such are the prospective dangers that possibly do not escape her.

The estimate which I have formed of the genius of this government, as well as of the characters of the men who direct, or who influence, all its operations, would lead me to fear that we are not as yet likely to witness any very material changes in the part which Britain has acted in the world for the past fifty years when the cause of freedom has been at stake; the part which she acted in 1774 in America which she has since acted in Europe and is now acting in Ireland. I shall therefore find it hard to keep from my mind the suspicion that the approaches of her ministers to me at this portentous juncture for a concert of policy which they have not heretofore courted with the United States, are bottomed on their own calculations. I wish that I could sincerely see in them a true concern for the rights and liberties of mankind. Nevertheless, whatever may be the *motive* of these approaches, if they give promise of leading to good *effects,* effects which the United States from principle and from policy would delight to hail, I grant that a dispassionate and friendly ear should be turned to them, and such shall be my aim in the duties before me.

In exhibiting the foregoing summary of the opinions which have been impressed upon me during my publick residence in this quarter, I would not have it inferred that I intend they should comprehend the imputation of any sinister motives towards the United States, as peculiar to the British cabinet as it is now composed. I am so far from thinking so that I believe the present cabinet to be as well disposed towards us permanently as any party in England and at this moment more cordially so than any other party. I believe that if Earl Grey and his associates were to come into power tomorrow that we should not get better terms if as good in our approaching negociation should it come on as from Mr. Canning and his associates.

In a further despatch, dated September 20th, Mr. Rush "gave an immediate and unequivocal refusal" to Canning's proposal of an agreement on the basis of a *"future* acknowledgement" by Britain of the Republics; and this negative brought the negotiations in London to a standstill.   On October 10th, Mr. Rush wrote of Britain:

This nation in its collective corporate capacity has no more sympathy with popular rights and freedom now than it had on the plains of Lexington in America; than it showed during the whole progress of the French revolution in Europe or at the close of its first great act, at Vienna, in 1815; than it exhibited lately at Naples in proclaiming a neutrality in all other events, save that of the safety of the royal family there; or, still more recently, when it stood aloof whilst France and the Holy Alliance avowed their intention of crushing the liberties of unoffending Spain, of crushing them too upon pretexts so wholly unjustifiable and enormous that English ministers, for very shame, were reduced to the dilemma of speculatively protesting against them, whilst they allowed them to go into full action.   With a king in the hands of his ministers, with an aristocracy of unbounded opulence and pride, with what is called a house of commons constituted essentially by this aristocracy and always moved by its influence, England can, in reality, never look with complacency upon popular and equal rights, whether abroad or at home.   She therefore moves in her natural orbit when she wars, positively or negatively, against them.   For their own sakes alone, she will never war in their favor.

In describing the "abrupt" postponement of further conversations, Mr. Rush made the comment on British policy:

It is France that must not be aggrandized, not South America that must be made free.

In the words of Henry Cabot Lodge:

In many respects a brilliant man, in all respects a very able man, Canning had larger views and a wider vision than any of the commonplace persons who had been governing England, who were all

Tories of a very narrow kind, and who also had reached a point where they were extremely afraid of being jostled or jarred by new ideas. Canning had never been a friend of the United States. As Canning's biographer, Mr. Philips, says: "He reaped in full measure the reward of those who do the right thing in the wrong way." But Canning was a man who could learn, he disliked the Holy Alliance, and he was now about to do the right thing, and if he had persisted in his original intent he would have done it in the right way.[1]

It is thus that we must interpret the famous declaration by Canning on Dec. 16th, 1826.

Contemplating Spain, such as our ancestors had known her, I resolved that if France had Spain, it should not be Spain with the Indies. I called the New World into existence to redress the balance of the old.

The popular idea that this splendid eloquence on the part of Canning was the birth of the Monroe Doctrine is, of course, mythical. The speech was delivered three years after the Doctrine had been promulgated at Washington. As a matter of fact, the speech suggests that Canning's approach to the public was essentially European and not American.

Let us now turn to what was happening in Washington. Many years afterwards, Senator Calhoun, addressing the Senate, said that Canning's communication to Mr. Rush, when it reached the United States, was received with joy, "for so great was the power of the Alliance that even we did not feel ourselves safe from its interpositions." Said Senator Calhoun:

I remember the reception of the dispatch from Mr. Rush as distinctly as if all the circumstances had occurred yesterday. I well recollect the great satisfaction with which it was received by the Cabinet. As was usual with Mr. Monroe upon great occasions, the papers were sent around to each member of the Cabinet, so that each might be duly apprised of all the circumstances and be prepared to give his opinion. The Cabinet met. It deliberated. There was long and careful consultation and the result was the declaration of the President. All this has passed away. That very movement on the part of England, sustained by this declaration, gave a blow to the Celebrated Alliance from which it never recovered. From that time forward it gradually decayed, till it utterly perished.

So far as we are aware, no authority has suggested that Mr. Rush has any title to share with Canning the credit for the original communication made by Great Britain to the United States. But the reports of Mr. Rush, illuminating as they are, and even fascinating to the historian, indicate that the United States Minister deserves a high place among the diplomats of his period.

Mr. Charles Francis Adams, Sr., moved by a just pride in the achievements of his father, has published a book claiming that John Quincy Adams, then Secretary of State, and later President, was the author of the Monroe Doctrine, as it was ultimately promulgated. It is a controversy to which we should be sorry to add further fuel. But we are bound to point out that it was President Monroe who, in fact, shouldered the responsibility for the Doctrine. Had the results of the Doctrine proved disastrous to the United States, we can hardly suppose that the Adams family would have published books claiming the credit or discredit for their illustrious ancestor. It is remarkable, indeed, that, in the Hall of Fame of the New York University, all the early Presidents, including John Quincy Adams, should have been honoured, except James Monroe, "whose Doctrine"—to quote the *New York World* of May 8th, 1927 —"has had world-wide significance for a century and never more than today." Several times Monroe's name has been submitted for election, but has never yet received the necessary votes!

President Monroe decided to take his predecessors, Jefferson and Madison, into his confidence. In the book setting out the case for John Quincy Adams, in which the diplomatic correspondence has been edited by Professor Ford, it is suggested that this action by Monroe was "unusual." Perhaps it was. But is that a criticism? Rather as it seems to us, it shows that President Monroe realized the grave importance of the situation with which he had to deal. We are all familiar with the view that President Wilson, under circumstances not less critical, would have been wise if he had consulted ex-President Taft or taken Mr. Root or Mr. Hughes with him to Paris.

The fact is, of course, that neither Monroe nor Jefferson and Madison who "sat in" with him and wrote words of approval and encouragement, nor Adams himself, were thinking of personal credit. There was glory enough for all of them.

Still, in a matter far transcending mere routine, there is no evidence that the proceedings were not directed by the President. Professor Ford admits that, when preparing memoranda for the President's annual message, Adams made no mention of Canning's proposition. When, however, he adds that it is not likely that the manuscript of the message is in existence, we can only disagree. We reproduce that original and in the actual handwriting of President Monroe.

Under the direction of the President, Secretary Adams was in charge of the negotiations. There were several other able men who took an active part in the proceedings of the cabinet, among them John C. Calhoun of South Carolina, already quoted, and the Attorney General, William Wirt, from Virginia.

The letter from President Monroe to Jefferson was as follows:

JOHN QUINCY ADAMS

Oakhill October 17th 1823

Dear Sir,—I transmit to you two despatches, which were receiv'd from Mr. Rush, while I was lately in Washington, which involve interests of the highest importance. They contain two letters from Mr. Canning, suggesting designs of the holy alliance, against the Independence of So America, & proposing a cooperation, Between G. Britain & the U States, in support of it, against the members of that alliance. The project aims in the first instance, at a mere expression of opinion, somewhat in the abstract, but which it is expected by Mr. Canning, will have a great political effect, by defeating the combination. By Mr. Rush's answers, which are also inclosed, you will see the light in which he views the subject, & the extent to which he may have gone. Many important considerations are involved in this proposition. 1st Shall we entangle ourselves, at all, in European politicks, & wars, on the side of any power, against others, presuming that a concert by agreement, of the kind proposed, may lead to that result? 2nd If a case can exist, in which a sound maxim may, & ought to be departed from, is not the present instance, precisely that case? 3d Has not the epoch arriv'd when G. Britain must take her stand, either on the side of monarchs of Europe, or of the U States, & in consequence, either in favor of Despotism or of liberty and may it not be presum'd, that aware of that necessity, her government, has seiz'd on the present occurrence, as that, which it deems, the most suitable, to announce & mark the commenc'ment of that career.

My own impression is that we ought to meet the proposal of the British govt, & to make it known, that we would view an interference on the part of the European powers, and especially an attack on the Colonies, by them, as an attack on ourselves, presuming that if they succeeded with them, they would extend it to us. I am sensible however of the extent, & difficulty of the question, & shall be happy to have yours, & Mr. Madison's opinions on it. I do not wish to trouble either of you with small objects, but the present one is vital, involving the high interests, for which we have so long & so faithfully, & harmoniously, contended together. Be so kind as to enclose to him the despatches, with an intimation of the motive. With great respect &c

JAMES MONROE

Recd Oct 23

Jefferson was not slow to appreciate the far-reaching significance of the affair:

The question presented by the letters you have sent me is the most momentous which has ever been offered to my contemplation since that of independence. That made us a nation; this sets our compass and points the course which we are to steer through the ocean of time opening upon us. And never could we embark upon it under circumstances more auspicious. Our first and fundamental maxim should be, never to entangle ourselves in the broils of Europe; our second never to suffer Europe to intermeddle with the cisatlantic affairs.

Under these circumstances, it is no wonder that, whereas Canning's definitive letter had been dated August 20th, it was not until November 29th that the reply of the United States, signed by Secretary Adams, was despatched. It is a pronouncement that clearly defines the attitude of the United States on the points raised:

The first of the *principles* of the British Government, as set forth by Mr. Canning is

1. We conceive the recovery of the Colonies by Spain to be hopeless. In this we concur.

The second is

2. We conceive the question of the Recognition of them as Independent States, to be one of time and circumstances.

We *did* so conceive it, until with a due regard to all the rights of Spain, and with a due sense of our responsibility to the judgment of mankind and of posterity, we had come to the conclusion that the recovery of them by Spain *was hopeless*. Having arrived at that conclusion, we considered that the People of those emancipated Colonies, were of *Right,* Independent of all other Nations and that it was our duty so to acknowledge them. We did so acknowledge them in March 1822. From which Time, the recognition has no longer been a question *to us*. We are aware of considerations just and proper in themselves which might deter Great Britain from fixing upon the same *Time,* for this recognition, with us; but we wish to press it earnestly upon her consideration, whether, after

having settled the point that the recovery of the Colonies by Spain
was hopeless—and after maintaining at the Cannon's mouth, commercial Relations with them, incompatible with their Colonial Condition while subject to Spain, the *moral* obligation does not necessarily
result of recognizing them as Independent States.

"3. We are however by no means disposed to throw any impediment in the way of an arrangement between them and the mother
Country, by *amicable Negotiation.*"

Nor are we. Recognizing them as Independent States we acknowledge them as possessing full power, to levy war, conclude peace,
contract alliances, establish commerce, and to do all other acts and
things, which Independent States may of right do. Among these an
arrangement between them and Spain, by amicable negotiation is one,
which far from being disposed to impede, we would earnestly desire,
and by every proper means in our power endeavour to promote
provided it should be founded on the basis of Independence.[1] But
recognizing them as Independent States, we do and shall justly and
(*provided their accommodation with Spain be founded on that basis*)
necessarily claim in our relations with them political and commercial
to be placed upon a footing of equal favour with the most favoured
Nation.

"4. We aim not at the possession of any portion of them ourselves."

"5. We could not see any portion of them transferred to any other
Power, with indifference."

In both these positions we fully concur.

On November 30th, 1823, Secretary Adams wrote a
further letter to Mr. Rush in which he emphasizes the value
of an agreement with Great Britain, provided that it be
based on a mutual recognition of the Republics:

We receive the proposals themselves, and all that has hitherto
passed concerning them, according to the request of Mr. Canning as
confidential. As a first advance of that character, which has ever
been made by the British Government, in relation to the *foreign*
affairs between the two Nations, we would meet it with cordiality,
and with the true spirit of confidence, which is candour. The
observations of Mr. Canning in reply to your remark, that the policy

[1] This phrase is taken from Monroe's amendments.

of the United States has hitherto been entirely distinct and separate from all interference in the complications of European Politics, have great weight, and the considerations involved in them, had already been subjects of much deliberation among ourselves. As a member of the European community Great Britain has relations with all the other Powers of Europe, which the United States have not, and with which it is their unaltered determination, not to interfere. But American Affairs, whether of the Northern or of the Southern Continent *can* henceforth not be excluded from the interference of the United States. All questions of policy relating to them have a bearing so direct upon the Rights and Interests of the United States themselves, that they cannot be left at the disposal of European Powers animated and directed exclusively by European principles and interests. Aware of the deep importance of united ends and councils, with those of Great Britain in this emergency, we see no possible basis on which that harmonious concert of measures can be founded, other than the general principle of South-American Independence. So long as Great Britain withholds the recognition of that, we may, as we certainly do concur with her in the aversion to the transfer to any other power of any of the colonies in this Hemisphere, heretofore, or yet belonging to Spain; but the principles of that aversion, so far as they are common to both parties, resting only upon a casual coincidence of interests, in a National point of view *selfish* on both sides, would be liable to dissolution by every change of phase in the aspects of European Politics.

The Government of the United States was thus prepared to agree that "a firm and determined stand could now be jointly taken by Great Britain and the United States in behalf of the *Independence of Nations,* and never in the History of Mankind was there a period when a stand so taken and maintained, would exhibit to present and future ages a more glorious example of Power, animated by Justice and devoted to the ends of beneficence."

No reply to a letter, despatched from Washington on November 29th, could have been received until the end of January, 1824. But on December 2nd, three days after the letter had been dated, President Monroe delivered his famous message. The actual words of the "Doctrine" are as follows:

In the wars of the European Powers, in matters relating to themselves, we have never taken any part, nor does it comport with our policy to do so. It is only when our rights are invaded or seriously menaced that we resent injuries or make preparation for our defense. With the movements in this hemisphere we are of necessity more immediately connected and by causes which must be obvious to all enlightened citizens and impartial observers.

. . . .

We owe it therefore to candor, and to the amicable relations between the United States and those powers, to declare that we should consider any attempt on their part to extend their system to any portion of this hemisphere as dangerous to our peace and safety. With the existing colonies or dependencies of any European Power we have not interfered and shall not interfere. But with the governments who have declared their independence and maintained it, and whose independence we have on great consideration and on just principles, acknowledged, we could not view any interposition for the purpose of oppressing them, or controlling in any other manner, their destiny, by any European Power, in any other light than as the manifestation of an unfriendly disposition toward the United States. In the war between these new governments and Spain we declared our neutrality at the time of their recognition, and to this we have adhered and shall continue to adhere, providing no change shall occur which, in the judgment of the competent authorities of this government, shall make a corresponding change on the part of the United States indispensable to their security.

It is impossible that the Allied Powers should extend their political system to any portion of either continent without endangering our peace and happiness; nor can anyone believe that our Southern brethren, if left to themselves, would adopt it of their own accord. It is equally impossible therefore, that we should behold such interposition, in any form, with indifference.

The Monroe Doctrine, implicit at first, was to be defined by the President in precise terms:

The occasion has been adjudged proper for asserting as a principle in which the rights and interests of the United States are involved, that the American Continents, by the free and independent condition which they have assumed and maintained, are henceforth not to be considered as subjects for future colonization by any European powers.

In the message of December 7th, 1824, President Monroe again referred to the Spanish American Republics as follows:

It is impossible for the European governments to interfere in their concerns (South America's) without affecting us; indeed, the motive which might induce such interference in the present state of war between parties, if war it might be called, would appear to be equally applicable to us. It is gratifying to know that some of the powers with whom we enjoy a very friendly intercourse, and to whom these views have been communicated have appeared to acquiesce in them.

The negotiations with Canning had been confidential. But here was an ultimatum, hinted directly at the head of the Holy Alliance, and without any guarantee of support from Great Britain. No free state in the Americas was to be used by Europeans for colonization. None was to be treated as a "springboard" from which a European power could land on our shores.

Of Canning's conduct, the view held by President Monroe seems to have been clear. He held that Canning was not in a position to make a joint declaration with the United States, based on a recognition of the Republics. The official advices, received from Mr. Rush, appeared to indicate that Great Britain was out of the matter.

Whatever view the historian may take of these cross-purposes, there is no doubt as to the result of them. To the United States, there is no more "favored nation" than Great Britain. But the temptation on the part of the United States to sign a formal treaty of alliance with Great

JAMES MADISON

Britain, or for that matter, any Old World nation, passed
with the default at execution of his proposal, by Mr. Canning. Ambassador Houghton and Ambassador Howard,
in behalf of both countries, have, in plain speeches in 1927
—speeches undoubtedly approved by their respective governments and the nations as a whole—disposed of this idea.

The fact that the principle of the Monroe Doctrine
originated with Great Britain is, we submit, of far-reaching
importance. Great Britain is bound, morally and in good
conscience, to respect her own initiative. For without cost
to her government or overt act and without impairing her
position in Europe, she obtained at the time of President
Monroe's message a full value for her enterprise.

In approaching the United States on behalf of Great
Britain, Canning had played the part of no mere altruist.
What had been his diplomatic objectives? He was endeavouring, through the aid of the United States, to protect
Canada from the menace (through Alaska) of England's
prospective opponent, the Russian bear; he was protecting
her West Indian colonies from Spain, backed up by the
"Holy Alliance"; and he was balking France, her traditional
and menacing rival, in other important spheres of policy.
Also, as Judge John Bassett Moore has pointed out, English merchants, like those of the United States, had developed a large trade with the Spanish-American countries—a
trade which, under the commercial system then in vogue,
their restoration to a colonial condition, whether under
Spain or any of the allies, would have cut off and destroyed.
She was, with the aid of the United States, definitely turning
the balance of world power and prestige against her foes
in the "Holy Alliance"; and by Mr. Canning's diplomacy
she succeeded in doing this without entering into any specific
engagement or officially challenging the "Holy Alliance."
This was what Canning meant by his famous statement in

1826—a date subsequent to the Monroe Doctrine by three years—that he had "called the New World into existence to redress the balance of the Old."

The position of Alaska should be fully appreciated. The province was a closely connected part of the Russian Empire. Through it, in 1823, Russia was advancing on Canada and so towards the United States. Great Britain and the United States were thus both threatened by the Russian Empire which might ultimately extend down the coast of North America through what is now California, and connect with Spain and the "Holy Alliance," and encircle not only the British colonies, but the United States, with the forces of the "Holy Alliance," formed to crush out democracies and maintain monarchistic governments throughout the world. This would have eventually embroiled the United States in the dynastic policies of Europe. The proclamation of President Monroe not only halted those "unholy" designs of Russia and the "Alliance," thus preventing perhaps a future world conflict between Monarchical Continental Governments and the two English-speaking countries for control of the Western World, but it eventually resulted in the United States buying Alaska outright. There stands Alaska today—United States territory, growing rapidly in strength and importance and barring the way to any Old World oppression.

Mr. Charles Francis Adams has suggested that President Monroe, in handling the situation in 1823, was "timid." We cannot agree. Imagine the actual situation of President Monroe, after he had gone through all the correspondence with London and with Jefferson and with Madison, and had actually drafted and written his now famous message. It was like representing two armies, acting jointly; Monroe was to hurl an ultimatum at an enemy stronger than the allied combination. To all intents and purposes, committed beyond recall, he looked around for his co-leader and the combined and supporting forces which were to defy continental and monarchical Europe; and both "General" Canning and his forces had disappeared. "General" Canning was over, so to speak, in the French Embassy negotiating to re-establish his relations with his continental friends. Under the circumstances, we submit that Monroe acted with great courage and decision.

What forced his hand appears to have been a communication from Russia. Of this he gives a graphic account in a letter to Jefferson which is among the historic documents of the period:

MONROE TO JEFFERSON

Washington, Decr, 1823

Dear Sir,—Shortly after the receipt of yours of the 24th of October, while the subject treated in it, was under consideration, the Russian minister, drew the attention of the govt to the same subject, tho' in a very different sense from that in which it had been done by Mr. Canning. Baron Tuyll, announced in an official letter, and as was understood by order of the Emperor, that having heard that the republic of Columbia had appointed a minister to Russia, he wished it to be distinctly understood that he would not receive him, nor would he receive any minister from any of the new govts de facto, of which the new world had been recently the theatre. On another occasion, he observ'd, that the Emperor had seen with great satisfaction, the declaration of this govt, when those new govts were recognized, that it was the intention of the U States, to remain neutral. He gave this intimation for the purpose of expressing the wish of his master, that he would persevere in the same policy. He communicated soon afterwards, an extract of a letter from the govt, in which the conduct of the allied powers, in regard to Naples, Spain, & Portugal, was reviewed, and that policy explain'd, distinctly avowing their determination, to crush all revolutionary movements, & thereby to preserve order in the civilized world. The terms "civilized world" were probably intended to be applied to Europe only, but admitted an application to this hemisphere also. These communications were received as proofs of candour, & a friendly disposition to the U States, but were nevertheless answer'd, in a manner equally explicit, frank, & direct, to each point. In regard to neutrality, it was observ'd, when that sentim't was declar'd, that the other powers of Europe had not taken side with Spain—that they were then neutral—if they should change their policy, the state of things, on which our neutrality was declar'd, being alterd, we would not be bound by that declaration but might change our policy also.[1] Informal notes, or rather a proces verbal, of what passed in conference, to such effect, were exchanged between Mr. Adams & the Russian minister, with an understanding however that they should be held confidential.

When the character of these communications, of that from Mr. Canning, & that from the Russian minister, is considered, & the time when made, it leaves little doubt that some project against the new govts, is contemplated. In what form is uncertain. It is hoped that the sentiments expressed in the message, will give a check to it. We certainly meet, in full extent, the proposition of Mr. Canning, & in the mode to give it the greatest effect. If his govt makes a similar decln, the project will, it may be presumd, be abandoned. By taking the step here, it is done in a manner more conciliatory with & respectful to Russia, & the other powers, than if taken in England, and as it is thought with more credit to our govt. Had we mov'd in the first instance in England, separated as she is in part, from those powers, our union with her, being marked, might have produced irritation with them. We know that Russia, dreads a connection between the UStates & G. Britain, or harmony in policy. Moving on our own ground, the apprehension that unless she retreats, that effect may be producd, may be a motive with her for retreating. Had we mov'd in England, it is probable, that it would have been inferr'd that we acted under her influence, & at her instigation, & thus have lost credit as well with our southern neighbours, as with the allied powers.

There is some danger that the British govt, when it sees the part we have taken, may endeavour to throw the whole burden on us, and profit, in case of such interposition of the allied powers; of her neutrality, at our expense. But I think that this would be impossible after what has pass'd on the subject; besides it does not follow, from what has been said, that we should be bound to engage in the war,

[1] To this point in thick lines; showing a change of pen, and presumably a change of time, what follows being written at a later day.

THOMAS JEFFERSON

in such event. Of this intimations may be given, should it be necessary. A messenger will depart for Engld with despatches for Mr.
Rush in a few days, who will go on to St Petersbg with others to
Mr. Middleton. And considering the crisis, it has occurr'd, that a
special mission, of the first consideration from the country, directed
to Engld in the first instance, with power, to attend, any congress,
that may be conven'd, on the affrs of So am: or Mexico, might have
the happiest effect. You shall hear from me further on this subject.

Very sincerely your friend
(no signature)

Endorsed "recd Dec. 11." [1]

It was under this threat by Russia that the Monroe Doctrine was finally formulated.

Not unlike an unwritten constitution, it has been developed, step by step—the one instrument over a thousand
years, the other over a century of rapid progress. It is
our belief that, at this moment, an evolutionary process is
in evidence which will merge the Monroe Doctrine and the
League of Nations into an institution which is neither, and
yet embodies in it the essence of both, that is, organized
co-operation between nations as between constituencies of
nations, to promote collective well-being. The Monroe
Doctrine rests on a recognition of the fact that a nation's
self-interest is dependent on the well-being of contiguous
nations. In any event, as Henry Cabot Lodge put it, "if
Canning could have lived a century longer, he would have
marveled indeed at the extent to which his celebrated declaration had expanded." As Daniel Webster said in the
Senate on April 24th, 1926:

Sir, I look on the message of December 23 as forming a bright
page in our history. I will help neither to erase it nor tear it out;
nor shall it be, by any act of mine, blurred or blotted. It did honor
to the sagacity of the Government, and I will not diminish that
honor. It lifted the hopes and gratified the patriotism of the people.

[1] From the Jefferson Papers in the Department of State, Washington, D. C.

Over those hopes I will not bring a mildew, nor will I put that gratified patriotism to shame.

There arises, finally, the question whether the Monroe Doctrine ought now to be acknowledged as an integral principle embodied in the common law of nations. By Article XXI of the Covenant of the League, it is laid down:

Nothing in this Covenant shall be deemed to affect the validity of international engagements such as treaties of arbitration or regional understandings like the Monroe Doctrine for securing the maintenance of peace.

It is true that the United States is not a party to the Covenant as a whole. But it is also true that Article XXI has been ratified by 53 sovereign Powers of the world, including the Latin American Republics other than Mexico. In February, 1928, there was signed in Washington a new arbitration treaty between the United States and France in which, for the first time in any such document, the Monroe Doctrine was mentioned and thus explicitly recognized. Questions within the Doctrine were excluded from the field of the arbitration contemplated in the treaty.

Of the validity of the Monroe Doctrine and its range, there has been much discussion. On May 30th, 1927, Señor Miguel Cruchaga, as Ambassador for Chile at Washington, spoke on the Monroe Doctrine as follows:

During the last twenty years it has been the chief topic of discussion among Chileans. The general sentiment, among the intellectual leaders of the country, the professors of international law, the members of the Senate and of our Chamber of Deputies and among public men generally is not against it. I am personally of the opinion that it makes the ties between Chile and the United States closer, that it assures mutual cooperation and friendship between our two countries and that it is a standing guarantee of our national independence.

It is true that Chile, unlike the United States, is a member of the League of Nations and that we need European help in the development of our country. It is also true that we speak of Spain as our "mother". But our tie with Spain is now largely a sentimental and cultural one. The United States is our closest relative commercially.

On January 22nd, 1928, Charles Evans Hughes, as the leading delegate of the United States at the Pan-American Conference held at Havana, insisted that there is an economic basis to the solidarity of the New World. The products of Latin America, so he argued, are of a kind that the United States is under the necessity of importing. On the other hand, there has developed in Latin America and particularly in Cuba a strong purchasing power of which the United States is the beneficiary. Since 1914, the exports from the United States to Latin America have increased from 302,000,000 dollars a year to 872,000,000 dollars a year while the imports from Latin America have increased from 435,000,000 dollars a year to 1,094,000,000 dollars.

On the other hand, this appreciation of the Monroe Doctrine is not universal in Latin America and on February 28th, 1928, the dissent was voiced at Geneva by Señor Valdez, the Minister of Argentina at Berne. His precise words were:

I feel bound from the point of view of historical accuracy to enter a protest against the wording of this article. It is really a discussion of a political principle which owes its origin to the days of the Holy Alliance, and which was enunciated as a means of opposing any attempt to carry out a predatory policy in our part of the world.

There is no doubt that the doctrine conferred a great service upon the American peoples in the early days of their existence and in that sense the Monroe Doctrine reflects great honor on the United States which has played so important a part in the history of the world in defense of ideals of liberty and justice. Nevertheless, it is not correct to refer, as Article 21 does, to "regional understandings like the Monroe Doctrine", because the Monroe Doctrine is not a regional agreement in the sense we understand that term. It is a unilateral declaration which could not be assimilated into regional agreements such as we are now discussing.

In his public statement to the Security Commission of the League, Señor Cantilo, the Argentine delegate, speaking on February 29th, 1928, said that "the Monroe Doctrine is a one-sided political agreement which never has been to my knowledge explicitly approved by other American countries."

It happened that at the moment of the pronouncement by Señor Valdez, Dr. Lindolfo Collor of the Brazilian Chamber of Deputies was a guest of the State of Virginia. Reported on March 2nd, 1928, he addressed the General Assembly and said:

Monroe . . . wrote a doctrine not restricted to the United States but (he) also expressed the true universal proclamation of rights that the new world had and has to govern itself without the interference of any foreign power. There is not a country in America which has not in its fight for independence, accepted the great doctrine as an intangible dogma. It does not appear to me as an acceptable and much less as a recommendable judgment that it be established as an international standard in America the possibility of renouncing today that which yesterday was a benefit. To all the Monroe Doctrine has not yet fulfilled its mission. However great are the services that it has given the continent, it will be by its continued reaffirmation that it will show the political character of America. It behooves us who accept it and who, today as in other times, have benefitted by its continental spirit, without a doubt, to cooperate with the United States in all their efforts to make it more and more respected by the rest of the world.

We submit that, after one hundred years of assent to the Monroe Doctrine, the time has come for incorporating its principles in the international jurisprudence of the world.

In the introduction to his great work, Grotius, the father of international law, according to Wheaton (Volume I, page 3) said:

I have used in favor of this law, the testimony of philosophers, historians, poets, and even of orators; not that they are indiscriminately to be relied on as impartial authority, since they often bend to the prejudices of their sects, the nature of their arguments or the interest of their cause; but where many minds of different ages and countries concur in the same sentiment, it must be referred to some general cause.

International Law is thus the product of human initiative, and in this initiative, the United States has played her part.

In a work entitled "International Law and the World War," James Milford Garner, Professor of Political Science in the University of Illinois, refers thus to the "Growth of Written Law of War":

The starting point in this development was promulgated in 1863, in the Instructions for the Government of the Armies of the United States in the field . . . . the instructions thus prepared and issued were distributed to the armies and rigorously enforced. They received high praise from International Jurists, and undoubtedly exerted an important place in the subsequent laws of war . . . . "Thus it was to the United States and to Lincoln," says Baron kMartens, "that the honor belongs of having taken the initiative to define and determine with precision the laws and usages of war."

The late W. E. Hall, one of the most eminent English writers on international law, has said that "the policy of the United States in 1793 constitutes an epoch in the development of the usages of neutrality." We can also point to the leadership of the United States in securing at the Hague Peace Conference of 1907 the adoption of the Porter Convention which forbids states to use armed force in collecting public debts owed by other countries to its citizens.

It would be an immense gain to the cause of peace if the Monroe Doctrine—another product of this country's initiative—could be removed from the category of national assertion and introduced into the category of international sanction. That sanction must be based upon the acceptance by the United States of the responsibilities to the world at large which are involved in the Monroe Doctrine. This logic is inescapable. As Secretary of State, Richard Olney said in effect that the Monroe Doctrine should be interpreted as any matter between individuals. John Hay, Elihu Root, and Charles E. Hughes said practically the same thing. Hay said further that we must follow the Golden Rule in our foreign affairs.

In 1905, Senator Root, when Secretary of State, defined the Monroe Doctrine thus:

It is an assertion of our right for our own interest to interfere with the action of every other nation in those parts of this hemisphere where others are sovereign . . . and to say, if you do thus and so, even by the consent of the sovereign, we shall regard it as an unfriendly act, because it will affect us injuriously. We arrogate to ourselves only the right to protect; what we will not permit the other great powers of Europe to do . . . we will not permit any American Republic to make it necessary for the great powers of Europe to do.

Mr. Charles E. Hughes, as Secretary of State of the United States, speaking at the American Academy of Political Science and the Philadelphia Forum on November 30th, 1923, to celebrate the centenary of the Monroe Doctrine, applied the principles directly to the protection of the Panama Canal in the following words:

We have certain special policies of the highest importance to the United States. We have established a waterway between the Atlantic and Pacific Oceans—the Panama Canal. Apart from obvious commercial considerations, the adequate protection of this Canal—its complete immunity from any adverse control—is essential to our peace and security. We intend in all circumstances to safeguard the Panama Canal. We could not afford to take a different position with respect to any other waterway that may be built between the Atlantic and Pacific Oceans. Disturbances in the Caribbean region are therefore of special interest to us, not for the purpose of seeking control over others, but of being assured that our own safety is free from menace.

By the Monroe Doctrine, therefore, the United States enforces a prohibition on other nations. She says that other nations shall be debarred from using all available methods, as hitherto understood, of protecting the lives and property of other citizens. The right to protect such citizens is a right acknowledged in international law and is strongly insisted upon by the United States herself in cases where her own citizens are concerned. If, then, other nations are to be asked to waive their rights under the common law of nations, it is surely obvious that the United States assumes a responsibility to make good the damages accruing from eventualities which may arise as the sequel to her attitude.

In certain quarters, it has been suggested that the United States should promulgate what has been called a Coolidge Doctrine, restating the Monroe Doctrine, for it would amount to this, by adding a provision that the United States would only intervene in the affairs of a Latin-American Republic after consultation with the other Latin-American nations and presumably approval by them. On this proposal, we would only say that obviously the time has not yet arrived for its serious consideration. A Pan-American Union, inclusive of Canada and organized into a genuine organ of common policy in the New World, may develop in time and perhaps is already developing. It would be in line with those regional compacts which European statesmen of the school of Edouard Benes of Czecho-Slovakia advocate.

In *Foreign Affairs* for April, 1927, Mr. Walter Lippmann, chief editorial writer in the *New York World,* summed up the position thus:

In a hundred years the Monroe Doctrine evolved from the simple prohibition of further colonization through the assumption of an international police power in the Caribbean to an insistence that governments in that region shall be, not only orderly, but friendly to the interests of the United States. This growth of American policy is however an evolution out of the principle of national security, and each new phase of it is consistent with that principle. That other motives played their part, that private interests may at times have created the situation, or made themselves the instruments and the beneficiaries, need not be denied. I shall not discuss here this aspect of what is popularly known as *"Dollar Diplomacy,"* because when in these disputed cases the United States Government acted, it appealed always, and I believe sincerely, to the principle of national security.

VIII

THE Monroe Doctrine may be defined, then, as a second Declaration of Independence, an all-American Bill of Rights or, to quote a phrase used by Representative Begg on Jan. 4th, 1928, as "the Holy Alliance of the New World."

Let us consider then, in practical terms, what has been the influence of the Monroe Doctrine on the destinies of the American nations.

In view of the difficulties, encountered by successive Presidents and their Secretaries of State in the conduct of Foreign Affairs, it is instructive to note how President Monroe's message was received in Congress.

Years before the Monroe Doctrine was promulgated, Henry Clay had been an eloquent advocate of the Spanish-America Colonies—"the eighteen millions of people, struggling to burst their chains and be free." His eloquence had encouraged their armies and no wonder. He said:

"We must pass sentence of condemnation upon the founders of our liberty, say that they were rebels, traitors, before we can condemn the cause of Spanish America. Our revolution was directed mainly against the theory of tyranny. We had suffered comparatively little. Spanish America has for centuries been doomed to the practical effects of an odious tyranny. If we were justified, she is more than justified."

Three years later, as Secretary of State, Clay saw, as he thought, his dream of a Pan-American league of free states coming true. For he had the satisfaction of despatching the

American delegates to the first Pan-American Congress.
This would in itself, he wrote, "form a new epoch in human
affairs." His agile imagination even touched the future
possibilities of the Panama Canal. "If the work should
ever be executed so as to admit of the passage of sea vessels
from ocean to ocean," he instructed the delegates, "the
benefits of it ought not to be appropriated to any one nation,
but should be extended to all parts of the globe upon payment of reasonable tolls."

Henry Clay failed at that time, however, to convince Congress and it was not until 1821 that the United States recognized the Republics.

Towards the Monroe Doctrine itself, Congress was no
more sympathetic.

On the 20th of January, 1824, Henry Clay introduced,
in the House of Representatives, a resolution to the effect
that the people of this country would view with inquietude
the forcible intervention by the Allied Powers, in behalf of
Spain, to reduce the Spanish American States to their
former subjection. This resolution and another of like
tenor did not even receive enough approval to get it out
of the Committee on Foreign Affairs. A majority of the
Committee must have been against it and the Monroe Doctrine thus failed to receive legislative sanction.

Could there be a better illustration of congressional attitude toward the President and State Department in Foreign
Affairs than such a record? We seem to be developing,
in regard to diplomacy, a traditional American policy, quite
different and distinct from the practice of any other nation.
It involves the opposition, at all times, of a sufficient number of senators (usually, but not always or necessarily, of
the opposite party to the President) who embarrass and
obstruct the State Department on any matter involving our
foreign relations, regardless of consequence. In view of the

later history of the Monroe Doctrine, a roll call of the senators and congressmen who opposed the Henry Clay Resolution might be valuable as a warning.

Surely a citizen may be pardoned, in this connection, for observing that, even in a country where statesmen strive for presidential nominations, and parties manœuvre for power, objections to presidential action inspired by partisanship, should "stop at the water's edge." Let us hope that it will some day come to be understood that no statesman can permanently advance himself by embarrassing the government in its foreign relations. It is a plea that we would apply with especial emphasis to the problems affecting the Isthmian Highway.

If the Federal Judiciary, appointed by the party in power, can be divorced from politics, so should the State Department be divorced from politics. As a rule, Presidents, when acting in a grave matter of diplomacy, are not moved by considerations of party. They have to face the public opinion of the world as well as the public opinion of the nation. To harass and obstruct them has been too long a pastime in which both parties have indulged. It seems as hard for a senator or a congressman—considering a small constituency—to approach a problem of foreign policy from a prudential standpoint as it is for a camel to pass through the eye of a needle. And this is the reason why it is recorded that, had the decision rested with Congress, there would have been no Monroe Doctrine at all. The argument that the Doctrine was outside the range of Congressional responsibility is, of course, too flimsy to be worth pursuing.

We have indicated that, in our view, Canning retreated from his original attitude towards the principles of the Monroe Doctrine. We hasten to add that the Doctrine received a support in the House of Commons which was a startling contrast to the coldness of Congress, just described.

At the time of its promulgation, we have Mr. Boughton, a member of the House, declaring:

The question with regard to Spanish America is now, I believe, disposed of, or nearly so, for an event has recently happened than which nothing ever dispersed greater joy, exaltation and gratitude over all the free men of Europe; that event, which is decisive on the subject, is the language held with respect to Spanish America in the message of the President of the United States.

Sir James Macintosh, whose position in the House of Commons was acknowledged, said:

This coincidence of the two great English-speaking Commonwealths (for so I delight to call them—and I heartily pray that they may be united forever in the cause of justice and liberty) cannot be contemplated without the utmost pleasure by every enlightened citizen of the earth.

The stand taken by the American Government, says Professor Moore, in his *International Law Digest*:

gave a decisive support to that of Great Britain, and effectually put an end to the designs of the absolutist powers of the Continent to interfere with the affairs of Spanish America. Those dynasties had no disposition to hazard a war with such a power, moral and material, as Great Britain and the United States would have presented, when united in the defense of independent constitutional governments.

What has been the attitude of Great Britain in more recent years? In 1904, the Duke of Devonshire said in the House of Lords:

"that Great Britain was accepting . . . frankly and without reserve, the Monroe Doctrine, to which the United States seems to attribute so much importance."

In 1902, Lord Cranborne in the House of Commons affirmed that "no nation has endeavored more than England to support the United States in the maintenance of the Monroe Doctrine."

Speaking at Liverpool, the Prime Minister, Mr. Balfour, stated in 1903:

"that the Monroe Doctrine has no enemies in England; that England neither desired colonization nor the acquisition of territory in the Western Hemisphere; that it had not the least intention of concerning itself with the mode of government of any portion of that continent."

We are satisfied that at the present date, no responsible British statesman of 1929 would repudiate these official utterances. Nor is it conceivable that in the future the attitude of Britain will change.

It has to be remembered that the United States has not always been either as important or as powerful as she has become in our own day. It is fair to Great Britain to say that, continuously from the year 1823, when the Doctrine was promulgated, it was understood by the Old World that her Navy stood between the continent of Europe and the principles of the Monroe Doctrine. Accepting and approving the Doctrine, Great Britain has said nothing to dispel the assumption by Europe that her sympathies, if tested, and her power on the sea would be found on the side of an assertion of the Doctrine.

It is a fact doubtless that we need no longer depend on the assistance of any other Power. Yet is there any one, save a madman, who would wish to violate the implied accord of which the Doctrine was the expression? Without friendship, treaties are apt to be "scraps of paper." And apart from treaties, a sympathetic coöperation is invaluable. The alternative is a mere nightmare. If friendly accord and understanding were to be broken down between the United States and Great Britain, a double line of nearly six thousand miles of Alaskan, Canadian and United States fortifications would have to be built. A race of armaments would take place that would make the incidents in Europe preceding the world war look small by comparison. Any such insanity on the part of statesmanship would be curbed, let us hope, by democracy itself.

Let us next consider what exactly has been meant by the enforcement of the Monroe Doctrine.

On November 30th, 1923, Secretary Hughes, with his accustomed lucidity, pointed out that the Doctrine, properly understood, is opposed to:

1. Any non-American action encroaching upon the political independence of the American States under any disguise.

2. Acquisition in any manner of control of additional territory in this hemisphere by a non-American power.

While generally accepted as a policy of defence and not of aggression, the Monroe Doctrine, in the opinion of Mr. Hughes:

. . . is distinctly an American policy, and this government reserves the right to formulate its definition, interpretation and application.

By the Monroe Doctrine in its simplest interpretation, the United States assumed the duty to defend the Latin-American Republics from aggression by any country, whether in Europe or Asia. More than once, our persistence in this policy has been tested by serious emergencies.

In the year 1848, President Polk warned both Spain and Great Britain to refrain from interfering in the controversy between the Republic of Yucatan and the Indians. It was in the Senate debate on the Yucatan Bill that Mr. Calhoun said:

Whether you will resist or not and the measure of your resistance —whether it shall be by negotiations, remonstrance, or some intermediate measure or by a resort to arms; all this must be determined and decided on the merits of the question itself. This is the only wise course. . . . There are cases of interposition where I would resort to the hazard of war with all its calamities. An. I asked for one? I will answer, I designate the case of Cuba.

It is enough to add that the warning was effective.

In 1861, Secretary Seward protested to Spain against the occupation of Santo Domingo and, once more, the warning was effective.

During those sixties, there arose a more serious crisis, affecting the Doctrine. The Union was rent in twain by Civil War. Even Great Britain in her official capacity sympathized with the South. Like New York City, the British were moved by reasons of business, for it was the South that supplied the great mills of Lancashire with cotton. Britain's motive was thus not so much to damage the Monroe Doctrine as such, but rather to assist the plantations on which she depended for raw material.

The fact remains, however, that Great Britain was found again flirting with countries on the continent of Europe— Spain, France and an unofficial Austria—which, contrary to the Monroe Doctrine, were desirous of intervention in Mexico.

The Emperor of Austria was anxious to strengthen the throne of his brother, Maximilian, who had been declared Emperor of Mexico, with the active support of France. In his *International Law Digest,* Professor Moore tells the story of what happened:

About the middle of July, 1860, the British Government, through Lord Lyons, its Minister at Washington, invited the United States to join Great Britain and France in addressing an identic note to the Miramon and Juarez governments of Mexico, advising the calling of a national assembly to settle their domestic difficulties upon some reasonable basis. This invitation was submitted to President Buchanan, and in due time Lord Lyons was advised that the general policy of the United States was "opposed to any interference, especially any joint interference, of other powers in the domestic affairs of an independent state."

It appears that after Lord Lyons delivered the invitation above mentioned, the French *Chargé d'Affaires* made a similar communication to the Department of State and, while giving an assurance that France had not the slightest idea of resorting to force in the matter, added that if the rights and interests of French citizens should be violated in Mexico, the government of France would feel at liberty to adopt such measures as might be deemed expedient. In reply Mr. Cass declared:

the permanent occupation of any part of the territory of Mexico by a foreign power, or any attempt in any manner forcibly to interfere in its internal concerns or to control its political destiny, would give great dissatisfaction to the United States. The policy of the United States on this subject was well known to all the powers in the question, and it should be "adhered to under all circumstances."

The British intervention may be dismissed, perhaps, as a diplomatic gesture. At an early stage of the business, England withdrew from it and without having committed any overt act. The venture was thus left to France, supported by the moral backing of Austria-Hungary.

We continue to quote from Professor Moore:

Toward the end of 1861 naval vessels of England, France and Spain sailed for Vera Cruz, with the avowed intention of taking possession of the custom houses of two or three Mexican ports for the purpose of satisfying the claims of their respective governments. Within a few weeks after the arrival of these ships and before the Allies had done much more than seize Vera Cruz, the English and Spanish commanders became dissatisfied with the course of the French. The English and Spanish forces withdrew in April, 1862, after an agreement had been reached with Mexico as to the claims of their governments. The triple alliance was thus dissolved. In spite of the fact that the three European powers had agreed to respect "the rights of the Mexican nation to choose and constitute freely the form of its government," the French, after the English and Spanish had retired from Vera Cruz, presented an ultimatum demanding payment of $27,000,000 and soon afterwards began a forced march toward the City of Mexico, which they entered in June, 1863. They then set up a provisional government, and later named an assembly of notables, which was almost exclusively composed of the enemies of the Juarez Constitutional Government. In July, 1863, the assembly met and without debate resolved, with only two dissenting votes, that an Empire should be established, that the throne be offered to the Archduke Maximilian of Austria, brother of Francis Joseph, and that if he should decline it, the Emperor of France should be asked to fill the vacancy. Maximilian expressed his willingness to accept, on certain conditions, and on April 10th, 1864 he finally accepted the crown. On the same day a convention was entered into between France and the Imperial Government, by which the latter agreed to pay the French claims and the past and future cost of intervention, under certain conditions, and France practically guaranteed Maximilian her military protection. He entered the City of Mexico in June, 1864, as Maximilian I.

The reports of Baron Wydenbruck, the Austrian Ambassador to the United States in 1866, recently unearthed in the Archives of the old Austrian Government by Professor Otto Ernst of Vienna, are interesting as giving the Austrian account of an episode in which the Austrian Government was supposed to have had no part. Said Baron Wydenbruck in a report of February 13, 1866:

Your Excellency will certainly remember that in my report of the 13th of last month I had the honor to describe the hostile attitude of the (American) Congress towards His Majesty, the Emperor Maximilian. Today I have the painful duty to report to your Excellency an analogous incident, but one of a far graver nature.

A short time ago, February 12 (that is yesterday), was fixed by the Senate as the memorial day in honor of the late President Lincoln. This solemnity was celebrated with the greatest possible splendor. The President of the United States, the Cabinet, the high officials of the State and the elite of the population participated. The foreign ambassadors, who received special invitations from the official heads of the Senate and of the Second Chamber, as well as from the Secretary of State, occupied the seats opposite to the tribune. The orator chosen by the Senate to eulogize Mr. Lincoln was Mr. Bancroft, former American Ambassador in London and subsequently Secretary of the Navy.

Mr. Bancroft, in a speech which seemed more like a review of recent political events than a panegyric of the late President, and in which he deemed it necessary to address sarcastic and bitter reproaches at those Governments whose representatives had been involved there, touched upon the Mexican question. I could scarcely believe my own ears, when I heard the speaker . . . several times call His Majesty, the Emperor of Mexico, first "the Austrian adventurer" and then "the adventurer Maximilian." Startled by the brutality of these terms, I was on the point of rising and leaving the hall. I did not do so only in view of the solemnity of the occasion and of the presence of the President of the United States.

Although I was resolved to make immediate protest because of the insult committed against the person of an august member of our imperial family, I thought it expedient to postpone this step until the next day, hoping that the President of the Senate or the Secretary of State would take the initiative and express their regret and disapproval of this occurrence. A few hours later I partook of a dinner given by the Prussian envoy, to whom I expressed my perplexity over the incident in the Senate. Mr. Seward was also among the guests. One moment before leaving the table Baron de Gerold (the Prussian envoy) came to me and persuaded me to occupy his seat beside the Secretary of State, to whom, as he said, he had mentioned my impression caused by the words of Mr. Bancroft. I was forced to accept his invitation and to talk to Mr. Seward about this matter. We were left alone. I commenced to tell him how painfully I was affected by the offensive expressions of Mr. Bancroft against the brother of my Sovereign. Mr. Seward quickly interrupted me, declaring that I had no right to complain of whatever had been said of the *Archduke* Maximilian, as the Viennese Government had declared its complete disinterestedness in Mexican affairs. I answered: "Yes, politically, but this abstention of my Government does not change the position of the Emperor Maximilian as a member of the Imperial family; and the Austrian Ambassador is entitled to protest against every insult against his person." The conversation lasted a few more minutes, remaining within this circle of ideas; and I must add with regret that Mr. Seward did not find one alleviating word; on the contrary, he seemed to approve of the conduct of Mr. Bancroft. He concluded in a most uncivil manner, saying: "I have nothing to do with the affair and Maximilian must quit Mexico." As I perceived the tone Mr. Seward used, I dropped the subject.

When the Austrian Emperor saw that the United States was resolved to enforce the Monroe Doctrine, he preferred to abandon Mexico "voluntarily" and informed Maximilian of this intention. Nevertheless, he tried to find a way to enable Maximilian to maintain his "empire," perhaps because he hoped that it would be possible to resume the Mexican enterprise later on.

Before he decided to evacuate Mexico, Napoleon wrote to Maximilian as follows:

I should like to point out to your Majesty the advantage which could be derived if your Majesty would organize a real army of Austrian troops. Then I could withdraw the greater part of my troops and *the American protest* would lose its force. . . . I request your Majesty to consider this possibility thoroughly; as for me, I see in this combination the best chance to strengthen your throne.

Baron Wydenbruck wrote on April 25, 1866, as follows:

Before the present report arrives in Vienna, your Excellency will be undoubtedly informed by Mr. Motley (the Ambassador of the United States in Vienna) of the unexpected phase into which the relations between our country and the United States have entered, because of the Austrian enrolments for Mexico. In the European mail of yesterday Mr. Seward sent an order to Mr. Motley to demand his passports the moment the first ship leaves the port with troops for Mexico and to notify the imperial Government that I receive my passports also, when this news arrives here.

In the evening of the same day (that is, yesterday evening) Mr. Seward declared himself in the presence of several persons literally in the same sense. One of the persons to whom I owe this communication added that the scornful frivolity of the tone with which Mr. Seward expressed himself, particularly in addressing Mr. Romero, the agent of Juarez, formed a singular contrast to the gravity of the subject, wherein nothing less is at stake than political rupture with one of the greatest Powers of Europe.

For several months I have not failed to keep your Excellency well informed about the tendency of the public sentiment to regard Austria as an enemy in the Mexican question. But I must confess that I was far from being prepared for the violence with which the Federal Government has acted in this matter: a violence which contrasts strangely with the prudence and reserve deemed necessary when negotiating the same question with France. France, however, in the eyes of this country, by reason of her proximity and her strong navy, is an enemy much more formidable than Austria—an essentially continental power.

This sudden change in the attitude of the Washington Government must be attributed to several causes. The first of these (as I had the honor to inform you in my last report) is the encouragement which they won for the recent concessions made by France to the demands of the American Government. These concessions are interpreted here in a most flattering sense, as a proof of the irresistible power of the United States. On the other hand, the conflict between the Government and the Congress, as well as the growing unpopularity of the President and the Secretary of State, induce them to make an effort to divert public attention from internal affairs and to regain popular favor by making some great political demonstration. Finally, the imminence of the Prussian war, which—this I can positively assert—has been greeted in advance with the greatest satisfaction by Mr. Seward, and which is limiting the liberty of action of Austria, seems to offer the occasion for which he has long been looking.

The arrogant behavior of Mr. Seward excludes all possibilities of negotiation over the present question, and I must wait until I receive my passports, if your Excellency does not give me in time an order to demand them myself so as to spare the envoy of Austria from the humiliation which menaces him now.

Facing this foreign and formidable defiance of the Monroe Doctrine, the country became, to some extent, united on its foreign policy, and the House of Representatives in 1864 voted unanimously that:

The Congress of the United States are unwilling by silence to have the nations of the world under the impression that they are indifferent spectators of the deplorable events now transpiring in the Republics of Mexico, and that therefore, they think fit to declare that it does not accord with the policy of the United States to recognize any Monarchial government erected on the ruins of any republican government in Mexico under the auspices of any European power.

In 1865, after the conclusion of the Civil War, 100,000 American troops were sent to the Texas frontier, and in November of that year our Minister in Paris was instructed to say to the French Government that the

presence and operations of a French army in Mexico and its maintenance of an authority there, which rested upon force and not the free will of Mexico, is a cause of serious concern to the United States—they still regard the effort to establish permanently a foreign imperial government in Mexico as disallowable and impractical.

In February, 1866, Mr. Seward demanded that the French troops set a time when they would withdraw. The French troops were reluctantly and unwillingly withdrawn.

This, as we suggest, was the crisis in which the Monroe Doctrine was most severely tested. In 1861, Secretary Seward had been compelled to admit the right of France to make war on Mexico and an army of 40,000 French troops had been actually landed on Mexican soil before the United States felt herself to be in a position to resist. A condition, imposed on France by Secretary Seward, was however that any government, set up in Mexico, should not be contrary to the principles of the New World. To this condition, France agreed and it was because the United States was not satisfied with the fulfilment of the condition that, at a later stage, she resisted the aggression. Under General Sheridan, an army of 100,000 men was organized and a navy was available in support of it. The French were informed that they must leave Mexico and they thought it well to acquiesce in what was substantially an ultimatum. In the words used by Secretary Seward in 1865:

It has been the President's purpose that France should be respectfully informed upon two points, namely: first, that the United States earnestly desires to continue and to cultivate sincere friendship with France; secondly, that this policy would be brought in imminent jeopardy unless France could deem it consistent with her honor to desist from the prosecution of armed intervention in Mexico to overthrow the domestic republican government existing there and to establish upon its ruins the foreign monarchy which has been attempted to be inaugurated in the capital of that country;

It was the last occasion when European armies effected an entrance on to Mexican soil.

We cannot but think that the handling of this affair by President Johnson, with whom was associated Secretary Seward, was a greater service to the country than the impeachment which was instigated against him by his critics.

It is possible to mention two occasions on which the Doctrine was applied to prevent what has come to be called the peaceful penetration of American territory by non-American powers. In 1848, Secretary Buchanan said:

The highest and the first duty of every independent nation is to provide for its own safety; and acting upon this principle, we should be compelled to resist the acquisition of Cuba by any powerful maritime state, with all the means which Providence has placed at our command.

In the following year, the warning was repeated by Secretary Clayton:

The news of the cession of Cuba to any foreign power would be in the United States the instant signal for war. No foreign power would attempt to take it that did not expect a hostile collision with us as an inevitable consequence.

Against negotiations for the sale of Cuba by Spain to France, Secretary Clay protested and, in consequence of these protests, France discontinued these negotiations.

The second illustration is not less instructive. A corporation purchased a tract of land in lower California proposing to work it with Japanese labour. The Government of Japan appeared to have no association with the project which therefore did not lead to an international incident. However, the principles of the Monroe Doctrine were jealously guarded by the Lodge Resolution of 1912, disapproving of the Colony, even as a private enterprise.

It will not be suggested that we entertain suspicions of Great Britain. Our view is that, in reference to the Panama Canal, she has played no unfriendly part. We must mention, however, a suggestion, appearing in January, 1927, that Britain might move her Naval Base in the West Atlantic from Bermuda to the West Indies—that is, the Caribbean. That Great Britain, like the United States, has special and substantial interests in the Americas—indeed, that she is the only European Power of which this is the fact— cannot be denied. Her interests, including her dominions and dependence on oceanic transit are, in a sense, as great as ours. If, however, she were to add a naval base in these regions to her present coaling and supply station at Bermuda, a situation, involving the Monroe Doctrine, undoubtedly would arise. It is not our belief, however, that Great Britain meditates any such challenge.

President Roosevelt in his message to Congress on December 5th, 1905, expresses the following warning:

That our rights and interests are deeply concerned in the maintenance of the Doctrine is so clear as hardly to need argument. This is especially true in view of the construction of the Panama Canal. As a matter of self defense we must exercise a close watch over the *approaches* to this canal; and this means that we must be thoroughly alive to our interests in the Caribbean.

The extent of British intervention under the Monroe Doctrine—for instance, the threat in 1861 to seize the customs houses of Mexico at Vera Cruz—has been slight and diminishing. The United States on her side has found ways through her bankers to cover claims on Latin-American Republics for debt or damage, the United States herself supervising the customs while the claims were being satisfied. We have recognized, as President Roosevelt would have said, that if we do not use "the big stick" when needed, other nations will demand the right to wield that weapon.

Here, then, we have in outline the body of precedent on which the Monroe Doctrine is based. We might have quoted at length from the masterly address delivered by Mr. Root in 1914 as President of the American Society of International Law, from the *International Law Digest,* of Professor John Bassett Moore, the United States Judge at the Hague, from Secretary Hughes and Chief Justice Taft's book on *Peace and War*. But, in general terms, we submit that the Monroe Doctrine, estimated with a "decent respect for the opinion of mankind," has now the force, if not the technical basis of international law.

The first essential to be appreciated was stated by Secretary Root in 1914; and with a classic authority:

> The Doctrine is not international law, but it rests upon the right of self protection and that right is recognized by international law. The right is a necessary corollary of independent sovereignty.

The Monroe Doctrine is not, in itself, recognized as international law but is based upon that right of self-defence which is a well established principle of international law.

As Professor Charles Cheney Hyde puts it:

The present importance of the Monroe Doctrine is derived, as Sir Frederick Pollock has pointed out, from continuous and deliberate approval of it by the Presidents of the United States. The doctrine, he declares, . . . is a living power because it has been adopted by the Government and the peoples of the United States, with little or no regard to party divisions for the best part of a century. (The Monroe Doctrine, Senate Document No. 7, 58th Congressional Sess. reprinted from the Nineteenth Century, October 1902.) It is the resolute, and what has come to be the habitual attitude expressed in behalf of the United States whenever the conduct of non-American States threatens to disregard the obligations of non-interference and of abstinence from acquisitions of territory, which it has sought to impose that sustain and invigorate its claim. The acquiescence of non-American States together with the devotion of the United States to the principles on which it rests, have united to cause the Monroe Doctrine to be regarded as a reasonable and lawful basis of restraint. Such a result could not have occurred had not the application of that doctrine wrought justice for the Western Hemisphere and done no harm to States outside of it.

It is not on force but on consent that the Doctrine has been based. As Representative Begg said on January 4th, 1928:

"It has been respected by the powers of the Old World, both great and small, since the day it was pronounced as the foreign policy of the United States.

"When President Cleveland said to Great Britain, the greatest sea power on the face of the earth, 'The peace of the world would be more secure if that government kept out of Central American affairs,' he had not a navy large enough to beat a good sized fleet of fishing smacks. But his commands were respected by Britain.

"The next serious threat against the sovereignty of the Monroe Doctrine was when Germany, which boasted the greatest military machine ever assembled in the history of the world, sent a fleet of war-ships to Venezuelan waters. Theodore Roosevelt gave the Kaiser a limited number of hours in which to withdraw those ships.

"Roosevelt had a navy no larger than Cleveland did, his army was less than 100,000 men, no match for the powerful war machine of the German War Lord, but his refusal to be bullied commanded the respect of the greatest military machine this world ever saw and the German fleet withdrew."

After a century of application, the authority behind the Monroe Doctrine is unsurpassed by that of any recognized principle by which international relations are guided.

The formal denial of the constitutional legality of the Doctrine lays the United States open to the suggestion that, acting outside the law, she is asserting merely her own interest without accepting a corresponding obligation to mankind as a whole. Until such arrangements, including the international conscience itself, is brought under the majesty of the law, there can be no permanent security.

As a matter of record, there has been one occasion, at least, when the Monroe Doctrine was declared on high authority to be international law. In 1895, President Cleveland delivered a Special Message to Congress. He was himself a lawyer of eminence. His Secretary of State was that eminent lawyer, Richard Olney. President Cleveland said:

"Practically the principle for which we contend has peculiar, if not exclusive relation to the United States. It may not have been admitted in so many words to the code of international law, but since in international councils every nation is entitled to the rights belonging to it, if the enforcement of the Monroe Doctrine is something we may justly claim, it has its place in the code of international law as certainly and as securely as if it were specifically mentioned; and when the United States is a suitor before the high tribunal that administers international law the question to be determined is whether or not we present claims which the justice of the code of law can find to be right and valid.

The Monroe Doctrine finds its recognition in those principles of international law which are based upon the theory that every nation shall have its rights protected and its just claims enforced."

GROVER CLEVELAND

Time has certainly not weakened the international principle laid down by President Cleveland any more than it has weakened the position in international affairs, of the United States. The proposition has been fortified, year by year, as a result of numerous diplomatic incidents; treaties, international conferences and agreements, such as the Covenant of the League of Nations; reservations by the United States, accepted internationally as a pre-requisite to entrance into the World Court of International Justice, and the recently renewed United States French Treaty. The Monroe Doctrine cannot, therefore, now be successfully challenged as a principle of Regional International Law, but must be reckoned with and respected by other nations, as actually as the provisions of the constitution itself of the United States. In fact, the principle underlying the Monroe Doctrine is now applied by Great Britain to her own far flung Empire.

At the same time, let us not be misunderstood. What experience and each succeeding diplomatic incident has demonstrated has been the obvious fact that the Monroe Doctrine, though emphasized in its authority, has been limited in the scope of its application to the section affecting the approaches to the Isthmian Highway, and the International Trusteeship of the United States in connection therewith; to the Caribbean Sea, to the West Indies and the Central American countries in the Zone of the Canal Littoral; to the responsibility, in short, of the United States, in the matter of order and sanitation in that well defined region.

Probably one reason why the Monroe Doctrine has not been generally acknowledged as international law, in spite of almost world-wide recognition of its basic principles, is that it has been differently interpreted and expanded by various Presidents and Secretaries of State.

The Doctrine depends on three arguments, first, the continuous insistence of the United States; secondly, the continuous acquiescence of the world at large; and thirdly, the fact that the Doctrine has not been so enforced as to create grievances.

If it is suggested that the Doctrine is an anomaly we may reply that it is an anomaly due to other anomalies. The world is not uniform nor is it administered on a uniform system of sovereignty.

There are various regional principles of international usage and law, which the world, as a whole, acknowledges and respects, and of which it takes, so to speak, judicial notice. There are, for instance, or there have been regions of the Old World in which monarchical, dynastic, and autocratic systems still exist and extend themselves—regions wherein government is from a crown downward, instead of from the people, in a democratic and directly representative manner, upward, with the consent of the governed. That is the accepted international usage and law as to that region, though the system is actually repugnant to the usages and customs of the New World. The United States has been compelled therefore to adjust its foreign affairs to a regional principle, already confronting her.

As an illustration, let us take an extreme case. Suppose that the Hohenzollerns, Hapsburgs, Wittelsbachs, Romanoffs, or Turkish Sultans were to be re-established as absolute rulers on the continent of Europe and in Asia, international law, growing out of custom and usage—and usage and custom eventually become regional law—would require that such a condition be treated as internationally and diplomatically acceptable to the nations of the New World. Such governments might not be approved but according to the terminology of international law they would have to be "recognized."

Now, it happens that the opposite governmental principle
—namely, democracy—is basic in the Western Hemisphere.
For one hundred years, therefore, the world has accepted
that basic principle as applying to government in the regions
of the New World.   Both conditions—the autocratic and
the democratic—are internationally lawful in a regional
sense, and in that sense, both are universally accepted by
responsible diplomacy.

In 1914, Senator Root declared:

> The scope of the Doctrine is strictly limited.   It concerns itself
> only with the occupation of territory in the New World to the
> subversion or exclusion of a preexisting American government.   It
> has not otherwise any relation to the affairs of either American or
> European states.   In good conduct or bad, observance of rights or
> violations of them, agreement or controversy, injury or reprisal,
> coercion or war, the United States finds no warrant in the Monroe
> Doctrine for interference.

Over the interpretation and enforcement of the Monroe
Doctrine, the United States has claimed and asserted a sole
jurisdiction.   It is a jurisdiction which has been safeguarded
with the utmost care.

In the first Hague Conference, the United States signed
the treaty of Arbitration which is to-day in force, with the
express reservation (which other powers unanimously
accepted):

> That nothing contained in this Convention shall be so construed
> as to require the United States of America to depart from its
> traditional policy of not entering upon, interfering with or entang-
> ling itself in the political questions or internal administration of any
> foreign State, nor shall anything contained in the said Convention be
> so construed as to require the relinquishment by the United States
> of America of its traditional attitude toward purely American
> questions.

Secondly, it is pertinent to repeat that in Article 21

of the Covenant of the League of Nations, most of the
States of the world have expressly recognized the Monroe
Doctrine and recognized it as an instrument for *"securing
the maintenance of peace."*

The circumstance that the Covenant was not ratified by
the Senate is merely incidental to the present argument.
The Treaty had been negotiated by a President of the
United States and signed by him.   In its allusion to the
Monroe Doctrine, it expressed the tradition which this
country has maintained since 1823.

On March 22, 1920, by a vote of 58 to 22, the Senate
adopted the following reservation, which was substantially
the same as the one that had been adopted the previous
November:

> The United States will not submit to arbitration or to inquiry by
> the assembly or by the council of the League of Nations, provided
> for in said treaty of peace, any questions which in the judgment of
> the United States depend upon or relate to its long-established policy,
> commonly known as the Monroe Doctrine; said Doctrine to be
> interpreted by the United States alone, and is hereby declared to
> be wholly outside the jurisdiction of said League of Nations, and
> entirely unaffected by any provision contained in the said treaty of
> peace with Germany.

Except for the brief mention in the Senate Resolution
of January 27, 1927, consenting to adhesion to the World
Court, this is the last official declaration made in regard
to the Monroe Doctrine, and with marked brevity it
declares the attitude of the United States.   If we ever join
the World Court of International Justice, or the League
of Nations, it should be only with an express reservation
as to that Doctrine, which should be affirmatively accepted
by the other members of the Court or by the League, as
a condition of our entrance.

IX

ORDER IN AMERICA

WE have seen that, by an unbroken record, extending over more than a century, presidents of the United States, Republican and Democrat, have supported the essential principles of the Monroe Doctrine and adapted it to circumstances. To this accepted principle, we must now apply what Chief Justice White in the Standard Oil Case has called "the rule of reason." On the anniversary of 1923, we indulged—and naturally—in a grand oratorical pæan of praise of the Doctrine. But the highest compliment that we can pay to President Monroe's message is to try to understand it in all its bearings.

As the sole trustee of the Monroe Doctrine, the United States has had a delicate duty to perform. It has not been only a problem of defending the Americas against European aggression. Indeed, this aspect of the case has receded somewhat into the background. To quote former President Taft:

In other words, the extent of our intervention to enforce the policy is a matter of our own judgment, with a notice that it may cover all America. It therefore follows that the Monroe Doctrine, as it applies to Argentina, Brazil and Chile, the so-called A B C governments of South America, is now never likely to be pressed, first because they have reached such a point that they are able to protect themselves against any European interference, and, second, because they are so remote from us that a violation of the doctrine with respect to them would be little harmful to our interests and safety.

The great republics, to which Mr. Taft alludes, are now standing firmly on their own feet. But there remain those problems of law and order which cannot be so briefly dismissed.

It is undeniable that the shores and islands of the Caribbean include some of the most disturbed territories on this planet. In their case, there arise problems of law and order which cannot be summarily dismissed. Of these smaller republics, Mr. Hughes, speaking at the Pan-American Conference of February, 1928, said:

Independence is not enough. Independence gives opportunity but stability is essential to take advantage of it.

It is idle to talk of the independence of a republic when the republic itself is in abeyance. In January, 1928, the realities of such a case were recognized even by so stalwart a member of the British Labour Party as Mr. H. N. Brailsford who, speaking at Washington, was reported as saying that no arbitration treaty could meet the problem of dealing with unorganized governments or governments considered to be below the condescension of great powers.

The case against intervention was developed early in the present century by Senor Luis M. Drago, then Foreign Minister in the Argentine. He urged that no American state should be subjected to armed intervention or occupation as a means of collecting a foreign debt. Dr. Pueyrredon, Argentine Minister at Washington, broadens the claim into the sentence that "no state may intervene in the internal affairs of another." He holds that "when a citizen leaves one country and goes into another he goes at his own risk."

The true principle was stated in 1916 by the American Institute of International Law, meeting at Havana under the presidency of Mr. Elihu Root. What Mr. Hughes has described as a "Magna Carta for the Western Hemisphere" reads:

"I think that if people want to invest their money outside their own country they should accept the risk involved. Why should the American people have to protect them?"

1. Every nation has the right to exist and to protect and conserve its existence; but this right neither implies the right nor justifies the act of the state to protect itself or to conserve its existence by the commission of unlawful acts against innocent and unoffending states.

2. International law is at one and the same time both national and international; national in the sense that it is the law of the land and applicable as such to the decision of all questions involving its principles; international in the sense that it is the law of the society of nations and applicable as such to all questions between and among the members of the society of nations involving its principles.

A deed committed within a country may be, therefore an offence against the just rights of another country.

It is an unchallengeable axiom of international law that a nation has a right to protect the property and persons of its citizens residing abroad. Nor can it be denied that such property and such persons, situated in Latin-America, have sometimes needed this protection. There has arisen the question, therefore, how European powers can fulfil their duty in these respects without infringing the Monroe Doctrine.

There have also been occasions, in the early history of the Doctrine when the United States refused to invoke the principle, when it would have been unfair and unjust on her part to do so. Secretary Henry Clay advised the Argentine Republic and the Republic of Brazil in 1825 that the United States would not intervene to protect them from an "obligation the performance of which foreign nations have a right to demand." Henry Clay knew wherein we crossed the line laid down by international law, or international justice, if one prefers to call it the latter.

This would not be a full and true record if we did not also state that the United States did not interfere when England blockaded Nicaragua in 1842, and again in 1884; and when, along with France, she blockaded Buenos Ayres in 1845 and Salvador in 1857. If the United States thus acquiesced, it may have been, in a measure, because, as we have suggested,

See p. 135

is a country of law and order."
"Aren't nicaraguans americans? somehow asked. "They're central americans."

the British navy in those early days was the most potential force behind the Doctrine. Apparently Great Britain intended by those blockades no actual violation of the principle, but merely to safeguard the interests of its nationals. Any nation would have a right to do so now, if we did not promptly do it for them. Besides, at that date, the Doctrine had not been interpreted to be as far-reaching as at present. The failure to intervene when Spain bombarded Valparaiso and Callao in 1866 may be attributed partly to the complications and distractions of the Civil War and partly to our belief that Spanish intervention would not result in any acquisition of territory, which was the point chiefly stressed by American statesmen, at least until the days of President Roosevelt.

Secretary Cass wrote, in 1858:

> With respect to the causes of war between Spain and Mexico, the United States have no concern, and do not undertake to judge them. Nor do they claim to interpose in any hostilities which may take place. Their policy of observation and interference is limited to the permanent subjugation of any portion of the territory of Mexico, or of any other American state, to any European Power whatever.

Secretary Seward wrote, in 1861, concerning the allied operation against Mexico:

> As the undersigned has heretofore had the honor to inform each of the plenipotentiaries now addressed, the President does not feel at liberty to question, and does not question, that the sovereigns represented have undoubted right to decide for themselves the fact whether they have sustained grievances, and to resort to war against Mexico for the redress thereof, and have a right also to levy the war severally or jointly.

So when Germany, Great Britain and Italy united to compel by naval force a response to their demands on the part of Venezuela, and the German Government advised the

"They call themselves americans."
"Well, they can also call themselves nicaraguans. We don't have anything else to call ourselves."
"Why don't we call ourselves Yankees"
"'Cause when your from Mississ..."

United States that it proposed to take coercive measures to enforce its claims for damages and for money against Venezuela, adding, "We declare especially that under no circumstances do we consider in our proceedings the acquisition or permanent occupation of Venezuelan territory," Mr. Hay replied that the Government of the United States although it "regretted that European Powers should use force against Central and South American countries, could not object to their taking steps to obtain redress for injuries suffered by their subjects, provided that no acquisition of territory was contemplated."

When President Roosevelt was called upon to interpret the Monroe Doctrine in connection with the Santo Domingo incident, he said:

This country would certainly decline to go to war to prevent a foreign government from collecting on defaulted debts; and since a temporary occupation by a European Power might turn into a permanent occupation, the only escape from these alternatives may at some time be that we must ourselves undertake to bring about some arrangement by which so much as possible of a just obligation shall be paid.

A test case was Venezuela, and it was a case which became acute on two occasions.

In the early nineties, there was a dispute between Venezuela and Great Britain over their mutual boundary. On July 20, 1895, Mr. Olney, then Secretary of State, sent a dispatch to Mr. Bayard, our ambassador in London, pressing for a settlement of the question, because, while the United States had no objection to any decision fairly rendered by an arbitral tribunal, the seizure of disputed territory in South America by a European power, unless the title to that territory was first determined by a judicial tribunal, was something not to be tolerated. In the course of the dispatch Mr. Olney said:

Today the United States is practically sovereign on this continent, and its fiat is law upon the subjects to which it confines its interposition.

All the advantages of this superiority are at once imperiled if the principle be admitted that European powers may convert American States into colonies or provinces of their own. The principle would be eagerly availed of, and every power doing so would immediately acquire a base of military operations against us.

The dispatch, which was a long and very able statement, had no result, and President Cleveland thereupon, on December 17, sent a message to Congress, laying before them the situation in Venezuela and pointing out that there must be a settlement. After proposing an American commission to settle the boundary dispute, he closed his message with the following language:

In making these recommendations I am fully alive to the responsibility incurred and keenly realize all the consequences that may follow.

I am, nevertheless, firm in my conviction that while it is a grievous thing to contemplate the two great English-speaking peoples of the world as being otherwise than friendly competitors in the onward march of civilization, and strenuous and worthy rivals in all the arts of peace, there is no calamity which a great nation can invite which equals that which follows a supine submission to wrong and injustice and the consequent loss of national self-respect and honor beneath which are shielded and defended a people's safety and greatness.

Mr. Cleveland also said in his message of December 17, 1895:

The doctrine upon which we stand is strong and sound because its enforcement is important to our peace and safety as a nation, and is essential to the integrity of our free institutions and the tranquil maintenance of our distinctive form of government. It was intended to apply to every stage of our national life and cannot become obsolete while our republic endures.

Richard Olney

This was as near to a breach of the accord over the Monroe Doctrine as the United States and Great Britain ever drifted. Our Atlantic Fleet was assembled at Porto Rico ready for action. But Great Britain on her side withdrew her war ships.

Thirty-five years have elapsed since the communication from Secretary of State Richard Olney to Lord Salisbury, and the message to Congress of President Cleveland, informing the world that the Doctrine, suggested in principle by a British Minister of Foreign Affairs, and proclaimed by President Monroe, still stood. There is no reason to suppose that Great Britain will seek modification now.

In 1902 Great Britain, Italy and Germany threatened to blockade Venezuela and seize territory on account of certain debts due to their subjects, and President Roosevelt actually ordered Admiral Dewey to assemble the fleet at Porto Rico, if the Germans, who were becoming arrogantly menacing, did not promptly withdraw their squadron. During the World War but before the United States entered it, ex-President Roosevelt, at his home in Oyster Bay, exhibited to the author a copy of the communication he had prepared to send to Admiral Dewey in regard to the threats of the German Admiral. The communication, as far as we know, has never gone on record—but it was direct and to the point, and in good Rooseveltian style.

At the moment of this interview, President Wilson was engaged in extensive note writing to Germany, of a more or less conventional diplomatic character. President Roosevelt drew a copy of the communication that he had written and then read it to the author and several other visitors to illustrate the only kind of communication the German Kaiser and his Imperial Government understood. The Colonel's judgment of the Kaiser turned out to be better than that of President Wilson.

The story of the German Venezuelan incident is told in Mr. Thayer's "Life and Letters of John Hay":

President Roosevelt did not shirk the test. Although his action has never been officially described, there is no reason for not describing it.

One day, when the crisis was at its height, he summoned to the White House Doctor Holleben, the German ambassador, and told him that unless Germany consented to arbitrate the American squadron under Admiral Dewey would be given orders by noon, 10 days later, to proceed to the Venezuelan coast and prevent any taking possession of Venezuelan territory. Dr. Holleben began to protest that his imperial master, having once refused to arbitrate, could not change his mind. The President said that he was not arguing the question, because arguments had already been gone over until no useful purpose would be served by repeating them; he was simply giving information which the ambassador might think it important to transmit to Berlin.

A week passed in silence. Then Dr. Holleben again called on the President, but said nothing of the Venezuelan matter. When he rose to go the President asked about it, and when he stated that he had received nothing from his government the President informed him in substance that in view of this fact Admiral Dewey would be instructed to sail a day earlier than the day he, the President, had originally mentioned. Much perturbed, the ambassador protested; the President informed him that not a stroke of a pen had been put on paper; that if the Emperor would agree to arbitrate, he, the President, would heartily praise him for such action, and would treat it as taken on German initiative; but that within 48 hours there must be an offer to arbitrate or Dewey would sail with the orders indicated. Within 36 hours Doctor Holleben returned to the White House and announced to President Roosevelt that a dispatch had just come from Berlin saying that the Kaiser would arbitrate. Neither Admiral Dewey (who with an American fleet was then maneuvering in the West Indies) nor anyone else knew of the step that was to be taken; the naval authorities were merely required to be in readiness, but were not told for what.

On the announcement that Germany had consented to arbitrate, the President publicly complimented the Kaiser on being so stanch an advocate of arbitration.

It was the telegram which President Roosevelt had drafted to send to Admiral Dewey in Caribbean waters, instructing Dewey what to do if the German Squadron did not move away in a certain number of hours, that did the trick in the German Venezuelan incident referred to by Mr. Thayer. We have often wondered what would have been the result if Roosevelt had been President in 1914, and had shown the German Ambassador a characteristic telegram by himself to some official abroad, indicating what the United States would undoubtedly do eventually. The Colonel knew the language of that tribe, the tribe of the Imperial Kaiser and his General Staff. If the telegram had been handed to the German Ambassador to read, with time to meditate before its despatch, it probably would never have had to be sent.

However, our main concern is with the Monroe Doctrine. Clearly, it was not to be expected that Germany would receive this Doctrine with the same enthusiasm with which it was received in England. However, something very similar to an explicit recognition is found in the *pro memoria* in which the Imperial Ambassador communicated to the United States Government the action which his government thought fit to take in Venezuela. The recognition may have been late and not altogether voluntary, but it is on record.

We consider it of importance to let first of all the Government of the United States know about our purpose so that we can prove that we have nothing else in view than to help those citizens who have suffered damage . . . We declare especially that under no circumstances do we consider, in our proceedings, the acquisition or the permanent occupation of Venezuelan territory.

It will be seen, then, that step by step, the United States has excluded other Powers from the task of maintaining order in Latin America. Yet there remains the right of other Powers to insist upon the protection of the persons and property of their citizens in territories outside their own sovereignty. It is an international right which, at this moment, the United States is upholding in China. In an address by President Coolidge, delivered in April 1927, it is expressly asserted. He said:

The recent period has brought America into a new position in the world. We shall have to bear the inevitable criticisms and try to discharge the inevitable obligations which arise from this condition. Because some others have pursued that course, it may be feared that we shall embark upon a program of military aggrandizement. Such, however, is not the spirit of the American people. If, even where our national interests and the protection of the rights of our citizens are involved, we attempt to assist in composing difficulties and supporting international law, we must expect to be charged with imperialistic motives. In our international intercourse we must hold ourselves up to high standards of justice and equity. We should be slow to take offense and quick to grant redress. The world knows that the whole genius of America always calls it to the support of the universal rights of humanity.

The civilization of the world has been accomplished by the acceptance and general observance of definite rules of human conduct. Our duty demands that it be clearly understood at home and abroad, that we are unwavering in our faith in those principles. Those who violate them cannot hope for our approbation. Our attitude toward all nations is one of friendship and good will. Toward those who are yet struggling to improve the conditions of their people and achieve a larger liberty it is especially one of forbearance. We support the demands of right and justice, but we are equally solicitous to observe the requirements of mercy and compassion. In the attempt of your Government to meet these great obligations by which alone an enlightened civilized society can be maintained a united America must constantly respond with service and sacrifice.

By inescapable logic, it follows that, if the United States attaches a full significance to the Monroe Doctrine, she must guarantee to the world at large that there shall be reasonable security for life and property within the sphere to

which the Doctrine applies. Candor compels us to add that
if we fail to achieve that security, we become liable in international equity for the damages which result from our omission. That undertaking does not mean alibis or post mor-
tems or diplomatic explanations in regard to disorderly incidents. It does not mean diplomatic expressions of regret
after Europeans are dead and their property destroyed—
while Congress debates and filibusters or junkets about,
automatically stirring up opposition to the State Department, and while anti-war petitions are being read, when there
is in fact no enemy to war against. Police duty by marines
is not war. If it is, every administration, Democratic and
Republican alike, during the last twenty years, has made
war below the Rio Grande. President Wilson actually sent
General Pershing at the head of an army into the heart of
Mexico and this country sustained him. When the United
States falters, foreign governments (as in the case of Great
Britain and Italy in 1927) have a right to assume that the
United States is abandoning the Monroe Doctrine and its
consequent traditional policy, and have a right, upon notice
(or in emergency) without notice, to act for themselves,
under the undisputed law of nations, regardless of the Monroe engagement. In regard to order, the United States cannot put itself in the place of even appearing as "the dog
in the manger." Since 1866 it has taken a strong and
unequivocal stand. The corollaries to that decision must be
accepted.

The circumstance that our obligations under the Monroe
Doctrine are implied and not explicitly stated in writing
suggests no release from their binding character. Whether
we can be held in international law to any particular inter-
polation of the Doctrine, is doubtful. But we stand before
the bar of international justice and must expect that public
opinion, arguing on the equities, will review strictly any

failure on our part to fulfil our duty to others than our-selves.

From those who have much, the world has a right to expect much. The greater and stronger we grow, the more will be expected of us by other nations. Our ideals and pre-tensions are unlimited. Not less acute must be our sense of international obligation.

To the great republics of South America, for instance, the Argentine, Brazil and Chili, the thesis that the power responsible for the Monroe Doctrine must keep order, has obviously no present application. On the contrary, the United States might well seek the co-operation of these re-publics in the task of administering the Monroe Doctrine elsewhere. Reduced to practical terms, the Monroe Doc-trine, as an agency of peace within the Americas, and in the world at large, is a principle now to be applied in actual policy to the Caribbean.

It is undeniable that the predominance of the United States has created a certain uneasiness in Latin-America, and especially among the smaller Latin-American nations. In order to allay these apprehensions, several able professors of history and government, associated with our universities, have urged that the time has come for us to abandon the Monroe Doctrine. We cannot agree. Our view is that the Monroe Doctrine will only be abandoned when we are ready to abandon the Constitution of the United States and the principles enumerated in the Bill of Rights. It is not by abdication but in equity that we should proceed to fulfil our destiny.

The question to be answered is whether apprehensions of an aggressive and imperialistic United States are well founded. Was such aggression, was such imperialism ever the object of the Monroe Doctrine?

We have written in vain unless we have shown beyond

contradiction that the governing principle of the Doctrine is that the Latin-American Republics are independent states, members of the family of nations, and not to be robbed of their independence by European powers. It must be remembered that the recognition of these then infant republics was one of the major issues which called forth the declaration from President Monroe. This basic principle rests upon the firmly established rule of international law that all states are equal. As Chief Justice Marshall said, "Russia and Geneva have equal rights." Bringing it down to date, we may say so have Paraguay and France. The Monroe Doctrine, therefore, was the announcement of the birth of new members of the family of nations and an assertion of the well-settled rule that as members of the family they should be respected as such. In this principle and its declaration by the United States, the nations of the world have acquiesced and for this reason we feel justified in calling it now a principle of international law.

The words of Chief Justice Marshall were:

No principle of general law is more universally acknowledged than the perfect equality of nations . . . It results from this equality that no one can rightfully impose a rule upon another.

In his message to Congress of December 3, 1906, President Roosevelt said:

In many parts of South America there has been much misunderstanding of the attitude and purposes of the United States toward the other American republics. An idea had become prevalent that our assertion of the Monroe Doctrine implied or carried with it an assumption of superiority and of a right to exercise some kind of protectorate over the countries to whose territory that doctrine applies. Nothing could be farther from the truth.

He quoted the words of the Secretary of State then in office, to the Pan-American Conference at Rio de Janeiro:

We deem the independence and equal rights of the smallest and weakest member of the family of nations entitled to as much respect as those of the greatest empire and we deem the observance of that respect the chief guaranty of the weak against the oppression of the strong. We neither claim nor desire any rights or privileges or powers that we do not freely concede to every American republic.

And the President then proceeded to say of these statements:

They have my hearty approval, as I am sure they will have yours, and I cannot be wrong in the conviction that they correctly represent the sentiments of the whole American people. I can not better characterize the true attitude of the United States in its assertion of the Monroe Doctrine than in the words of the distinguished former minister of foreign affairs of Argentina, Doctor Drago . . . "the traditional policy of the United States without accentuating superiority or seeking preponderance condemned the oppression of the nations of this part of the world and the control of their destinies by the great Powers of Europe.

In his message of December 2nd, 1902, President Roosevelt spoke not less clearly:

No independent nation in America need have the slightest fear of aggression from the United States. It behooves each one to maintain order within its own borders and to discharge its just obligations to foreigners. When this is done they can rest assured that, be they strong or weak, they have nothing to dread from outside interference.

There was one reason alone that might lead to forcible intervention. In his message of December 6th, 1904, President Roosevelt said:

Chronic wrongdoing, or an impotence which results in a general loosening of the ties of civilized society, may in America, as elsewhere, ultimately require intervention by some civilized nation, and in the Western Hemisphere, the adherence of the United States to the Monroe Doctrine may force the United States, however reluctantly, in flagrant cases of such wrongdoing or impotence, to the exercise of an international police power.

In his message to Congress, December 3, 1901, President Roosevelt said that by the Monroe Doctrine

"we do not guarantee any state against punishment if it misconducts itself, provided that punishment does not take the form of the acquisition of territory by any non-American power."

A country like the United States which has assumed these responsibilities, should look to her first principles. She cannot ignore "the imponderables" of justice and good faith.

To Secretary Hay, when he discussed the matter, American diplomacy was or should be simply the application of the "Golden Rule." His ideal was put into definite terms by Secretary Root:

"We must be sure that, in all our international intercourse, the view which we propose is both right and just, and the test of justice is such as we ourselves would accept if the situation were reversed."

From a slightly different point of view, President Grover Cleveland expressed the same idea:

"The rules of conduct governing individual relations between citizens or subjects of a civilized state are equally applicable as between enlightened nations."

The weaker the nation with which we are dealing, the surer we should be of the application of these principles.

The above definition of American diplomacy by a Republican like Hay and by a Democratic President like Grover Cleveland, should be taken with the recent (1927) declaration of President Coolidge, a Republican, that "America cherishes no imperialistic designs," and that the country is "content within its own territory to prosper through development of its own resources."

President Wilson, a voice from the Democratic Party, addressed the South Commercial Congress at Mobile in

October, 1913 and emphasized the attitude of the country in words of decisive meaning. He said:

The United States will never again seek one additional foot of territory by conquest.

Senator Root, as we have seen, has based the Monroe Doctrine on the rule of self defence which is recognized in international law. To this factor, Senator Borah has added the phrase, "special interest," which certainly supplements the more legal plea. Yet Senator Borah, in his statement in the Senate on February 19th, 1927, declared:

We are under every obligation to respect the sovereignty of these Republics and to build up that confidence and foster that friendship which inevitably springs from right conduct upon the part of a strong nation. The respect and consideration due to these peoples is the same respect and consideration due to great and unassailable powers.

These are solemn declarations which commit the nation; they are of the highest diplomatic authority; and their sincerity is not to be challenged. If studied in a dispassionate spirit, they are calculated to reassure Latin America and contribute to a better understanding of the motives which inspire the United States in any action that it may be necessary for her to take in the Caribbean area. The Isthmian Highway is of a common benefit to North, to Central and to South America. The interests of all concerned are identical, and it is only as a trustee for those interests that the United States applies the Monroe Doctrine.

In 1914, Senator Root said:

It happens, however, that the United States is very much bigger and more powerful than most of the other American republics. And when a very great and powerful state makes a demand upon a very small and weak state, it is difficult to avoid a feeling that there is

JOHN HAY

an assumption of superior authority involved in the assertion of superior power, even though the demand be based solely upon the right of equal against equal. An examination of the various controversies which the United States has had with other American powers will disclose the fact that in every case the rights asserted were rights not of superiority but of equality. Of course it can not be claimed that great and powerful states shall forego their just rights against smaller and less powerful states. The responsibilities of sovereignty attach to the weak as well as to the strong, and a claim to exemption from those responsibilities would imply not equality but inferiority. The most that can be said concerning a question between a powerful state and a weak one is that the great state ought to be especially considerate and gentle in the assertion and maintenance of its position; ought always to base its acts not upon a superiority of force, but upon reason and law; and ought to assert no rights against a small state because of its weakness which it would not assert against a great state notwithstanding its power. But in all this the Monroe Doctrine is not concerned at all.

Professor Alejandro Alvarez, Secretary General of the American Institute and himself a South American, has shown that South American nations have not only from time to time approved the Monroe Doctrine, but invoked it, and appealed to the United States for protection under it, when threatened by European countries. As Professor Moore shows in his *Digest of International Law,* the Doctrine, as a matter of fact, has been invoked more in the interest of South and Central America than in the interest of the United States—a view supported by authorities and state papers. With the advent, however, of our Isthmian Highway responsibilities, we are beginning to hope for a more mutual result and to expect the necessary treaties and full coöperation for that purpose from those countries.

It is not easy to imagine any development in Central America to which the Monroe Doctrine in some of its many phases would not apply.

As the Isthmian Highway binds North and South America

together geographically at the Isthmus of Panama, it can also split them apart, physically and otherwise; and can be the ending of the Monroe Doctrine. The use or misuse of the Canal as an instrumentality of transport or of other highways across the Isthmus whatever they may be, is thus vital to the principles of the Doctrine. *It, therefore, follows as a matter of course, that the Canal and the Highway in general, stand or fall with the Monroe Doctrine; and the Monroe Doctrine stands or falls, in future, with the ability of the United States fully to control and adequately to defend the Highway. One is no stronger than the other.* As the world stands, no international principle or interest, in the last analysis, exists in safety unless there is power and determination somewhere to defend it. Good intentions and high-sounding words, as President Roosevelt so often observed, are worth nothing without action, or preparation for action, with the necessary potential power behind it.

In the Eighteen Sixties, as we have seen, the Civil War and its problems diverted our energies for a few years from the discharge of our responsibilities under the Doctrine. Today, our preëminence as a great power is known to the world. Also, the world knows that, as far as possible, we limit our responsibilities to the Western world. All the more is it incumbent upon us to carry out those responsibilities without flinching from our task.

X

THE FREEDOM OF THE SEAS

Over a period of more than a century, we have traced the development and the application of the Monroe Doctrine. We have seen that, in its very nature, it was regional and limited in its range to the Americas and to the American waters surrounding these continents.

We have now to consider a principle, distinct from the Monroe Doctrine and of a wholly different character—a principle not of limited application but universal in its scope. That principle, asserted also by the United States, is known to diplomacy as the freedom of the seas.

Over this phrase there has been much controversy, but the principle, so named, may be defined, broadly, as the right of all nations to make equal use of all seas and maritime waterways in pursuance of lawful trade.

Even in time of war, neutral shipping should be immune from seizure and confiscation, except where the vessel is carrying admitted contraband to a belligerent or is endeavouring to break through an effective blockade.

In his deservedly popular *History of Mankind*, recently published, Hendrik Van Loon described the origin of the phrase, freedom of the seas:

Early in the seventeenth century a Dutch Captain by the name of van Heemskerk, a man who had made himself famous as the head of an expedition which had tried to discover the North Eastern Passage to the Indies and who had spent a winter on the frozen shores of the island of Nova Zembla, had captured a Portuguese ship in the Straits of Malacca. You will remember that the Pope had divided the world into two equal shares, one of which had been given to the Spaniards and the other to the Portuguese. The Portuguese quite naturally regarded the water which surrounded her Indian Islands as part of their own property and since, for the moment, they were not at war with the United Seven Netherlands, they claimed that the captain of a private Dutch trading company had no right to enter their private domain and steal their ships. And they brought suit. The directors of the Dutch East India Company hired a bright young lawyer, by the name of De Groot or Grotius, to defend their case. He made the astonishing plea that the ocean is free to all comers. Once outside the distance which a cannon ball fired from the land can reach, the sea is or (according to Grotius) ought to be, a free and open highway to all the ships of all nations. It was the first time that this startling doctrine had been publicly pronounced in a court of law. It was opposed by all the other seafaring people. To counteract the effect of Grotius' famous plea for the "Mare Liberum", or "Open Sea", John Selden, the Englishman, wrote his famous treatise upon "Mare Clausum" or "Closed Sea" which treated of the natural right of a sovereign to regard the seas which surrounded his country as belonging to his territory."

The United States was born a nation without an Empire which, none the less, desired to carry on a foreign trade. In insisting on the freedom of the seas as in other of her international relations, this country was adopting a policy, dictated doubtless by self-interest.

But the policy is one of which the results are equally advantageous to the rest of mankind. The freedom of the seas is no more than an extension of that equality of opportunity which is the very basis of American enterprise. From this equality on the ocean, the whole world has derived an incalculable benefit.

The Republic was in its mere infancy when the problem of maritime security had to be faced. The Barbary States of Northern Africa captured merchant vessels and held them for ransom. Faced by other embarrassments, Washington had, perforce, to submit to these exactions and, under treaty, several millions of dollars of what may be described as blackmail were paid.

During Jefferson's administration, the Administration felt strong enough to end the menace. Jefferson sent a fleet against the pirates, captured Tripoli and after a complete victory, negotiated a treaty which secured to persons engaged in commerce the assurance of safety without the payment of tribute.

As an assertion of freedom on the high seas, this was an important achievement. But freedom on the seas was not enough. An effective charter of maritime commerce must include a similar freedom for all nations alike to use those natural channels which connect sea with sea and ocean with ocean. Such restricted waters, belonging exclusively to no one sovereign state, must be made fully available for peaceful use on equal terms by all nations.

Here also, the United States, as a country whose interests were commercial alone and not territorial, led the way. Of restricted waters, there was a conspicuous example in the channels which connect the North Sea with the Baltic. On vessels and cargoes passing through those channels, Denmark was exacting dues which were justified by the Danish government on the ground of immemorial usage sanctioned by a long succession of treaties, and of benefits conferred on shipping by the policing and lighting of these waters. They nevertheless bore heavily on shipping, and the United States after appropriate diplomatic remonstrances, gave notice that it would not submit to them any longer. This action led to the calling of a conference. The United States declined to take part in it, but afterwards co-operated by a treaty with Denmark which gave effect to a plan whereby the dues were to be capitalized and extinguished by compensation to Denmark for vested interests surrendered.

The United States insisted on the neutralization of the Strait of Magellan. In 1879 William M. Evarts, Secretary of State, declared that this country would not tolerate exclusive claims to that channel and would hold the nation responsible which attempted to lay any impost or put any check whatsoever on the commerce of the United States using it. It is interesting to add that in 1916, a British Prize Court laid it down that "the Strait must be considered free for the commerce of all nations passing between the two oceans."

Of an importance comparable with the freedom of the seas and of the natural channels, is the free navigation of international rivers, that is, rivers which are navigable within two or more countries. In logic, such rivers come under the same principles as natural channels and were so treated in the regulations adopted by the Congress of Vienna for the navigation of the Rhine. Here again the United States consistently advocated the principle of equality and, in several treaties, it has been embodied in slightly different forms. An instance is the Peace of Paris which, in 1856, included the inauguration of the Danube Navigation Commission.

When the British Government sought to deprive the inhabitants of this country of the commercial use of the St. Lawrence River, Henry Clay, as Secretary of State, appealed to the regulations of the Congress of Vienna, which should, he declared

"be regarded only as the spontaneous homage of man to the superior wisdom of the paramount Lawgiver of the universe by delivering His great works from the artificial shackles and self-contrivance to which they had been arbitrarily and unjustly subjected."

The free navigation of the St. Lawrence River was temporarily secured by the reciprocity treaty of 1854 and in perpetuity by the treaty of Washington in 1871. The latter treaty also declared that the Yukon, Porcupine and Stikine Rivers should be forever free and open to citizens of the United States and of Canada for purposes of commerce. By a series of treaties, the free use of international rivers in South America was secured.

It will be seen that the object of the United States throughout these affairs was the advancement of equal opportunity for the oversea commerce of all nations, the abridgement of privilege and the removal of obstacles to free transport from shore to shore.

Between a natural channel, like the Strait of Magellan, and an artificial channel, like the Suez or Kiel Canal, a distinction has to be drawn. But in the year 1826, Henry Clay, as Secretary of State did not hesitate to reason by analogy. He declared that if a canal to unite the Pacific and Atlantic Oceans should ever be constructed, the benefits of it ought not to be appropriated by any one nation, but should be extended to all mankind upon the payment of a charge which will give a reasonable return on the actual investment of the owner.

It would be difficult to overestimate the importance of this pronouncement. At that early date, the United States did not propose, herself, to construct an Isthmian Highway nor did she ask that the control of such a highway be vested in herself. But she did insist that no such exclusive control should be exercised by any foreign power, except on conditions approved by the United States, which conditions were to be in accord with the principles known as the freedom of the seas.

The views of Secretary Clay are formulated into a definite policy to be applied to any canal that might be built over the territory of New Granada, as Colombia was then called.

In the year 1835, during the administration of President Jackson, the Senate of the United States unanimously adopted a resolution, as follows:

That the President of the United States be respectfully requested to consider the expediency of opening negotiations with the Governments of other nations, and particularly with the Governments of Central America and New Granada, for the purpose of effectually protecting, by suitable treaty stipulations with them, such individuals or companies as may undertake to open a communication between the Atlantic and Pacific Oceans by the construction of a ship canal across the isthmus which connects North and South America, and of securing forever by such stipulations the free and equal right of navigating such canal to all such nations on the payment of such reasonable tolls as may be established to compensate the capitalists who may engage in such undertaking and complete the work.

In 1839, the House of Representatives, by a unanimous vote, adopted a resolution of similar import. In it the President was requested:

to consider the expediency of opening or continuing negotiations with the Governments of other nations, and particularly with those the territorial jurisdiction of which comprehends the Isthmus of Panama, and to which the United States have accredited ministers or agents, for the purpose of ascertaining the practicability of effecting a communication between the Atlantic and Pacific Oceans by the construction of a ship canal across the Isthmus and of securing forever by suitable treaty stipulations the free and equal right of navigating such canal by all nations.

Hence, the difference between a natural and an artificial waterway was clearly defined. In both, there was to be unrestricted navigation, on equal terms for all nations. But in the case of a canal, a charge might be made on shipping which would cover the cost of administration and of a reasonable return on capital invested, whether by a corporation or a sovereign state.

These were the principles then, which Secretary Clay stated and Congress endorsed. It was during the forties that the time came when the principles had to be applied.

Over the future of the Isthmus, there was a certain friction or, at any rate, a rivalry between the United States and Britain. In his book, *The British Empire and the United States*, Dunning puts the case thus:

British and American diplomats had been diligently fishing in the murky waters of Latin-American politics for a controlling position in respect to any possible Isthmian canal. In the early forties a British official formally asserted that the territory of the Mosquito Indians included the port of San Juan de Nicaragua, which would be the terminus of any canal that should be cut across Nicaragua. As the Mosquitos were held to be a kingdom under the protection of Great Britain, the bearing of the claim on their behalf was obvious.

．　　　．　　　．　　　．　　　．　　　．　　　．

In New Granada, at about the same time, the American *chargé d'affaires* displayed a like activity, and in 1846, without instructions, concluded with the government of that state a treaty of far-reaching importance. By its provisions the government and citizens of the United States and their property secured freedom of transit across the Isthmus of Panama in return for a guarantee by the United States of the neutrality of the Isthmus, and the further guarantee of the sovereignty and property of New Granada in the said territory. This treaty remained pending in the Senate until after the British movements in Nicaragua in 1848. In June of that year the treaty, with the advice and consent of the Senate, was duly ratified.

The terms of the Treaty with New Granada were as follows:

Any modes of communication that now exist, or that may be hereafter constructed, shall be open and free to the Government and citizens of the United States, and for the transportation of any articles of produce, manufactures or merchandise of lawful com-

merce belonging to the citizens of the United States; no other tolls
or charges shall be levied or collected upon the citizens of the
United States, or their said merchandise thus passing over any road
or canal that may be made by the Government of New Granada,
or by the authority of the same, than is, under like circumstances,
levied upon and collected from the Granadian citizens.

Such provisions deserve the most careful scrutiny. That
the United States undertook a special responsibility, is manifest. She guaranteed the neutrality of the Isthmus, and the
sovereignty of New Granada over the Isthmus.

But in return for this guarantee, she received no special
privilege. Her right of passage over any lines of communication then in existence across the Isthmus, or thereafter to
be constructed, was no more than a common right which any
nation might enjoy. The principle was accepted that the
proprietor of the means of such transit was to receive his
compensation through a non-discriminatory charge for his
services.

The Treaty was concluded between the United States and
New Granada alone. But in submitting it to the Senate for
ratification, President Polk left no doubt as to his readiness
for its general application. He said:

In entering into the mutual guaranties proposed by the thirty-
fifth article, neither the Government of New Granada nor that of
the United States has a narrow or exclusive view. The ultimate
object . . . is to secure to all nations the free and equal right of
passage over the Isthmus.

Let us review, then, the precise position at which the
United States had arrived when the forties were drawing to
a close. She had asserted and assented to a doctrine clearly
recognized under the descriptive title, "The Freedom of the
Seas." Within this doctrine, there were embodied the following rights:

First, an unimpeded navigation of the ocean.

Secondly, the free and equal right to use restricted but maritime waterways.

Thirdly, the equal use, on reasonable terms, of international rivers.

Fourthly, the equal use, on reasonable terms, of any canal which might be constructed across the Isthmus of Panama.

It is at this point that we encounter the negotiation of the Clayton-Bulwer Treaty.

The responsibility for initiating the treaty should be clearly appreciated. The negotiations were begun not by Britain but by the United States. Mr. Clayton, who was Secretary of State at the time, sent Mr. Rives, our Minister in France, to London for the purpose of urging upon Lord Palmerston the making of the treaty. The treaty was made by Great Britain as a concession to the urgent demands of the United States.

Mr. Rives, in his letter to Secretary Clayton of September 25, 1849, describes an interview with Lord Palmerston and states that in pursuance of his instructions he had said to him:

that the United States, moreover, as one of the principal commercial powers of the world, and the one nearest to the scene of the proposed communication, and holding besides, a large domain on the western coast of America, had a special, deep and national interest in the free and unobstructed use, in common with other powers, of any channel of intercourse which might be opened from one sea to the other; . . . that the United States sought no exclusive privilege or preferential right of any kind in regard to the proposed communication, and their sincere wish, if it should be found practicable, was to see it dedicated to the common use of all nations on the most liberal terms and a footing of perfect equality for all; . . . that the United States would not, if they could, obtain any exclusive right or privilege in a great highway which naturally belonged to all mankind.

By this document, the United States emphasized two points of permanent significance, first, the obvious geographical fact that she is specially interested in a waterway which connects her Atlantic and her Pacific seaboards; secondly, that she will insist on this waterway being open for the free and equal use by all nations.

In his work, entitled *American Diplomatic Questions,* Henderson makes it clear that, in the correspondence between Mr. Clayton and Messrs. Bancroft and Lawrence, successive American Ministers in London, and also in the records of interviews between Mr. Clayton and Mr. Crampton, the British Minister at Washington, the attitude of the United States was definitely stated—"Under no circumstances would the United States permit Great Britain or any other power to exercise exclusive control of any isthmian transit route"—which was one side of the picture. But, "upon the other hand, he (Secretary Clayton) did not seek for his own country the exclusive control he denied to others, and in assuming his position, he followed the universally accepted theory of the complete neutrality of ship canals." Henderson adds:

When it was understood by both Mr. Clayton and Lord Palmerston, as revealed by their correspondence, that neither power actually sought monopoly power over the canal, the way was cleared of the most formidable obstacle to the conclusion of a treaty. . . .

The Clayton-Bulwer Treaty of April 1850 is printed as an appendix. It was signed in Washington by Secretary Clayton and Sir Henry Lytton Bulwer, acting as Envoy Plenipotentiary "for the aforesaid purpose," and a clear understanding of its provisions is essential to this narrative.

By the preamble, it is held to refer to "any means of communication by ship canal which may be constructed between the Atlantic and the Pacific Oceans by the way of the river

San Juan de Nicaragua and either or both of the lakes of Nicaragua or Managua, to any point or place on the Pacific Ocean." In other words, the Treaty applied in the first instance to the Nicaraguan Canal.

But, as will be immediately seen, the scope of the provisions extended beyond that particular route and included Panama—a fact of enormous importance to the future of the Isthmus.

For by Article I, the signatories promise to refrain from any attempt, whether by themselves or through allies, to "occupy, or fortify, or colonize, or exercise any dominion over Nicaragua, Costa Rica, the Mosquito Coast or any part of Central America." The neutralization is not limited to Nicaragua. It is general to the entire range of the Isthmus.

Also "any rights or advantages in regard to commerce or navigation through the said (Nicaraguan) canal must be offered on the same terms to both nations."

By Article II, it is laid down that in the event of war between the United States and Great Britain, vessels of the two powers shall be exempt from "blockade, detention or capture by either of the belligerents"—a very strong assertion of the freedom of the seas.

By Article III, they who contract to make the canal "upon fair and equitable terms" shall be "protected" jointly by the United States and Great Britain "from unjust detention, confiscation, seizure or any violence whatsoever."

By Article IV, the two powers agree "to facilitate the construction of the said canal by every means in their power" and "to use their good offices, wherever and however it may be most expedient, in order to procure the establishment of two free ports, one at each end of the said canal."

Article V assures to the canal, when completed, a joint guarantee of protection by the two powers. But with one significant reservation. "The protection and guarantee may be withdrawn by both governments or either government" if the management of the canal "adopt or establish such regulations concerning the traffic thereupon as are contrary to the spirit or intention of this convention, either by making unfair discriminations in favor of the commerce of one of the contracting parties over the commerce of the other, or by imposing oppressive exactions or unreasonable tolls upon the passengers, vessels, goods, wares, merchandise or other articles." The application of maritime freedom to the canal must continue without evasion.

By Article VI, the two powers invite other countries to join in the treaty "to the end that all other States may share in the honor and advantage of having contributed to a work of such general interest and importance as the Canal herein contemplated." The Canal was to be regarded as an international communication.

By Article VII, it was said to be "desirable that no time should be unnecessarily lost in commencing and constructing the said Canal." The two powers agree, therefore, "to give their support and encouragement to such persons or company as may first offer to commence the same, with the necessary capital," and on the agreed conditions of equality.

Finally, we have the famous Article VIII which extends the entire treaty into "a general principle," applicable to the case of any other canal that might be projected whether at Tehuantepec or Panama.

Article VIII

The Governments of the United States and Great Britain having not only desired, in entering into this convention, to accomplish a particular object, but also to establish a general principle, they hereby agree to extend their protection, by treaty stipulations, to any other practicable communications, whether by canal or railway, across the isthmus which connects North and South America, and especially to the interoceanic communications, should the same prove to be practicable, whether by canal or railway, which are now proposed to be established by the way of Tehuantepec or Panama. In granting, however, their joint protection to any such canals or railways as are by this article specified, it is always understood by the United States and Great Britain that the parties constructing or owning the same shall impose no other charges or conditions of traffic thereupon than the aforesaid Governments shall approve of as just and equitable; and that the same canals or railways, being open to the citizens and subjects of the United States and Great Britain on equal terms, shall also be open on like terms to the citizens and subjects of every other State which is willing to grant thereto such protection as the United States and Great Britain engage to afford.

This, then, was the famous and, some would say, the ill-fated Clayton-Bulwer Agreement or Treaty of the year 1850, on the significance of which there has been written a library of comment, favourable, unfavourable and explanatory. The case against the Treaty was stated by Senator Lodge in an article appearing in *Scribner's Magazine* for October 1923. He held that the Treaty was

a derogation from the Monroe Doctrine by making an agreement with Great Britain in regard to the building of an Isthmian Canal. We ought never to have recognized the right of any power or powers outside the American continents to have part or lot in that great undertaking. I do not mean by this to exclude a corporation composed of foreigners, in the nature of a private enterprise, from undertaking to construct an Isthmian Canal, but no foreign government should ever have been permitted to share with the United States in this direction upon an equal footing. Very fortunately the Clayton-Bulwer Treaty was never put into practical operation.

Considering the situation of the two countries in 1850, and the great and special interests of Great Britain in North and Central America, and considering particularly her vital requirements as to such a world highway, or possible highways, of trade of an international character, it is hard to understand how that country could have been treated otherwise than she was by the United States in the Clayton-Bulwer Treaty. We were not then in a position to dictate terms to the world as to such a matter, had we desired to do so. At any rate the full record shows—and we must be historically fair—that the United States has always received full coöperation and sympathetic support from Great Britain in connection with the Monroe Doctrine and the Panama Canal.

It is quite true that the United States had asserted the Monroe Doctrine which, by its very nature, is unilateral. But she had also insisted on the freedom of the seas which, as a principle, is essentially universal.

Hence, she had to guarantee the same freedom of the seas within the sphere of the Monroe Doctrine that she demanded of other nations outside that sphere. In other words, the freedom of the seas for which the United States herself contended, gave to other nations a certain standing in the maritime equities of the Americas of which standing the Clayton-Bulwer Treaty—whether considered to be perfect or imperfect—was an expression.

XI

THE CHARTER OF THE CANAL

WE have seen that, in 1850, there was concluded the Clayton-Bulwer Treaty between the United States and Great Britain. It was a treaty that foreshadowed an Isthmian Highway, constructed and neutralized under the joint guarantee of the two Powers, and under the political control of the sovereign state whose territory it traversed.

In actual fact, no such enterprise was undertaken. At the idea of so stupendous a venture, private capital was staggered. For half a century therefore, the Clayton-Bulwer Treaty represented no more than an unfulfilled possibility.

The fact is that the Clayton-Bulwer Treaty raised very serious and unwelcome questions. The case against joint control was put by Secretary Fish (1869-1875) in his negotiations with Colombia:

The proposal of a protectorate over the Canal, in which other maritime powers should be joined with the United States in equal control, would probably remove many obstacles to the grant, and may secure the ratification of a treaty by the Colombian Government. But in the present state of international law, such a joint protectorate would be a source of future trouble, and while it might facilitate the concession by the Colombian Government, it would be viewed with apprehension in this country, and might probably prove an obstacle to the ratification by the United States Senate of a treaty on the subject. Apart, however, from the latter consideration of expediency, the President is disinclined to enter any entanglement in participation of control over the work with other powers. He regards it as an American enterprise, which he desires to undertake under American auspices, to the benefit of which the whole commercial world should be fully admitted.

President Harrison in his inaugural message of March 4th, 1889, again set forth the policy:

It is so manifestly incompatible with those precautions for our peace and safety which all the great powers habitually observe and enforce in matters affecting them that a shorter waterway between our eastern and western seaboards should be dominated by any European power, that we confidently expect that such a purpose will not be entertained by any friendly power.

It cannot be said that the subject ever lapsed. For instance we have the statement of Secretary Cass who, in 1857, said to Great Britain:

The United States, as I have before had occasion to assure your Lordship, demand no exclusive privileges in these passages, but will always exert their influence to secure their free and unrestricted benefits, both in peace and war, to the commerce of the world.

In 1881, Secretary Blaine sought a modification of the Clayton-Bulwer Treaty. His aim was to obtain the consent of Great Britain to a canal, controlled by the United States alone. But he emphasized the pledge that there should be equality among nations in the commercial use of the Canal. In a letter dated June 24th, 1881, he asked Minister Lowell to state to Lord Granville:

The United States recognizes a proper guarantee of neutrality as essential to the construction and successful operation of any highway across the Isthmus of Panama, and in the last generation every step was taken by this Government that is deemed requisite in the premises. The necessity was foreseen and abundantly provided for long in advance of any possible call for the actual exercise of power. . . . Nor, in time of peace, does the United States seek to have any exclusive privileges accorded to American ships in respect to precedence or tolls through an interoceanic canal any more than it has sought like privileges for American goods in transit over the Panama Railway, under the exclusive control of an American corporation. The extent of the privileges of American citizens and ships is measurable under the treaty of 1846 by those of Colombian citizens and ships. It would be our earnest desire and expectation to see the world's peaceful commerce enjoy the same just, liberal and national treatment.

At a later date, Secretary Blaine amplified his earlier views as follows:

Nor does the United States seek any exclusive or narrow commercial advantage. It frankly agrees, and will by public proclamation declare at the proper time, in conjunction with the Republic on whose soil the canal may be located, that the same rights and privileges, the same tolls and obligations for the use of the canal, shall apply with absolute impartiality to the merchant marine of every nation on the globe; and equally in time of peace the harmless use of the canal shall be freely granted to the war vessels of other nations.

In simple and adequate terms, we have here a statement of the case—namely that there be a strategic control of the Canal by the United States alone, with a guarantee of equal use by all nations. The "general principles" embodied in the Clayton-Bulwer Treaty would be retained, but the single trusteeship of one power would be substituted for a joint trusteeship.

About this "general principle," there was never a misunderstanding. Richard Olney, Secretary of State under President Cleveland thus referred to the Clayton-Bulwer Treaty:

As Article VIII expressly declares, the contracting parties by the convention desired not only to accomplish a particular object, but to establish a general principle. This general principle is manifested by the provisions of the first seven articles, and is that the interoceanic routes there specified should, under the sovereignty of the States traversed by them, be neutral and free to all nations alike.

The views of President Cleveland are expressed in his annual message of 1885:

The lapse of years has abundantly confirmed the wisdom and foresight of those earlier administrations which, long before the conditions of maritime intercourse were changed and enlarged by the progress of the age, proclaimed the vital need of interoceanic transit across the American Isthmus and consecrated it in advance to the common use of mankind by their positive declarations and through the formal obligations of treaties. Toward such realization the efforts of my administration will be applied, ever bearing in mind the principles on which it must rest and which were declared in no uncertain tones by Mr. Cass, who, while Secretary of State in 1858, announced that what the United States wants in Central America next to the happiness of its people is the security and neutrality of the interoceanic routes which lead through it.

In 1888, there was created a precedent which could not be ignored. A Convention at Constantinople arrived at an international guarantee of the Suez Canal. The entire Treaty, signed by Great Britain, Germany, Spain, France, Italy, the Netherlands, Russia and Turkey, is printed as an appendix. By Article I,

The Suez Maritime Canal shall always be free and open, in time of war as in time of peace, to every vessel of commerce or of war, without distinction of flag.

Consequently, the High Contracting Parties agree not in any way to interfere with the free use of the Canal, in time of war as in time of peace.

The Canal shall never be subjected to the exercise of the right of blockade.

It is stated in Article IV that even the ships of war of belligerents may use the Canal—a liberty obviously of difficult application. The safeguards which accompany this right are significant. There is to be committed "no act of hostility nor any act having for its object the free navigation of the Canal." Such neutralization shall extend to the "ports of access" and to "a radius of three marine miles from these ports, even though the Ottoman Empire (the owner of the territory which the Canal traverses) should be one of the belligerent Powers." Also

ARTICLE V

In time of war belligerent powers shall not disembark nor embark within the Canal and its ports of access either troops, munitions or materials of war. But in case of an accidental hindrance in the Canal, men may be embarked or disembarked at the ports of access by detachments not exceeding one thousand men, with a corresponding amount of war material.

ARTICLE VI

Prizes shall be subjected, in all respects, to the same rules as the vessels of belligerents.

ARTICLE VII

The powers shall not keep any vessel of war in the waters of the Canal (including Lake Timsah and the Bitter Lakes).

Nevertheless, they may station vessels of war in the ports of access of Port Said and Suez, the number of which shall not exceed two for each power.

This right shall not be exercised by belligerents.

[It may here be mentioned that, during the Russo-Japanese War, a portion of the Russian fleet, on its way from the Baltic to the Far East, did, during the year 1903, pass through the Suez Canal.]

In form this Treaty was international. In fact, it placed the Suez Canal under the control of a single power. By Article VIII we read:

The agents in Egypt of the Signatory Powers of the present Treaty shall be charged to watch over its execution.

These "agents" were and are Great Britain.

Here then there was a clear case of an artificial waterway, owned in effect by a single Power but by a Power acting as a Trustee for the world as a whole; and the rule of this Canal was to be a free and equal use. By Article XII

The High Contracting Parties, by application of the principle of equality as regards the free use of the canal, a principle which forms one of the bases of the present treaty, agree that none of them shall endeavor to obtain with respect to the canal territorial or commercial advantages or privileges in any international arrangements which may be concluded. Moreover, the rights of Turkey as the territorial power are reserved.

It was the opening of the Spanish American War that precipitated the decisions affecting the Isthmian Highway. The country awoke to the fact that it had two ocean fronts, widely separated by navigable distance. When the war broke out, the *Oregon* had to double Cape Horn, and the importance of a channel whereby the navy could pass from one ocean to the other was emphasized by a dramatic object lesson.

It was seen that if the Canal should prove successful as a commercial venture as it was believed it would, we would secure a factor in national security at little or no unremunerative cost. The indirect commercial benefits would be a clear gain if the enterprise bore its own burden, which was an additional reason that impelled the United States to enter upon the project. The Canal would be a self-supporting commercial enterprise usable by the United States for its military purposes to the exclusion of the enemy; and assuming that the policy, so anticipated, were carried out in administration, no expense need fall on the current revenues of the United States Treasury.

Over the negotiations which followed, there were heated controversies in Congress and serious delays. But, regarded in the perspective of history, the ultimate interests of the United States and of Great Britain—we might add the world as a whole—are seen to have been still identical. Both countries wanted the Canal to be built for commercial reasons. To the United States, as to Britain at Suez, an additional reason was naval and military strategy. The Hay-Pauncefote Treaty, now to be considered, gave to the

WILLIAM McKINLEY

two countries precisely what each wanted, that is, national security on the one side and equality of mercantile use on the other.

On the British side, there was no doubt as to the position. In a communication to the Department of State, Henry White, Secretary of the U. S. Embassy in London and chargé d'affaires, who acted on instructions from Secretary Hay, thus tells the result of his first conference with Lord Salisbury:

A brief, informal conversation followed, during which Lord Salisbury said nothing to leave me to suppose that he is unfavorably disposed—much less hostile—to the construction of the Canal under our auspices, provided that it is open to the ships of all countries on equal terms.

In a letter to Henry White, the ambassador responsible in London, Mr. Choate, defined the position as follows:

I wrote to the chairman of the committee, Senator O'Gorman, inclosing to him, by the express permission of the Secretary of State, a copy of my letters to Secretary Hay between August 3 and October 12, 1901, the same that you have. To my mind they establish beyond question the intent of the parties engaged in the negotiation that the treaty should mean exactly what it says, and excludes the possibility of any exemption of any kind of vessels of the United States. Equality between Great Britain and the United States is the constant theme, and especially in my last letter of October 2, 1901, where I speak of Lord Lansdowne's part in the matter, and say "He has shown an earnest desire to bring to an amicable settlement, honorable alike to both parties, this long and important controversy between the two nations. In substance, he abrogates the Clayton-Bulwer Treaty, gives us an American canal—ours to build as and where we like, to own, control, and govern—on the sole condition of its being always neutral and free for the passage of the ships of all nations on equal terms, except that if we get into a war with any nation we can shut its ships out and take care of ourselves.

It was during the administration of President McKinley that negotiations for a new treaty were begun. In his message to Congress for 1898, he declared that the Canal had become "a national necessity." His views were reported by Secretary Hay to Senator Cullom in the following words:

He (the President) not only was willing but earnestly desired that the "general principle of neutralization" referred to in the preamble of this treaty and in the eighth article of the Clayton-Bulwer Treaty should be perpetually applied to this canal.

Again to quote Secretary Hay:

The President was, however, not only willing but desirous that the "general principle" of neutralization referred to in the preamble of this treaty should be applicable to this canal now intended to be built, notwithstanding any change of sovereignty or of international relations of the territory through which it should pass. This "general principle" of neutralization had always in fact been insisted upon by the United States.

In other words, the United States was to build the Canal, but there was to be a right of equal use in the pursuit of commerce for the rest of the world. In the relevant words of Clause VIII of the Clayton-Bulwer Treaty:

It is always understood by the United States and Great Britain that the parties constructing or owning the Canal shall impose no other charges or conditions of traffic thereupon than are just and equitable; and that the said Canal, being open to the citizens and subjects of the United States and Great Britain on equal terms, shall also be open on like terms to the citizens and subjects of every other State.

The first Hay-Pauncefote Treaty, when submitted to the Senate, was amended and, in its amended form, was rejected by Great Britain. In 1901, a second treaty was negotiated. President Roosevelt had succeeded McKinley and, in his first utterance, as Chief Executive, had endorsed the policies of his predecessor.   In transmitting the second Treaty to President Roosevelt, Secretary Hay wrote:

I submit for your consideration . . . a convention . . . to remove any objection which may arise out of the . . . Clayton-Bulwer Treaty . . . without impairing the "general principle" of neutralization established in Article 8 of that convention.

President Roosevelt, in submitting this treaty to the Senate said:

I transmit, for the advice and consent of the Senate to its ratification, a convention signed November 18, 1901 . . . to remove any objection which may arise out of the convention of April 19, 1850, . . . to the construction of such canal under the auspices of the Government of the United States without impairing the "general principle" of neutralization established in Article 8 of that convention.

The "general principle" referred, not to the control of the Canal, but to the commercial right to use it.   There was no doubt that the control was to be vested in the United States alone.   In his message to the Senate, President Roosevelt said:

It specifically provides that the United States alone shall do the work of building and assume the responsibility of safeguarding the Canal and shall regulate its neutral use by all nations on terms of equality without the guaranty of interference of any outside nation from any quarter.

Again he said, on January 4, 1904, in a special message:

Under the Hay-Pauncefote Treaty it is explicitly provided that the United States should control, police and protect the Canal which is to be built, keeping it open for the vessels of all nations on equal terms.   The United States thus assumes the position of guarantor of the Canal and of its peaceful use by all the world.

In a note, Secretary Hay on the following day, states:

The Clayton-Bulwer Treaty was conceived to form an obstacle, and the British Government therefore agreed to abrogate it, the United States only promising in return to protect the Canal and keep it open on equal terms to all nations, in accordance with our traditional policy.

Among the Appendices, the two treaties are printed in full and the amendments to the first of them, made by the Senate, are indicated. It is worth while to examine these documents with some care.

In effect the preamble as finally adopted was the preamble originally submitted. This preamble states that the United States and Great Britain are "desirous to facilitate the construction of a ship canal to connect the Atlantic and Pacific Oceans, *by whatever route may be considered expedient*, and to that end to remove any objection which may arise out of the convention of the nineteenth of April, 1850, commonly called the Clayton-Bulwer Treaty, to the construction of such canal under the government of the United States without impairing the 'general principle' of neutralization established in Article VIII of that convention."

The only change is the insertion of the words in italics which permits the construction of the Canal by any route that may be "considered expedient." It is doubtful whether these words change the sense. The important point is that the "general principle of neutralization" is retained.

Article I is not in the original draft. It states that "the High Contracting Parties agree that the present treaty shall supersede" the Clayton-Bulwer Treaty, and therefore the idea of a jointly controlled canal.

In his article in *Scribner's Magazine* for October, 1923, Senator Lodge states that "the Clayton-Bulwer Treaty . . . was superseded by the Second Hay-Pauncefote Treaty." Technically, this is true. But the Hay-Pauncefote Treaty, while superseding its predecessor, perpetuated the "general principle" of neutralization which had been agreed to by Clayton and Bulwer.

Indeed, in the second and ratified version of the treaty the "general principle" is yet further explained by Article IV:

It is agreed that no change of territorial sovereignty or of international relations of the country or counties traversed by the before-mentioned canal shall affect the general principle of neutralization or the obligation of the High Contracting Parties under the present treaty.

Moreover there were written into the second treaty the words

Such conditions and charges of traffic shall be just and equitable.

Article II, authorizing the construction and financing of the Canal by the United States alone, and granting to the United States "the exclusive right of providing for the regulation and management of the canal" was, save for a verbal change that need not detain us, unamended.

Article III contains changes of wording and of substance. But in both the versions, "the basis of the neutralization of such ship canal" is to be "the following rules, substantially as embodied in the convention of Constantinople, signed the twenty-eighth of October, 1888, for the free navigation of the Suez Canal." The "rules" are:

1. The canal shall be free and open to the vessels of commerce and of war of all nations observing these rules, on terms of entire equality, so that there shall be no discrimination against any such nation, or its citizens or subjects, in respect of the conditions or charges of traffic or otherwise. Such conditions and charges of traffic shall be just and equitable.

2. The canal shall never be blockaded, nor shall any right of war be exercised nor any act of hostility be committed within it. The

United States, however, shall be at liberty to maintain such military police along the canal as may be necessary to protect it against lawlessness and disorder.

3. Vessels of war of a belligerent shall not revictual nor take any stores in the canal except so far as may be strictly necessary; and the transit of such vessels through the canal shall be effected with the least possible delay in accordance with the regulations in force, and with only such intermission as may result from the necessities of the service.

Prizes shall be in all respects subject to the same rules as vessels of war of the belligerents.

4. No belligerent shall embark or disembark troops, munitions of war, or warlike materials in the canal, except in case of accidental hindrance of the transit, and in such case the transit shall be resumed with all possible dispatch.

5. The provisions of this article shall apply to waters adjacent to the canal, within three marine miles of either end. Vessels of war of a belligerent shall not remain in such waters longer than twenty-four hours at any one time, except in case of distress, and in such case shall depart as soon as possible; but a vessel of war of one belligerent shall not depart within twenty-four hours from the departure of a vessel of war of the other belligerent.

6. The plant, establishments, buildings and all works necessary to the construction, maintenance and operation of the canal shall be deemed to be part thereof, for the purposes of this treaty, and in time of war, as in time of peace, shall enjoy complete immunity from attack or injury by belligerents, and from acts calculated to impair their usefulness as part of the canal.

The changes here, insofar as they are of substance, consist of two omissions. First, the words "in time of war as in time of peace" have disappeared from Section I. This means that, if there were war, the United States, at its discretion, might close the canal.

Secondly, the words, "no fortifications shall be erected commanding the canal or the waters adjacent," have been eliminated. The United States has the right to erect such fortifications.

LORD PAUNCEFOTE OF PRESTON

One article was dropped:

The High Contracting Parties will, immediately upon the exchange of the ratifications of this convention, bring it to the notice of the other powers and invite them to adhere to it.

The Hay-Pauncefote Treaty, like the Clayton-Bulwer Treaty, is a bond between the United States and Great Britain alone.

The acceptance of the principle of commercial equality between all nations using the Canal was thus strictly in line with the foreign policy of the United States the wide world over. It was the policy adopted in the case of the Suez Canal. It was a profoundly wise policy.

By some statesmen of authority like Senator Root, the franchise enjoyed by the United States over the Isthmus of Panama has been described by the term "mandate" which has become so familiar to the League of Nations at Geneva. Of its character, there can be no doubt. It is fully set out in the Messages delivered to Congress by President Roosevelt on Dec. 7th, 1903, and Jan. 4th, 1904. It will be realized that Mr. Roosevelt was in office and therefore responsible to the nation and to the world when he made these pronouncements. Perhaps his most conclusive words were:

That our position as the mandatory of civilization has been by no means misconceived is shown by the promptitude with which the powers have, one after another, followed our lead in recognizing Panama as an independent State.

[The Powers in question were, he added, France, Germany, Denmark, Russia, Sweden, and Norway, Nicaragua, Peru, China, Cuba, Great Britain, Italy, Costa Rica, Japan and Austria Hungary.

According to a distinguished foreign authority, Dr. Diena, who challenges the contrary view of a not less "highly esteemed writer," Oppenheim, the rights of mankind in the Panama Canal are not based merely on customary use over a given period of time. They are based on specific treaties.

The Canal has been constructed under two engagements, one implied, that is, the Monroe Doctrine, and the other specific, that is, the Hay-Pauncefote Treaty. Indeed, it would be, perhaps a just tribute to two notable American statesmen if one entrance to the Canal were to be guarded by a statue of the President who said to the Old World, "thus far shalt thou go and no further," and the other entrance by a similar monument to William McKinley who founded the enterprise on a compact with Britain unshakable as a rock and of world-wide significance.

We submit that, obviously, when a specific point at issue arises, it should be the terms of the treaties, and not an interpretation of the Monroe Doctrine which should be paramount over the decision.

By making it clear that the Panama Canal was managed on the principle that all nations should enjoy the same opportunity to live and grow, the United States removed all possible cause of grievance against her control of the Canal and so contributed to the security of her strategic position. To quote from the masterly communication addressed by Secretary Hay to Mr. de Obaldia, Minister from Panama to the United States, dated October 24th, 1904,

The Isthmian Canal is an instrumentality of commerce—a measure for the promotion of peace.

XII

THE TOLLS

In the year 1912, the United States found herself exercising the *de facto* sovereignty over the Panama Canal, then approaching completion and over the adjacent zone of territory.

For the due discharge of this important trust, it was necessary for Congress to make a statutory provision and legislation was submitted.

All legislatures are human. Congress could not be unaffected by what Sir Edward Grey called "the interest which this great undertaking has aroused in the New World and the emotion with which its opening is looked forward to by United States citizens." Here was admittedly an American achievement of the first magnitude.

Moreover, there was still the sense that, in the Hay-Pauncefote Treaty, based as it was upon obligations, assumed under the previous Clayton-Bulwer Treaty, the United States had been driven to a close bargain. There was a strong desire that the mercantile marine of the United States should be assisted in its uphill competition with British shipping. Also, there was no great inclination to "check up" the record of diplomatic engagements and discussions which formed the international background to the latest position.

In the picturesque language of the period, there was asked the question, "Why cannot we do as we please with our own Ditch?"

On the question how far the Panama Canal is an asset to

the United States, various opinions might be quoted. We have this from a former Secretary of the Navy:

Nor can it be for a moment conceded that the Panama Canal will double the efficiency of the fleet, as it has often been stated. The efficiency of the Canal will increase the efficiency of the fleet somewhat because it will reduce the time necessary to move a given number of ships from one coast to another, but this rapidity of movement is not the equivalent of a numerical increase of units. The actual advantage of the Canal and its value to our navy is something that can be deduced only in theory, for it involves problems of strategy and warfare.

On the other hand, if a private company had constructed the Canal, the United States would have been compelled in perpetuity to pay for the use of the Canal by its public vessels. As matters stand, we are exempt from such payment. Nor may our enemies use the Canal against us.

Nor is this all. We have shown that, out of the revenues of the Canal, the capital invested in it may be amortized. When this capital is repaid, the Canal, as a military and naval asset, will have cost the United States nothing except the bare cost of the fortifications organized in its defence. The suggestion that, in the Hay-Pauncefote Treaty, we made a bad bargain, is thus only well founded if we fail to apply to the Canal a just system of accounting.

For a hundred years the ship of state had been navigated according to a certain chart. President Monroe, with the advice and coöperation of former Presidents, Jefferson and Madison, drew up the chart in the first instance. President Cleveland, with Richard Olney as his Secretary of State, was compelled to invoke that chart and to guide his course in a diplomatic conflict with Great Britain over what became known as the Venezuelan affair. President Cleveland followed the course laid down in the chart. President Roosevelt, as the captain of the ship, kept the craft on a safe and true course in the controversy with Germany and Great Britain over Venezuela. Sometimes the sailing has been exciting but the helm of the great ship has always been held by a steady hand.

But there now arose the question whether or not Congress would carry out the policy and the pledges of the United States according to which the charges on ships using the Canal would be levied at rates absolutely the same in all respects for the tonnage of every nation.

As it emerged from Congress, the Panama Canal Act contained a clause in which only too clearly it was apparent that discrimination had been authorized. These famous provisions were as follows:

That the President is hereby authorized to prescribe and from time to time change the tolls that shall be levied by the Government of the United States for the use of the Panama Canal: *Provided,* That no tolls, when prescribed as above, shall be changed, unless six months' notice thereof shall have been given by the President by proclamation. No tolls shall be levied upon vessels engaged in the coastwise trade of the United States.

Tolls may be based upon gross or net registered tonnage, displacement tonnage, or otherwise, and may be based on one form of tonnage for warships and another for ships of commerce. The rate of tolls may be lower upon vessels in ballast than upon vessels carrying passengers or cargo. When based upon net registered tonnage for ships of commerce, the tolls shall not exceed one dollar and twenty-five cents per net registered ton, nor be less, other than for vessels of the United States and its citizens, than the estimated proportionate cost of actual maintenance and operation of the canal.

The differentiation between the shipping of the United States and the shipping of other countries was defined by Senator Root in terms which may be thus paraphrased:

(1) On foreign vessels, using the Canal, the rate was to be not less than 75 cents a ton and not more than $1.25 a ton.

(2) On American vessels, the President was "authorized to impose no tolls" at all.

(3) On American vessels, engaged on coastwise trade, the President was "required to impose no tolls."

To the Monroe Doctrine, the freedom of the seas, including oceanic waterways, had been an indispensable accompaniment. Yet, little as it may have been realized, the freedom of the seas was clearly infringed by the discriminatory tolls. The United States was abandoning a principle which she herself had been the first among nations to emphasize, a principle which was the guarantee of her right on equal terms to use other waterways.

A test case had been the Welland Canal. In a masterly speech, delivered in favour of repealing the tolls-exemption provision of the Panama Canal Act, Senator Burton drove home the cogency of this precedent. He said:

> The Canadian Government in council had in substance decreed that while the tolls on cargoes carried through the Welland Canal should be twenty cents per ton on eastbound freight, yet if the boat went as far as Montreal there should be a rebate of eighteen cents a ton, leaving the net toll only two cents. This gave a preference to the port of Montreal as compared with the ports of the United States on Lake Ontario, the St. Lawrence River, and, in fact, upon the North Atlantic seaboard. Its manifest object was to increase the importance of Montreal as a port for the export of grain and other commodities.

The result was a controversy which continued from 1888 to 1892 when it was ended by the proclamation of August 18th, 1892, wherein President Harrison announced measures of retaliation. Under this pressure, the Government of Canada by Order in Council, revoked its regulation and so granted equal privileges to the ships and commerce of both nations.

According to Senator Burton, there were two reasons why

the complaint against discriminating tolls on the Panama Canal was more strongly supported by argument than had been the complaint against the discrimination along the Welland Canal.

First, a comparison of the treaties revealed how much more definite was the Panama clause than the Welland clause. By the Hay-Pauncefote Treaty:

The Canal shall be free and open to the vessels of commerce and of war of all nations observing these rules on terms of entire equality, so that there shall be no discrimination against any such nation, or its citizens or subjects, in respect of the conditions or charges of traffic, or otherwise.

This is a mandatory and a precise stipulation. But in the case of the Welland Canal, we have:

The Government of Her Britannic Majesty engage to urge upon the Government of the Dominion of Canada to secure to the citizens of the United States the use of the Welland, St. Lawrence and other canals in the Dominion on terms of equality with the inhabitants of the Dominion.

The only pledge is to "urge" what is described in quite general language as "terms of equality."

Secondly, in Senator Burton's words, we have this:

There is no question of territory involved in Canadian canals, either the Welland or those below Lake Ontario beside the rapids along the St. Lawrence River. They are all within the Dominion of Canada. It was not necessary to acquire the land through which they pass to build a canal as "a trust for the world." The argument in favor of the right of exclusion is, we must admit, much stronger than it is in the case of the Panama Canal; yet when a discrimination in tolls, which it was alleged was not altogether against our ships, was attempted, we demanded that it should be done away with, because it discriminated against our citizens and diverted trade and transportation which naturally belonged to our own country in another direction. Can we afford to assert the principle of equality in the use of channels when it benefits us and our trade, and at the same time establish another and entirely opposite rule when the canal or route belongs to us?

Canada was not a trustee, acting for international interests in a foreign country; she was a sovereign power dealing with her own country.

The answer to the unanswerable advanced in Congress was that, if Canada gave way, it was not because she admitted that she had been wrong, but only on grounds of expediency. Not that this rejoinder, so Senator Burton contended, altered the facts. As he says:

We made an insistent demand, not merely by diplomatic notes, but by action of Congress and by a retaliatory proclamation expressing our interpretation of the principles involved in the treaty relating to the Welland Canal and asserting the observance of our traditional policy.

Broadly it is agreed throughout the world that a national, a state, or a municipal utility must charge all its customers at the same rate for identical units of service. Railroads, gas and water and electricity corporations—they all accept this principle as axiomatic. Discriminations have been outlawed by numerous tribunals, including the Supreme Court of the United States. There are laws on our statute books making it a crime punishable by imprisonment for railroad corporations to discriminate between localities and persons, whether by rebates or otherwise. Secret advantages of all kinds are prohibited.

The decision in respect of the Panama Canal thus affected the control of canals throughout the world. As Sir Edward Grey pointed out, it was directly contrary, not only to the policy applied to the Suez and to the Welland Canals but to the Boundary Waters Treaty of 1909 between the United States and Great Britain which contained the following:

The high contracting parties agree that the navigation of all navigable boundary waters shall forever continue free and open for the purposes of commerce to the inhabitants and to the ships, vessels, and boats of both countries equally, subject, however, to any laws and regulations of either country, within its own territory, not inconsistent with such privilege of free navigation, and applying equally and without discrimination to the inhabitants, ships, vessels, and boats of both countries.

It is further agreed that so long as this treaty shall remain in force this same right of navigation shall extend to the waters of Lake Michigan and to all canals connecting boundary waters and now existing, or which may hereafter be constructed on either side of the line. Either of the high contracting parties may adopt rules and regulations governing the use of such canals within its own territory, and may charge tolls for the use thereof; but all such rules and regulations and all tolls charged shall apply alike to the subjects or citizens of the high contracting parties, and they . . . shall be placed on terms of equality in the use thereof.

Reduced to its simple terms, the question was whether the words "all countries" in the Hay-Pauncefote Treaty did or did not include the United States. What was the intention of the negotiators at the time of the negotiations? To quote Representative Stevens:

In the construction of the controverted clauses of any document it is always of prime importance to know exactly what the persons themselves intended by the language which is subject to dispute; and when they have set forth their own ideas as to its intention and meaning and have given good reasons for it, usually such facts have been conclusive as to the construction whenever the language has fairly allowed.

Let us see, then, what the men said who had been in actual touch with the negotiations.

We will begin frankly with the opinion of Theodore Roosevelt. With his usual candor, he stated it to his editorial friends on the *Outlook:*

I believe that under the arbitration treaty of 1908 the United States is honorably bound to arbitrate the question raised by Sir Edward Grey on behalf of Great Britain in reference to the canal tolls, provided the question cannot be settled in some other way satisfactory to both Powers.

I believe that the position of the United States is proper as regards the coastwise traffic. I think that we have the right to free *bona fide* coastwise traffic from tolls. I think that this does not interfere with the rights of any other nation because no ships but our own can engage in coastwise traffic, so that there is no discrimination against other ships when we relieve the coastwise traffic from tolls. I believe that the only damage that would be done is the damage to the Canadian Pacific Railway. Moreover, I do not think that it sits well on the representatives of any foreign nation, even upon those of a power with which we are, and I hope and believe will always remain, on such good terms as Great Britain, to make any plea in reference to what we do with our own coastwise traffic; because we are benefiting the whole world by our action at Panama. and are doing this where every dollar of expense is paid by ourselves. In all history I do not believe you can find another instance where as great and expensive a work as the Panama Canal undertaken not by a private corporation but by a nation, has ever been as generously put at the service of all the nations of mankind.

Moreover, I quite admit that it would be a difficult thing to get an arbitral tribunal which will not have some bias against us. Switzerland is almost the only community which has not some commercial interest in the Panama Canal.

Nevertheless I hold that these considerations in no way affect our moral obligations to arbitrate the question if Great Britain so insists. It is to be presumed that we made the promise with our eyes open, and were aware that it might not be wholly pleasant to keep it. I was certainly alive to this fact, but the very fact that the promise may not be easy to keep is the reason why we make it with the solemnity attending a treaty. A promise to arbitrate is worthless unless we mean to keep it on the precise occasions when it is unpleasant for us to do so. Moreover, this arbitration must be, if Great Britain so desires, at the Permanent Court at The Hague, unless we are prepared to violate our solemn arbitration treaty proclaimed by our Government on June 5, 1908. Article I of this treaty explicitly states that "differences relating to the interpretation

THEODORE ROOSEVELT

of treaties existing between the two contracting parties" shall be referred to The Hague Court "provided that they do not affect the vital interests or the independence, or the honor of the two contracting states." It seems to me impossible to argue that the question of tolls on our coastwise traffic is one which affects either the vital interests of America or its independence or its honor. Such being the case, I hold that it is a matter of honorable obligation on our part to live up to that arbitration treaty in spirit and letter, and that therefore, if the question cannot be settled in some other way, we must refer it to The Hague Court for arbitration.

The whole incident illustrates well the folly of those Americans who a year or two ago endeavored to commit this country to general arbitration treaties under which they would have been bound to arbitrate everything. A general arbitration treaty is nothing whatever but a promise, and surely every man in private life understands that the worth of a promise consists in its being kept, or that it is deeply discreditable for any man to make a promise when there is reasonable doubt whether he can keep it. A merchant who loosely promises all kinds of things without serious thought as to whether he will be able to keep his promise is in grave jeopardy of losing both his fortune and his good name. The same thing is true of a nation. We should understand that the time to weigh, and to weigh well and thoroughly, the full import of a promise is the time when it is desired to make that promise and not the time when it is desired to break that promise.

What is going on in connection with this canal treaty now illustrates well the truth of this position. I have always advocated the arbitration of such questions as the interpretation of the Hay-Pauncefote Treaty. When I negotiated the arbitration treaties in 1908, I acted in accordance with what seemed the practically unanimous desire of our people, and with what certainly was the almost practically unanimous desire of the representatives of the people in the Senate and the lower House of Congress.

Now, when I made that treaty I understood entirely that under it we might be obliged to arbitrate questions where we thought that our side was absolutely right, and where nevertheless it was possible that a court might decide against us. This is precisely one of those cases. We are right, and yet the court may decide against us. But, with our eyes open, we have agreed to arbitrate just such cases as this and we must not go back on that agreement. I believe in being cautious about making promises. I believe in refusing to make foolish and sweeping general promises, which it would be impossible, and improper, to keep. But when we have deliberately and solemnly made a promise, then I most emphatically believe that this Nation should keep that promise, just as an honorable man would do as regards a private promise of the same type. Therefore I believe it to be the bounden duty of this Nation to arbitrate the question of the Canal tolls under the provisions of our arbitration treaty.

Mr. Roosevelt's position was thus broadly that the United States had a right to discriminate the tolls, but that she should submit the issue to arbitration. Evidently, he suspected that, on an arbitration, the verdict would go against this country.

The suggestion of the *Outlook* has been that, since the general Arbitration Treaty and the Hay-Pauncefote Treaty were ratified during Mr. Roosevelt's Administration, his interpretation of them had "a semi-official and arbitrative character." It is, perhaps, enough to say that the Hay-Pauncefote Treaty was negotiated through all save its final stages under President McKinley, and that, as Vice-President, Mr. Roosevelt had no direct contact with the negotiations. He became President on September 14th, 1901. He approved the final Treaty on September 21st, only seven days later.

Yet even so, he seems to us to be a witness against his own later view.

In transmitting the second Hay-Pauncefote Treaty to the Senate for its consideration, President Roosevelt stated:

I am glad to be able to announce to you that our negotiations on this subject (construction of an Isthmian Canal) with Great Britain, conducted on both sides in a spirit of friendliness and mutual good-will and respect, have resulted in my being able to lay before the Senate a treaty which if ratified will enable us to begin preparations for an Isthmian Canal at any time, and which guarantees to this nation every right that it has ever asked in connection with the Canal. In this treaty, the old Clayton-Bulwer Treaty, so long recognized as inadequate to supply the base for the construction and maintenance of a necessarily American ship canal, is abrogated. It specifically provides that the United States alone shall do the work of building and assume the responsibility of safeguarding the Canal and shall regulate its neutral use by all nations on terms of equality without the guarantee or interference of any outside nation from any quarter.

Again, he said, on January 4, 1904, in a special message:

Under the Hay-Pauncefote Treaty it was explicitly provided that the United States should control, police and protect the canal which was to be built, keeping it open for the vessels of all nations on equal terms. The United States thus assumes the position of guarantor of the Canal and of its peaceful use by all the world.

Secretary Hay stated in a note on the following day:

The Clayton-Bulwer Treaty was conceived to form an obstacle, and the British Government therefore agreed to abrogate it, the United States only promising in return to protect the Canal and keep it open on equal terms to all nations, in accordance with our traditional policy.

Mr. Willis Fletcher Johnson, as a journalist, interviewed Colonel Hay:

I asked Colonel Hay plumply if the treaty meant what it appeared to mean on its face, and whether the phrase, "vessels of all nations," was intended to include our own shipping, or was to be interpreted as meaning "all other nations." The Secretary smiled, half indulgently, half quizzically, as he replied:

"All means all. The treaty was not so long that we could not have made room for the word 'other' if we had understood that it belonged there. All nations means all nations, and the United States is certainly a nation."

"That was the understanding between yourself and Lord Pauncefote when you and he made the treaty?" I pursued.

"It certainly was," he replied. "It was the understanding of both governments, and I have no doubt that the Senate realized that in ratifying the second treaty without such an amendment it was committing us to the principle of giving all friendly nations equal privileges in the canal with ourselves. That is our Golden Rule."

Ambassador Choate confirms this construction of the Hay-Pauncefote Treaty in the following:

It is true that I had something to do with the negotiation of this Treaty. In the summer of 1901—you will remember that the Treaty was ratified by the Senate in November, 1901—I was in England until October and was in almost daily contact with Lord Pauncefote and was also in very frequent correspondence with Mr. Hay, our Secretary of State, under whom I was acting.

As the lips of both of these diplomats and great patriots, who were each true to his own country, and each regardful of the rights of others, are sealed in death, I think it is quite proper that I should say what I believe both of them, if they were here, would say today, that the clause in the Panama Canal bill exempting coastwise American shipping from the payment of tolls is in direct violation of the Treaty. I venture to say now that in the whole course of the negotiation of this particular treaty, no claim, no suggestion, was made that there should be any exemption of anybody.

Senator McCumber put to former Ambassador Choate the following questions:

First. Was it understood by the State Departments of the two countries that the words "vessels of commerce and war of all nations" included our own vessels?

Second. Was it understood that these words also included our own vessels engaged in the coastwise trade?

Ambassador Choate replied:

I answer both of these questions most emphatically in the affirmative. The phrase quoted, "vessels of commerce and war of all nations," certainly included our own vessels, and was so understood by our own State Department and by the foreign office of Great Britain. It was understood by the same parties that these words also included our own vessels engaged in the coastwise trade.

When we came to the negotiation of this last treaty, that of 1901, there was no question that, as between the United States and Great Britain, the Canal should be open to the citizens and subjects of both on equal terms, and that it should also be open on like terms to the citizens and subjects of every other state that brought itself within the category prescribed. On that point there was really nothing to discuss, and in the whole course of the negotiations there was never a suggestion on either side that the words "the vessels of commerce and of war of all nations" meant anything different from the natural and obvious meaning of these words. Such language admitted of the exemption or exception of no particular kind of vessels of commerce and of war of any nation, whether of vessels engaged in foreign trade or coastwise trade.

In a letter to Secretary Hay, ex-Ambassador Choate summarized the result of the negotiation of the Hay-Pauncefote Treaty and threw an interesting sidelight on its construction:

I am sure that in this whole matter, since the receipt by him of your new draft, Lord Lansdowne has been most considerate and more than generous. He has shown an earnest desire to bring to an amicable settlement, honorable alike to both parties, this long and important controversy between the two nations. In substance he abrogates the Clayton-Bulwer Treaty, gives us an American canal, ours to build as and where we like, to own, control and govern, on the sole condition of its being always neutral and free for the passage of ships of all nations on equal terms, except that if we get into a war with any nation, we can shut its ships out and take care of ourselves.

Senator Root was equally explicit:

The only two things in Article VIII of the Clayton-Bulwer Treaty are the equality of service and of charge between the vessels of the United States and those of Great Britain and the extension of that to other countries that come in and the obligation of protection. The great object of the negotiation of the Hay-Pauncefote Treaty was to make over to the United States alone the duty and right of protection. That was the difference between the Hay-Pauncefote Treaty and the Clayton-Bulwer Treaty—that Great Britain was to surrender the right of protection, to be relieved from the duty of protection, and no other countries were to be permitted to come in and exercise the right of protection. The United States was to put itself on the platform that Blaine laid down in 1881 as the sole protector of the Canal. What, then, was there to be preserved unimpaired in the eighth article of the Clayton-Bulwer Treaty? Nothing except the basis of equality, equality between the United States and Great Britain, equality measured by the treatment of the nationals of one country for the nationals of the other. Nothing else was left to be preserved unimpaired.

Again:

Whatever else the Hay-Pauncefote Treaty means, it means to secure absolutely the general principle of neutralization contained in the eighth article of the Clayton-Bulwer Treaty, which was, according to the understanding of the makers of the Hay-Pauncetote Treaty, the absolute equality of the ships, the citizens and the subjects of all nations with the ships and the citizens of the United States and of Great Britain; and we are not at liberty to spell out any different meaning of the Hay-Pauncefote Treaty.

While the controversy was proceeding, Senator McCumber inquired of Mr. Henry White whether the negotiators of the Hay-Pauncefote Treaty understood that coastwise shipping could be relieved from the payment of tolls imposed on the shipping. Mr. White replied promptly and emphatically:

There is but one way in which I can answer the inquiry contained in your letter—as to the understanding of Mr. Hay and Lord Pauncefote on the question of the use of the canal by vessels engaged wholly in the coastwise trade—to wit:

(1) That the exemption of our coastwise shipping from the payment of tolls was never suggested to, nor by, anyone connected with the negotiation of the Hay-Pauncefote treaties in this country or in England;

(2) That, from the day on which I opened the negotiations with Lord Salisbury for the abrogation of the Clayton-Bulwer Treaty until the ratification of the Hay-Pauncefote Treaty, the words "all nations" and "equal terms" were understood to refer to the United

States as well as to all other nations, by every one of those, whether American or British, who had anything to do with the negotiations whereof the Treaty last mentioned was the result.

Of Mr. White's first hand knowledge, there can be no doubt. As Secretary to the Embassy in London, he witnessed the entire drama. Ambassador Choate wrote of him to Secretary Hay:

> As I do not see anything likely to be required of me that may not be just as well done by Mr. White, who knows your mind and mine exactly, and has been fully advised of all that has been done, I propose to keep my long-cherished purpose of sailing on the *Philadelphia* on Saturday.

The question next to be answered was what was the understanding of the matter in the Senate itself? It happens that we are left in no uncertainty over that aspect of the case. Senator Bard of California proposed an amendment to the Hay-Pauncefote Treaty which contained the provision:

> The United States reserves the right in the regulation and management of the Canal to discriminate in respect of the charges of traffic in favor of vessels of its own citizens engaged in coastwise trade.

The amendment was defeated and for a reason which the then Senator Fairbanks makes clear:

> The Bard amendment was voted down, after full discussion, not because it was regarded as surplusage, but because in the opinion of a large majority of the Senate it was violative of the spirit of equality, which had been expressed in the treaty.

As Senator Bacon, who voted for the Bard amendment, and so becomes a decisive witness, put it:

> I wish to say, if the Senator will pardon me a moment, in this connection, as I am one of those recorded as voting in favor of the

Bard amendment, that my idea at that time was not that any part of the merchant marine of the United States should have free transportation or free right of passage through the canal, but I was standing simply upon the ground that I thought the United States should have the right to control whatever tolls were imposed and discriminate in favor of our own citizens if we saw fit to do so.

. . . .

What the Senate of the United States then did was to decline even to make that demand upon Great Britain. We declined to say that we would contend for that. We not only by that action, in fact, recognized that there was an obligation of that kind under the Clayton-Bulwer treaty, but we declined to contend that that should be surrendered by Great Britain and that a new contract should be made, to which they would not have agreed.

The Senate refused to exempt coastwise trade from the tolls for the express reason that it would be a contradiction of the rest of the Treaty.

Evidence of this character must be cumulative to be conclusive. As the commercial provisions of the first and second Hay-Pauncefote treaties are the same, expressions of senators in connection with the consideration of either of these treaties serve as evidence. We will introduce them with the following citation from the majority report by Cushman K. Davis of the Committee on Foreign Relations in presenting the first Hay-Pauncefote Treaty to the Senate for its consideration:

The Suez Canal makes no discrimination in its tolls in favor of its stockholders . . . and, taking its profits or the half of them as our basis of calculation, we will never find it necessary to differentiate our rates of toll in favor of our own people in order to secure a very great profit on the investment.

No American statesman, speaking with official authority or responsibility, has ever intimated that the United States would attempt to control this canal for the exclusive benefit of our Government or people. They have all, with one accord, declared that the canal

was to be neutral ground in time of war and always open on terms of impartial equality to the ships and commerce of the world.

．　　　　．　　　　．　　　　．　　　　．　　　　．　　　　．

The United States cannot take an attitude of opposition to the principles of the great act of October 22, 1888 (Suez Canal Convention) without discrediting the official declarations of our Government for fifty years on the neutrality of an isthmian canal and its equal use by all nations, without discrimination.

That the United States sought no exclusive privilege or preferential right of any kind in regard to the proposed communication, and their sincere wish, if it should be found practical, was to see it dedicated to the common use of all nations on the most liberal terms and on a footing of perfect equality for all.

That the United States would not, if they could, obtain any exclusive right or privilege in a great highway which naturally belongs to all mankind.

Senator Morgan submitted a minority report. It agrees with the report of the majority that this treaty provided for equality of opportunity in the commercial use of the projected Isthmian Canal.

All that is left of this general treaty is the general principle provided in Article VIII of the Clayton-Bulwer treaty. That is, that the vessels of all nations using the canal should be treated with exact equality, without discrimination in favor of the vessels of any nation.

．　　　　．　　　　．　　　　．　　　　．　　　　．　　　　．

Then this convention, in Article II, proceeds to define and formulate into an agreement, intended to be world-wide in its operation, "the general principle of neutralization," established in Article VIII of the Clayton-Bulwer treaty.

．　　　　．　　　　．　　　　．　　　　．　　　　．　　　　．

Nothing is given to the United States in Article II of the convention now under consideration, nor is anything denied to us that is not given or denied to all other nations.

Senator Lodge was equally emphatic:

Whatever our opinion may be as to the strict legal interpretation of the rules governing the matter of tolls imposed upon vessels passing through the canal, we cannot and we ought not to overlook the understanding of those who negotiated the treaty as to the intent and effect of the rules which they framed. As to the nature of the understanding we have direct testimony. Mr. Henry White, who first laid before the British Government the desire of the United States to enter into negotiations for the supersession of the Clayton-Bulwer treaty, has stated that Lord Salisbury expressed to him the entire willingness of England to remove all obstacles which the Clayton-Bulwer treaty put in the way of the construction of the canal, and desired only to maintain equality of tolls imposed upon all vessels, including those of the United States. Mr. Choate, who completed the negotiations which resulted in the second Hay-Pauncefote treaty, has publicly stated that the understanding at that time of both parties was the same as that given by Mr. White. The only other American concerned in the actual negotiation of the treaty was the late Mr. Hay, at that time Secretary of State. I know that Mr. Hay's view was the same as that of Mr. Choate and Mr. White. It is therefore clear on the testimony of our three negotiators that the negotiations as they were begun and as they were completed in the second Hay-Pauncefote treaty proceeded on the clear understanding that there was to be no discrimination in the tolls imposed as between the vessels of any nation, including the vessels of the United States.

This phase of our argument can be brought to a close by citations from an address by Senator McCumber in favour of the repeal of the tolls-exemption provision of the Panama Canal Act. They are conclusive and final as to what the Senate understood when it ratified the Hay-Pauncefote Treaty:

I have presented this much of the proceedings in the Senate at the time of the adoption of the Hay-Pauncefote treaty to demonstrate beyond any possible contention that the Senate as a whole, those who listened to the debate or took part in it, did comprehend and clearly comprehend that the treaty was being pressed for adoption upon the theory of construction that it bound the United States to claim no privileges for its own vessels of any kind that it did not accord to other vessels.

On the British side, the understanding of the issue was not less clear.

The views of Lord Lansdowne, Minister for Foreign Affairs for Great Britain and of Ambassador Choate are contained in a despatch by the latter to Secretary Hay dated September 21, 1901. In it he stated that Lord Lansdowne contended that we (United States):

might in the future acquire all the territory on both sides of the canal; that we might then claim that a treaty providing for the neutrality of a canal running through a neutral country could no longer apply to a canal that ran through American territory only; and he again insisted that they must have something to satisfy Parliament and the British public that, in giving up the Clayton-Bulwer treaty, they had retained and reasserted the "general principle" principle of it; that the canal should be technically neutral, and should be free to all nations on terms of equality, and especially that in the contingency supposed, of the territory on both sides of the canal becoming ours, the canal, its neutrality, its being free and open to all nations on equal terms, should not be thereby affected.

Three exceptions to the rule of equality had been admitted and—themselves not of great importance—may be here mentioned and so eliminated from the controversy.

(1) By Treaty with Colombia, her public vessels were permitted to use the Canal, free of toll. This was a concession which might be described as an offset against rental due in equity on the Colombian territory which had been alienated for the use of the Canal. The concession emphasized the clear title to the Zone engaged by the United States.

(2) The public vessels of Panama are allowed a free use of the Canal, see Article XIX of the Treaty:

The Government of the Republic of Panama shall have the right to transport over the canal its vessels and its troops and munitions of war in such vessels at all times without paying charges of any kind.

(3) Certain public vessels owned by the United States enjoyed this privilege. Indeed, the privilege was cited by Senator Walsh as proof that equality of tolls was never contemplated by the Treaty:

It is advanced that the duty of maintaining the neutral character of the Canal, so far as it is neutral, being by the treaty imposed upon the United States, and upon it alone, it is implied that its vessels of war may pass through the Canal free, since it is presumed that they are in the discharge of the duty thus cast upon our Government, it being impossible to differentiate between service which falls within that duty and such as is beyond its scope, and because, if it were, the naval authorities ought not to be called upon to disclose the particular mission in pursuit of which the Canal is opened for the reception of our fleet or any part of it.

But what is this argument but an admission that, by reason of the peculiar relations our Government sustains to the Canal, its vessels of war, so far as payment of tolls is concerned, are not included in the expression used in the treaty, "vessels of commerce and of war of all nations observing these rules"?

This line of argument is not applicable, however, to a great variety of craft in the Government service, such as revenue cutters, light-house tenders, and such as carry officers of the Coast and Geodetic Survey and employees of the Bureau of Fisheries, and the like.

It is enough to say here that, where a corporation uses traffic in its own service, it is not customary to charge the cost to revenue and then to expenses so swelling both sides of the account. The ledger is simplified by omitting the item on both sides.

Senator Walsh asked whether a fleet of vessels, owned by the United States and in some cases naval in character, but employed on carrying workers and supplies to Alaska for the construction of railroads, would be liable for tolls.

Reference to the practice of transportation companies in similar situations will again furnish the answer. Traffic on an interurban railway to a summer resort of which it is the owner must pay the same fare it would have to pay on another interurban line or that it would have to pay if its destiny was another or competitive resort. This principle is almost as securely established in the regulation of domestic corporations as are the fundamental principles of constitutional law. Applying this principle to the questions raised in the foregoing citations, it at once becomes clear that insofar as the United States is itself engaged in business, its traffic through the Canal must be charged the same rate as the traffic of nationals and non-nationals of the same character.

Not that these comparatively minor issues affected the situation as a whole. It was the discrimination on mercantile marine that upset the world. It was a repudiation of the entire structure of policy and pledges, elaborated by the United States since the days of George Washington—the Monroe Doctrine, the freedom of the seas and the equal rights of all nations in restricted waters and in artificial highways, like the Suez and the Welland Canals, were dealt a staggering blow.

In his Farewell Address, George Washington had adjured "a great nation to give to mankind the magnanimous and too novel example of a people always guided by an exalted justice and benevolence." Yet, for the sake of a paltry $2,000,000 a year—an Esau's mess of pottage— these high purposes were to be abandoned.

The truth must be plainly stated. Before the United States acquired a title-deed to the Canal Zone, its desires and those of the world at large were substantially the same.

In that environment our statesmen formulated the traditional American policy that an Isthmian Canal should be
at the service of mankind on equal terms. As the United
States grew in numbers and wealth—in self-conscious importance—its desire altered so as to include political control
without commercial advantage. After a title-deed had been
secured and construction was nearing completion, its desires
changed so as to include commercial advantage. The tolls-
exemption provision of the Panama Canal Act was the
result of this change in American desire fostered by the
consciousness of superior power, untempered by the spirit
of brotherhood. The United States changed from the
humble pleader that she had been when conscious of the
strength of the other party in interest—that is, Great
Britain—to an autocrat, exulting in her sudden accession
of world power.

XIII

On general grounds of equity, it was the world as a whole that had reason to complain of the discriminatory tolls, expressed under the Panama Canal Act. But the specific treaties which had been infringed were treaties made between the United States and Great Britain; as a maritime power, therefore, second to none at that period, Great Britain entered her protest.

We submit not only that she was justified, but that if she had omitted to take this initiative, she would have failed in her duty as the leading representative of nations, other than the United States who were to use the Canal.

The date of the protest—February 8th, 1912—is significant. It reached Washington while the debates in Congress, dealing with the Panama Tolls, were in progress. The terms of the protest were tentative, therefore, and, as we submit, inconclusive.

We think it well to set out the document as it stands:

The attention of His Majesty's Government has been called to the various proposals that have from time to time been made for the purpose of relieving American shipping from the burden of the tolls to be levied on vessels passing through the Panama Canal, and these proposals, together with the arguments that have been used to support them have been carefully considered with a view to the bearing on them of the provisions of the treaty between the United States and Great Britain of November 18, 1901.

The proposals might be summed up as follows:

(1) To exempt all American shipping from the tolls; (2) to refund to all American ships the tolls which they may have paid;

(3) to exempt American ships engaged in the coastwise trade; (4) to repay the tolls to American ships engaged in the coastwise trade.

The proposal to exempt all American shipping from the payment of the tolls would, in the opinion of His Majesty's Government, involve an infraction of the treaty, nor is there, in their opinion, any difference in principle between charging tolls only to refund them and remitting tolls altogether. The result is the same in either case, and the adoption of the alternative method of refunding the tolls in preference to that of remitting them, while perhaps complying with the letter of the treaty, would still contravene its spirit.

It has been argued that a refund of the tolls would merely be equivalent to a subsidy and that there is nothing in the Hay-Pauncefote treaty which limits the right of the United States to subsidise its shipping. It is true that there is nothing in that treaty to prevent the United States from subsidizing its shipping, and if it granted a subsidy His Majesty's Government could not be in a position to complain. But there is a great distinction between a general subsidy, either to shipping at large or to shipping engaged in any given trade, and a subsidy calculated particularly with reference to the amount of user of the canal by the subsidized lines or vessels. If such a subsidy were granted it would not, in the opinion of His Majesty's Government, be in accordance with the obligations of the treaty.

As to the proposal that exemption shall be given to vessels engaged in the coastwise trade, a more difficult question arises. If the trade should be so regulated as to make it certain that only bona fide coastwise traffic which is reserved for United States vessels would be benefited by this exemption, it may be that no objection could be taken. But it appears to my Government that it would be impossible to frame regulations which would prevent the exemption from resulting, in fact, in a preference to United States shipping and consequently in an infraction of the treaty.

Put into simple language, this meant

(1) that to exempt all American shipping from the tolls would be "an infraction of the treaty."

(2) that to refund the tolls to American shipping would be an artifice not less contrary to "the obligations of the treaty."

(3) that to exempt coastwise shipping only would be

PHILANDER C. KNOX

"impossible." No regulations could be framed which would not be evaded. Presumably, a vessel proceeding from a foreign port or to a foreign port would make itself "coastwise" by touching at an American port.

A lawyer of President Taft's eminence was not slow in picking out the flaws in this reasoning. In a memorandum, added to the Panama Canal Act, on signature, he insisted on two points.

First, in his view, the ships of all nations, mentioned in the Hay-Pauncefote Treaty did not include ships of the United States:

The Article is a declaration of policy by the United States that the canal shall be neutral, that the attitude of this Government towards the commerce of the world is that all nations will be treated alike and no discrimination made by the United States against any one of them observing the rules adopted by the United States. The right to the use of the Canal and to equality of treatment in the use depends upon the observance of the conditions of the use by the nations to whom we extended that privilege. The privileges of all nations to whom we extend the use upon the observance of these conditions were to be equal to that extended to any one of them which observed the conditions. In other words, it was a conditional favored nation treatment, the measure of which in the absence of express stipulation to that effect, is not what the country gives to its own nationals, but the treatment it extends to other nations.

Thus it is seen that the rules are but a basis of neutralization, intended to effect the neutrality which the United States was willing should be the character of the canal and not intended to limit or hamper the United States in the exercise of its sovereign power to deal with its own commerce using its own canal in whatsoever manner it saw fit.

Secondly, the contention that the United States was debarred from refunding the tolls, could only mean an infringement of her essential sovereignty.

If there is no "difference in principle between the United States charging tolls to its own shipping only to refund them and remitting tolls altogether," as the British protest declares, then the irresistible conclusion is that the United States, although it owns, controls and has paid for the Canal is restricted by treaty from aiding its own commerce in the way that all the other nations of the world may freely do.

If it is correct then to assume that there is nothing in the Hay-Pauncefote Treaty preventing Great Britain and the other nations from extending such favors as they may see fit to their shipping using the canal, and doing it in the way they see fit, and if it is also right to assume that there is nothing in the Treaty that gives the United States any supervision over, or right to complain of such action, then the British protest leads to the absurd conclusion that this Government in constructing the Canal, maintaining the Canal, and defending the Canal, finds itself shorn of its right to deal with its own commerce in its own way, while all other nations using the Canal in competition with American commerce enjoy that right and power unimpaired.

The British protest, therefore, is a proposal to read into the treaty a surrender by the United States of its right to regulate its own commerce in its own way and by its own methods, a right which neither Great Britain herself, nor any other nation that may use the Canal, has surrendered or proposes to surrender.

On the merits, President Taft assumed that competition between American and foreign shipping was not in question:

The policy of exempting the coastwise trade from all tolls really involves the question of granting a Government subsidy for the purpose of encouraging that trade in competition with the trade of the trans-continental railroads. I approve this policy. It is in accord with the historical course of the Government in giving government aid to the construction of the trans-continental roads. It is now merely giving Government aid to a means of transportation that competes with those trans-continental roads.

President Taft admitted that the Act authorized the President to discriminate tolls in favour of general as well as coastwise American shipping, but he added:

There is nothing in the Act to compel the President to make such a discrimination. It is not, therefore, necessary to discuss the policy

of such discrimination until the question may arise in the exercise
of the President's discretion.

The British rejoinder was dated November 14th, 1912.
If we do not quote it at any length, it is because it reviews
broadly the ground which, in previous pages, we have
already covered. Great Britain argued:

The effect of these provisions is that vessels engaged in the coastwise trade will contribute nothing to the upkeep of the Canal.
Similarly vessels belonging to the Government of the Republic of
Panama will, in pursuance of the treaty of 1903, contribute nothing
to the upkeep of the Canal. Again, in the cases where tolls are
levied, the tolls in the case of ships belonging to the United States
and its citizens may be fixed at a lower rate than in the case of
foreign ships and may be less than the estimated proportionate cost
of the actual maintenance and operation of the Canal.

The reply of Secretary of State Philander C. Knox was,
as might have been expected, brilliant in its dialectical
ability. He insisted that, in fixing the tolls, the President
limited discrimination strictly to coastwise shipping, and
that no other question had arisen. He reminded Sir
Edward Grey that, by the terms of her original protest,
Great Britain had admitted in principle that coastwise shipping might be exempt under the treaty, on which his comment was:

that obviously the United States is not to be denied the power to
remit tolls to its own coastwise trade because of a suspicion or possibility that the regulations yet to be framed may not restrict this
exemption to bona fide coastwise traffic.

On the general question whether the tolls, declared by
the President, are "just and equitable," Secretary Knox
disclosed the data on which they were calculated:

If the British contention is correct that the true construction of
the treaty requires all traffic to be reckoned in fixing just and

equitable tolls, it requires at least an allegation that the tolls as fixed are not just and equitable and that all traffic has not been reckoned in fixing them before the United States can be called upon to prove that this course was not followed, even assuming that the burden of proof would rest with the United States in any event, which is open to question. This Government welcomes the opportunity, however, of informing the British Government that the tolls fixed in the President's proclamation are based upon the computations set forth in the report of Professor Emory R. Johnson, a copy of which is forwarded herewith for delivery to Sir Edward Grey, and that the tolls which would be paid by American coastwise vessels, but for the exemption contained in the act, were computed in determining the rate fixed by the President.

By reference to page 208 of Professor Johnson's report, it will be seen that the estimated net tonnage of shipping using the canal in 1915 is as follows:

	Tons
Coast to coast American shipping	1,000,000
American shipping carrying foreign commerce of the United States	720,000
Foreign shipping carrying commerce of the United States and foreign countries	8,780,000

Here the argument was that, in fixing the tolls, coastwise shipping had been taken into the reckoning and that the failure to collect these tolls merely represented a loss to the United States. The concession to Colombia was part of the consideration which secured to the United States a clear title to the use of the Canal Zone and was thus not only in the nature of rent but was also intended to remove all doubts as to the right of way.

The Secretary of State also observed that as Great Britain had not protested against free transit to the public vessels of the Republic of Panama when the Hay-Bunau-Varilla Treaty was under consideration, she was guilty of *laches* and any rights that she may have had ceased during the interim of 1904 and 1912, owing to acquiescence in the *status quo* created by the last mentioned treaty.

Sir Edward Grey pointedly observed:

Unless the whole volume of shipping which passes through the Canal, which benefits all equally by its services, is taken into account, there are no means of determining whether the tolls chargeable upon a vessel represent that vessel's fair proportion of the current expenditure properly chargeable against the Canal; that is to say, interest on the capital expended in construction and the cost of operation and maintenance. If any classes of vessels are exempted from tolls in such a way that no receipts from such ships are taken into account in the income of the Canal, there is no guaranty that the vessels upon which tolls are being levied are not being made to bear more than their fair share of the upkeep.

Hence, according to Sir Edward Grey, a differentiation of tolls means, *ipso facto,* that there had been an infringement of the stipulation that the amount of the tolls "shall be just and equitable."

To make the point plain, let us suppose that a public utility requires an income of $150,000 a year and that it serves 1500 customers. On the average, each customer must supply $100 of revenue. What happens, then, if 300 customers are exempted from charge? The other 1200 customers must find between them an average of $125, and this addition of $125 may exceed what is just and reasonable.

Our foreign policy from and after 1899 in relation to the open door in the spheres of influence acquired in China by other powers is very persuasive as to the kind of equality for which our Department of State was then negotiating. Insofar as this policy is of significance in this discussion, it is contained in the article of the statement of principles communicated by Secretary Hay to Russia for its approval. This article requested that it agree:

That is will levy no higher harbor dues on vessels of another nationality frequenting any port in such "sphere" than shall be levied on vessels of its own nationality, and no higher railroad charges over lines built, controlled or operated within its "sphere" on merchandise belonging to citizens or subjects of other nationalities transported through such "sphere" than shall be levied on similar merchandise belonging to its own nationals transported over equal distances.

The United States sought to obtain and actually did obtain equality of opportunity in the use of the ports and in the use of railroads in the pursuit of trade in these spheres of influence.

There arises here a point of some subtlety on which a word must be said. It was argued in Congress that the world had no reason to protest against a differentiation of the tolls because the method of differentiation was so adjusted as to lay no additional burden on nations other than the United States. The rate of toll, so it was argued, was calculated not on foreign tonnage alone but all tonnage using the Canal, including that of the United States whether coastwise or other. Hence, an exemption of coastwise tonnage only meant that the United States herself would have to make up the difference. It was a way of drawing a subsidy for shipping out of the Treasury.

On this we can only say that, assuming the argument to be sound, it was a very bad way of attaining the end in view. The statistical and accounting jugglery only would have meant that the taxpayers would have been called upon to accept a burden, not frankly disclosed to them. Moreover, the slipshod arrangement, so outlined, would have laid the United States open to insinuations on the part of other countries to which she would have been unable to give a clear and lucid reply.

With the protests of Great Britain received and published, there arose the question what, if any steps, should be taken to adjust the controversy. The proposal of Sir

WOODROW WILSON

Edward Grey was arbitration. The proposal split parties at Washington into three groups.

First, there were those, Democrats as well as Republicans, who took the ground that there was no basis for arbitration because the question was clear and undoubted, that the provision of our score or more of treaties providing for arbitration when the construction of a treaty was involved did not apply because in this matter there were involved the vital interests of the country.

A second group held with former President Roosevelt that while, in fact, we have the right under the Hay-Pauncefote Treaty to exempt our coastwise ships from toll, yet, as the Panama Canal Act involved the construction of treaties, it was our duty to arbitrate if arbitration was demanded by Great Britain.

A third group, led by Senator Root, whose two speeches in the Senate will be treasured as classics in our congressional debates, maintained that the Panama Canal Act was so plainly in violation of our treaty obligations both in letter and in spirit that it must be amended.

The reply of Secretary Knox to Great Britain was, in effect, that no cause for arbitration could arise until it had been shown that British shipping had suffered a genuine injury.

One suggestion, included by President Taft in his Memorandum of August 12th, raises an interesting question of constitutional procedure. His idea was that all persons and especially British subjects, aggrieved under the terms of the Panama Canal Act, might seek redress by litigation before the Supreme Court of the United States. By Article 2, Section 1, of the Constitution, the laws of the United States and treaties made under the authority of the United States are the supreme law of the land. But, on many occasions, the Supreme Court has had to determine

a discrepancy between a treaty and a later act of Congress.
If read apart from the specific issues involved, such decisions
are apt to be confusing and I shall content myself with
quoting from Justice Miller's decision in the Supreme Court,
in the Head Money Cases, 112 U. S. He says:

A treaty is primarily a compact between independent nations. It
depends for the enforcement of its provisions on the interest and the
honor of the Governments which are parties to it. If these fail, its
infraction becomes the subject of international negotiations and
reclamations, so far as the injured party chooses to seek redress,
which may in the end be enforced by actual war. It is obvious that
with all this the judicial courts have nothing to do and can give no
redress.

This was the situation, then, at the moment when, on
March 31st, 1913, Woodrow Wilson was inaugurated as
president. How he handled it is history. Refraining from
all argument, he made a simple appeal to the dignity of a
great nation. It was an appeal which was prompted by
great courage. It was dated March 5th, 1914:

I have come to state to you a fact and a situation. Whatever
may be our own differences of opinion concerning this much debated
measure, its meaning is not debated outside the United States.
Everywhere else the language of the treaty is given but one interpretation, and that interpretation precludes the exemption I am
asking you to repeal. We consented to the treaty; its language we
accepted, if we did not originate it; and we are too big, too powerful,
too self-respecting a nation to interpret with a too strained or refined
reading the words of our own promises just because we have power
enough to give us leave to read them as we please. The large thing
to do is the only thing we can afford to do, a voluntary withdrawal
from a position everywhere questioned and misunderstood. We
ought to reverse our action without raising the question whether we
were right or wrong, and so once more deserve our reputation for
generosity and for the redemption of every obligation without quibble
or hesitation.

In a communication to the author of these pages, the Hon. Oscar S. Straus, Ambassador to Turkey under President Cleveland, a Cabinet Minister and Member of The Hague Court, wrote:

The debates in Congress upon the subject of repeal proved to be of a quality in learning, ability and eloquence in keeping with the best traditions of our national legislature. Some of the leading Democratic members of the opposition effectively supported the President.

It was Senator Root who summed up the issue in terms of uncompromising candour. Speaking in the Senate, he said:

So, far from our being relieved of the obligations of the treaty with Great Britain by reason of the title that we have obtained to the Canal Zone, we have taken that title impressed with a solemn trust. We have taken it for no purpose except the construction and maintenance of a canal in accordance with all the stipulations of our treaty with Great Britain. We cannot be false to those stipulations without adding to the breach of contract a breach of the trust which we have assumed, according to our own declarations, for the benefit of mankind as the mandatory of civilization.

Senator Lodge's contribution to the debate contained the following:

When the year 1909 opened, the United States occupied a higher and stronger position among the nations of the earth than at any period in our history. Never before had we possessed such an influence in international affairs, and that influence had been used beneficiently and for the world's peace in two conspicuous instances— at Portsmouth and at Algeciras. Never before had our relations with the various States of Central and South America been so good. It seemed as if the shadow of suspicion which, owing to our dominant and at times domineering power, had darkened and chilled our relations with the people of Latin America, had at last been lifted. A world power we had been for many years, but we had at last become a world power in the finer sense, a power whose active participation and beneficent influence were recognized and desired by the other nations in those great questions which concerned the welfare and happiness of all mankind. This great position and this commanding influence have been largely lost. I have no desire to open up old questions or to trace the steps by which this result has come to pass, still less to indulge in criticism or censure upon anyone. I merely note the fact.

It is enough to add that Congress responded. The Hay-Pauncefote Treaty was affirmed as a world pact, to be held without modification as long as the Panama Canal endures.

President Wilson's attitude toward the tolls-exemption clause of the Panama Canal Act was reaffirmed in his 1914 Fourth of July address at Independence Hall. It is reported as follows:

I say that it is patriotic sometimes to prefer the honor of the country to its material interest. Would you rather be deemed by all nations of the world incapable of keeping your treaty obligations in order that you might have free tolls for American ships? The treaty under which we gave up that right may have been a mistaken treaty, but there was no mistake about its meaning.

When I have made a promise as a man I try to keep it, and I know of no other rule permissible to a nation. The most distinguished nation in the world is the nation that can and will keep its promises even to its own hurt. And I want to say, parenthetically, that I do not think anybody was hurt. I cannot be enthusiastic for subsidies to a monopoly, but let those who are enthusiastic for subsidies ask themselves whether they prefer subsidies to unsullied honor.

The high moral purpose of this memorable message was recognized abroad. Sir Edward Grey, the British Foreign Secretary, complimented it in a speech in the House of Commons:

It is due to the President of the United States and to ourselves that I should so far as possible clear away misrepresentation. It was stated in some quarters that the settlement was the result of bargaining or diplomatic pressure. Since President Wilson came into office no correspondence has passed, and it ought to be realized in the United States that any line President Wilson has taken was not because it was our line, but his own.

President Wilson's attitude was not the result of any diplomatic communication since he has come into power and it must have been the result of papers already published to all the world.

It has not been done to please us or in the interests of good relations, but I believe from a much greater motive—the feeling that a government which is to use its influence among the nations to make relations better, must never when the occasion arises flinch or quail from interpreting treaty rights in a strictly fair spirit.

Viscount Bryce, former British Ambassador to the United States, speaking at the Independence Day dinner of the American Society in London on July 4, 1914, paid this tribute to President Wilson:

Courage is a virtue rare among politicians. What we have all admired in the President is his courage in the matter of the canal tolls.

Absolutely no pressure was brought to bear by Great Britain to obtain repeal of the tolls-exemption clause of the Panama Canal Act.

Ambassador Page added that the last British letter to the United States Government relating to the Canal was written by Ambassador Bryce before the end of the Taft administration.

On September 4th, 1914, Secretary Bryan wrote to the author a letter, in which he thus recorded his view of President Wilson's action.

The position taken by the President on the tolls question aroused more opposition at that time than it would arouse today, subsequent events having completely vindicated the wisdom of his action.

The enviable position which our nation occupies today is due, in part, to the fact that it has allowed no doubt to exist as to its purposes to live up to the stipulations of its treaty.

There were economic considerations which weighed heavily in

favor of the repeal of the free tolls law, but these were less important than those which affected the international standing of our nation.

A government must be above suspicion in the matter of good faith; no pecuniary advantage, even where such an advantage actually exists, can for a moment justify the violation of a treaty obligation, and violation must be the more scrupulously avoided if the question is one which is not to be submitted to arbitration.

In international matters the question is not whether we are ourselves certain of our Government's purpose in the position taken, but whether other nations, also, have confidence in our rectitude.

The President set a high standard and the support given to him in the Senate and the House was as creditable to Congress as it was complimentary to him. The popular approval which is now accorded to both the President and Congress on this subject is proof positive that the people can be trusted to pass judgment upon the merit of international, as well as domestic questions.

I may conclude this record with a letter which Lord Bryce wrote to me in acknowledgment of our earlier book. Of "the admirable example set by President Wilson of the spirit in which questions affecting the faith of treaties ought to be handled," Lord Bryce wrote:

No praise can be too high for the rectitude and the courage which he showed on this occasion. Wisdom also he showed and clear foresight. He perceived that one of America's greatest assets is her reputation for righteous dealing and for loyalty to the international obligations she has undertaken. He understood the mind and conscience of the American people, and knew that when an appeal was made to them in the name of good faith they would respond. The result vindicated his judgment.

Your book calls attention to the testimony borne by the British Foreign Secretary and by myself (for I was Ambassador at Washington when Mr. Wilson entered the White House) to the fact that no pressure whatever was exerted by the British Government in the matter. To this I may add that when I reported to my Government the last conversation I had with Mr. Wilson in which the subject was mentioned, I expressed to them the confident belief that whenever the President had time to study and master the issues involved he would do whatever he felt to be right, and would not was mentioned. I explained to them my confident belief that whenever the President had time to study & master the issues involved, he would do whatever he felt to be right, and would not be diverted by any political considerations from what he thought to be the course that honour prescribed.

Those of us in England who know America best & love her most rejoiced at the approval which she gave to the President's policy in this matter, not on account of any British interest involved, but because it shewed that to be true which we had often declared — that no nation in the world has a keener love of peace & goodwill or a higher sense of international honour than have the American people. — I am

Hugh Gordon Miller Esq,   Faithfully yours
                              James Bryce

LORD BRYCE: A LETTER COMMENDING PRESIDENT WILSON

be diverted by any political considerations from what he might hold
to be the course that honor prescribed.

Those of us in England who know America best and love her most
rejoiced at the approval which she gave to the President's policy in
this matter, not on account of any British interest involved but
because it showed that to be true which we had often declared—
that no nation in the world has a truer love of peace and good will
or a higher sense of international honor than have the American
people.

The comment of the *New York World* on this letter
was:

No higher tribute has perhaps ever been paid an American President by a foreign statesman.

The only question that remained for time to answer was
whether the demon of inequality had been killed or merely
scotched. At a later date, the proposal to exempt the shipping of the United States from tolls was revived in Congress. On October 10th, 1921, a Bill of this kind was
sponsored by Senator Borah and passed the Senate by
47 to 37 votes. The Disarmament Conference was pending and Senator Lodge told the Senate plainly that the
measure would expose the United States to "implications
of bad faith." The bill did not become law.

XIV

THE CREATION OF PANAMA

WE have shown that the control of the Isthmian Highway is subject to two equities—first, the rights of the *de facto* sovereign, namely, the United States, and secondly, the rights of mankind.

There is a third equity that has now to be considered—namely, the rights of the *de jure* sovereign, that is, of the Central American Republics concerned with the Highway and particularly of Colombia, Panama and Nicaragua.

The total population of Central America is under 6,000,000, but the six Republics, though small, are sensitive and their susceptibilities affect a wider area than their own, that is, Latin America as a whole.

Indeed, there is another reason why a clear statement of the position, taken by the United States, is now essential. The war has changed many things. One of its results has been to create an international opinion—indeed, vigilance—to which every country, however powerful, must pay respect. It is recognized more fully than ever before that as an institution, the State can only fulfil its true function by aiming at the betterment of social conditions, not only in the domestic but in the international sphere. To accomplish a purpose, thus far-reaching, has always been and will always be a matter of great difficulty. In an enterprise, world wide in its importance, such accomplishment is only possible when a state enjoys the confidence—indeed, the good opinion—of mankind.

To chronic critics of the United States Administration,

whether at home or abroad, whatever party be in power,
we have nothing to say. Our appeal must be limited to
the responsible opinion for which the Fathers of the Republic, in the Declaration of Independence, expressed a "decent
regard"—the opinion which was defied in 1914, with such
tremendous results, by Imperial Germany. We are bound
to agree that, if it be really true that the United States in
her relations with Latin-America were following a similar
path of aggression, the prospects of peace for the world
as a whole would be overshadowed. But our submission
is that it is not true. It is a submission all the more important because the case of Panama no longer stands alone.
There is also Nicaragua.

On April 1st, 1927, the New York *Herald-Tribune*
quoted a speech in which Lord Bryce informed the House
of Lords that, among the things the citizens of the United
States held dear are "international law and practice." It
is by this severest of all standards that the policy of the
United States must be judged. International Law defines
the rights and duties of nations, the one to the other, and
we have accepted explicitly the principle that the Latin-
American Republics enjoy a status identical with our own.

On November 30th, 1923, Secretary Hughes, speaking
at Philadelphia, declared that "we recognize the equality
of the American Republics and their equal rights under the
law of nations." He disclaimed any desire to deprive these
Republics of self-government, or to reduce them to the
subordination of a protectorate.

That this has been the traditional attitude of the United
States towards the Latin American Republics cannot be
denied. In his Farewell Address, George Washington said:

The great rule of conduct for us in regard to foreign nations is,
in extending our commercial relations, to have with them as little
political connections as possible. But even our commercial policy

should hold an equal and impartial hand, neither seeking nor granting exclusive favors or preferences; consulting the natural course of things; diffusing and diversifying by gentle means the streams of commerce, but forcing nothing.

On December 7th, 1824, James Monroe added this:

The new (Spanish American) States are settling down under governments elective and representative in every branch, similar to our own. In this, their career, however, we have not interfered, believing that every people have a right to institute for themselves the government which, in their judgment, may suit them best.

On December 4th, 1827, John Quincy Adams thus referred to the New American republics:

In reference to the new Spanish American States disclaiming alike all right and all intention of interfering in those concerns which it is the prerogative of their independence to regulate as to them shall seem fit, we hail with joy every indication of their prosperity, of their harmony, of their persevering and inflexible homage to those principles of freedom and of equal rights which are alone suited to the genius and temper of the American nations.

Finally, we have the address delivered by President Wilson at Mobile in October, 1913, when he spoke thus:

The future is going to be very different for this hemisphere from the past. These states lying to the south of us, which have always been our neighbors, will now be drawn closer to us by innumerable ties, and, I hope, chief of all, by the tie of a common understanding of each other. Interest does not tie nations together; it sometimes separates them. But sympathy and understanding does unite them, and I believe that by the new route (the Panama Canal) that is just about to be opened, while we physically cut two continents asunder, we spiritually unite them. It is a spiritual union which we seek.

Enlarging upon the relations between the United States and the states of Central and South America, President Wilson said:

CHARLES EVANS HUGHES

We must prove ourselves their friends and champions upon terms of equality and honor. You cannot be friends upon any other terms than upon the terms of equality. You cannot be friends at all except upon the terms of honor. We must show ourselves friends by comprehending their interest whether it squares with our own interest or not. It is a very perilous thing to determine the foreign policy of a nation in the terms of material interest. It not only is unfair to those with whom you are dealing, but it is degrading, as regards your own actions.

Comprehension must be the soil in which shall grow all the fruits of friendship, and there is a reason and a compulsion lying behind all this which is dearer than anything else to the thoughtful men of America. I mean the development of constitutional liberty in the world. Human rights, human integrity, and opportunity as against material interests—that, ladies and gentlemen, is the issue which we now have to face. I want to take this occasion to say that the United States will never again seek one additional foot of territory by conquest. She will devote herself to showing that she knows how to make honorable and fruitful use of the territory she has, and she must regard it as one of the duties of friendship to see that from no quarter are material interests made superior to human liberty and national opportunity. I say this, not with a single thought that any one will gainsay it, but merely to fix in our consciousness what our real relationship with the rest of America is. It is the relationship of a family of mankind devoted to the development of true constitutional liberty. We know that that is the soil out of which the best enterprise springs. We know that this is a cause which we are making in common with our neighbors, because we have had to make it for ourselves.

The only question is whether, under the pressure of events, the United States has abandoned these principles. The case is presented clearly and concisely in a cable to the *New York Times:*

LONDON, March 6, 1927.—In its penetration of Nicaragua and other Central American republics, the United States has followed the methods by which the British Empire was built up, according to the London *Times.*

"The American Government," declares the newspaper, "has been led step by step through all the processes familiar to us in our own country as the flag has followed trade. What distinguishes present events in Nicaragua is the quantity and nature of public comment they have aroused."

The correspondent sees the American Government embarrassed in its effort to preserve the *"mandate"* it has assumed over Nicaragua by the growth of critical public opinion in Latin-America. American critical opinion, according to the editorial, is influenced by "any Central American buccaneer who learns the simple vocabulary of sovereignty."

This opinion, based on the belief that representative government can flourish everywhere, "cuts across the traditional path of unostentatious domination that the Executive desires to follow," because such critical opinion has great influence in the Senate, which can block the President's actions. Therefore "it is not unnatural that the Executive should in self-defence seek his ends by means which the Senate cannot control."

It is this challenge that the defenders of the policy of the United States have to meet.

We cannot agree that the action of the United States in the Caribbean stands on all fours with "the mandates" administered under the League of Nations. How do European countries themselves regard those "mandates"? In arguing a case before the World Court in 1923, the French Government said that one of the "new mandates of the League of Nations" was "very like a Protectorate." *Yet when President Diaz of Nicaragua asked for such a Protectorate by the United States, he was in effect refused it by the Administration at Washington.*

The interpretation put upon a mandate by the League of Nations is indicated further in the following quotation taken from the opening address to the Legislative Council of Tanganyika Territory by Sir Donald Cameron, the Governor:

> There is no provision in the mandate for its termination or transfer. It constitutes merely an obligation and not a form of temporary tenure under the League of Nations. This obligation does not make British control temporary, any more than other treaty obligations (such as those under the Berlin and Brussels Acts or the convention revising those acts) render temporary British control over Kenya or Uganda, which are no more and no less likely to remain under that control than is the Tanganyika Territory.
>
> I make this statement with the full authority of His Majesty's Government. And let this not escape the attention of all who may hear it or read it. There are others in the territory to whom I speak besides the non-natives; there is the huge body of chiefs and native inhabitants of the territory. To them I have repeatedly stated in the many barazas I have held during the last eighteen months that Tanganyika is a part of the British Empire and will remain so; to them the words I am now using will be repeated. To them these words are a pledge.

That language is a complete contrast to the definite recognition of independent sovereignty on which the relations between the United States and the Latin-American republics have been based.

A test case is Cuba. As a result of the war with Spain, the island came under the control of the United States—to quote President McKinley—"through the hand of Providence." To suggest that Governor-General Wood talked to the citizens of Cuba in the language used by the Governor-General of Tanganyika would be to falsify history. Of her own initiative, the United States handed to Cuba an independence which, heretofore, she had never enjoyed, and under her own sovereignty.

Except for minor political disturbances, Cuba has been peaceful, and she has been increasingly prosperous in terms of commerce. A commercial treaty with the United States, negotiated soon after the establishment of the republic, has encouraged trade between the two countries to such an extent that now she is the sixth best customer of the United States.

That there are reservations to the complete sovereignty of Cuba is true enough. They are contained in the Platt Amendment to the Cuban Constitution, the terms of which, though familiar, may be here quoted:

I. That the government of Cuba shall never enter into any treaty or other compact with any foreign power or powers which will impair or tend to impair the independence of Cuba, nor in any manner authorize or permit any foreign power or powers to obtain by colonization or for military or naval purposes or otherwise, lodgment in or control over any portion of said island.

II. That said government shall not assume or contract any public debt, to pay the interest upon which, and to make reasonable sinking-fund provision for the ultimate discharge of which, the ordinary revenues of the island, after defraying the current expenses of government, shall be inadequate.

III. That the government of Cuba consents that the United States may exercise the right to intervene for the preservation of Cuban independence, the maintenance of a government adequate for the protection of life, property, and individual liberty, and for discharging the obligations with respect to Cuba imposed by the treaty of Paris on the United States, now to be assumed and undertaken by the government of Cuba.

These provisions, defending Cuba against alliances with powers other than the United States, against contracting debts which would lead to insolvency and against certain domestic difficulties, have left the Cubans wholly at liberty to develop their nationhood in all the essentials of organized human life.

That there was an occasion when the United States intervened in Cuba is quite true. But what was the occasion? The Cubans had held their second election. In 1906 Presi-

VISCOUNT BRYCE, O.M.

dent Palma was re-elected, but José Miguel Gomez, the defeated Liberal candidate, charging that there had been fraud, began a rebellion and the destruction of foreign property. President Roosevelt sent troops, and a Provisional Government under Charles E. Magoon was set up. In the elections that were held under American supervision Palma was defeated and Gomez elected, and the troops were withdrawn in 1909. It meant that in Cuba, at any rate, the Latin-American habit of treating the ballot as a preliminary to the bullet was definitely outlawed.

In *Foreign Affairs* for July, 1927, there is a very fair summary of the record of the United States as a leading Power in Central America:

Undoubtedly the American Government has made mistakes in its dealings with the smaller Latin American nations, although I believe these mistakes have been more in taste than in morals. Undoubtedly American business interests have not always played fair. But when the credit and debit columns of the ledger are set against each other I believe that the credit column will be very large and the debit very small. In spite of the critics, the whole story, growingly in its later phases, is an admirable chapter in American foreign policy.

We have from time to time sent marines into some of these countries. Wilson sent them to Haiti and Santo Domingo, and these little nations are peaceful and happy and prosperous as they have never been before. Taft sent them into Nicaragua, where they remained, a few of them, for years, until Coolidge thought it safe to take them away. Are the thousands of lives and the millions of dollars saved by their presence no justification for "interference in the domestic affairs of other nations?" The answer would seem to be inevitably in the affirmative, especially since the United States has always made it clear that their presence pointed not at all toward eventual annexation.

There are Central Americans, of course, who resent any American interference. They learn the language in which they express themselves publicly from the professional anti-imperialists of the United States, but what they really resent is the fact that they no longer dare to carry on pillage and murder for their own political advancement. As a rule they are supremely and entirely selfish, caring nothing for national tranquility and prosperity because it interferes with their own selfish purposes. The first and only idea of most Central American *"reformers"* is to bring about a revolution which will put them personally into power. This was illustrated when the little company of American marines was withdrawn from Managua. The country has been in the throes of revolution ever since, and the recent peace brought about by President Coolidge's representative would be wholly illusory if the American guarantee of peace were withdrawn. Yet already our critics are busy showing the wickedness of this peace for the reason that the coming elections are to be supervised by Americans to insure fairness. Political labels in Latin-America are as meaningless as they are elsewhere, but I have often wondered whether Secretary Kellogg would have been so violently attacked if Diaz had happened to call himself a Liberal.

I have argued that the United States is subject to the opinion of mankind. This means that the Central American republics are not less subject to that opinion. The mere fact that they are small in area and population does not exempt them from a rule which applies to great Powers. There are small nations also in Europe. But those nations, though independent, are and must be a part of the continental system.

Indeed, it has been argued that the small nation in Europe is by no means so independent in its sovereignty as the small nation in the Americas. Addressing the American Society of International Law at its first meeting in 1907, Secretary of State Richard Olney said:

It has not been uncommon to treat the predominance of the European concert and the American primacy of the United States under the Monroe Doctrine as things of substantially the same matter. But, except as the United States and the European concert each outclass all probable antagonists of their respective policies in point of military strength, there is no real resemblance. The European concert practically has charge of the international relations of such smaller states and of their domestic affairs to the extent required by such international relations. The United States under the Monroe Doctrine has never undertaken and does not now undertake anything of that sort.

In the New World, there has been no use of the small states as a pawn in the great game of diplomacy and war known as "the balance of power."

Let us now examine in precise outline the steps by which the United States obtained control of the Panama Canal. It is common ground that the territory traversed by the Canal was owned in absolute fee simple by the Republic of Colombia. But what is ownership? However good it may be in law. it is always subject to limitations, both of time and necessity.

In law, apart from limitations of time, the Indians have a better claim to Colombia than even Spain had, Spain had a better claim than the Colombians themselves, and Colombia has a better claim than the Republic of Panama. But such law is limited by a right known to the law as eminent domain. It is by this right that the United States has acted. The right of eminent domain—to apply the words of Cicero—"was never written and was never taught but was drawn from nature itself."

By the right of eminent domain, the property of the private citizen may be acquired by the state compulsorily provided that it be needed for a public purpose. In the development of cities, railroads, water supply, electricity, and other amenities of civilization, the right of eminent domain is invoked every day of the week in every modern community. In Article V of the Constitution of the United States, it is stated, "nor shall private property be taken for public use without just compensation," words which imply an admission that, given "just compensation," private property may be taken for public use.

The only question, here relevant, is whether it is legitimate to apply the principle of eminent domain to international utilities and especially to such utilities as the Isthmian Highway. Here, the League of Nations furnishes in its Covenant a decisive judgment. We read:

> The members of the League will make provision to secure and maintain freedom of communications and transit.

To that declaration, no fewer than 53 countries are committed, including all the republics in Latin-America except Mexico. When I was in Geneva (August, 1927), there was sitting a Committee on "Communications and Transit" of which a report was entitled thus:

> Verbatim Records and Texts relating to the Convention on the Régime of Navigable Waterways of international concern and the Declaration recognising the Right to a Flag of States having no Sea-Coast. Geneva, 1921.
>
> *Contents:* Part I, Statement by Dr. Mineitciro Adatci (vice-president of the conference) on the question of navigable waterways and general discussion in conference, 11th-13th meetings, March 22-24, 1921; Part II, Discussion in committee (Dr. Mineitciro Adatci in the chair) of the draft convention on the international régime of navigable waterways, 1st-18th meetings, March 30-April 18, 1921; Part III, Report of the committee to the conference. Discussion and adoption of the convention on the régime of navigable waterways of international concern, 28th-30th meetings, April 18-19, 1921.

The authority of the League of Nations is thus absolutely behind the principle that communications and the "securing" or opening up of communications are a legitimate international interest which individual nations must respect.

In the New York *Evening Post* of April 4th, 1927, there was enunciated an academic dilemma:

> In his address before the Pan-American Commercial Conference last evening, President Coolidge made a statement which must have

startled the members of the Conference: "Our associates in the
Pan-American Union," he said, "all stand on an absolute equality
with us." May we expect then, that Nicaragua will be landing
marines at New Orleans or New York if at any time there is serious
disorder in this country?

To this we reply that if New York or New Orleans
covered a territory astride, or abutting, or in the area or
littoral, of a world inter-oceanic communication across any
isthmus that has been a world highway of commerce, in
one way or another, from time immemorial in a manner
like that of the Isthmian Highway between the Atlantic
and Pacific Oceans, and if any such South or Central American Republic had spent about five hundred million dollars
in building a canal for the commercial use of all the world,
and might have to spend over a billion dollars more to
make a further and additional canal through a similar
isthmus and in the territory of the United States, called
either New York or New Orleans; and if such other country
had assumed the implied obligations in general of the Monroe Doctrine to aid in defending the area, and preserving
order in that littoral, plus such written obligations as the
Hay-Pauncefote Treaty, and the United States diplomatic
representations leading up to it, in connection with the
canals; and had assumed what is in effect, a trusteeship in
behalf of world commerce; and was interested also through
a more direct and inherent concern in the defence of the
Canal, as a part of its own vital national defence; and if
such other country were involved in a traditional policy of
the *"open door"* for commerce, trade, and inter-oceanic
communications on equal terms for all the world; and
further if conditions in the New York or New Orleans
(supposed) canal area, were such as they have been (as
an illustration) in Nicaragua (a part of the highway
through which a new canal has been arranged for) during

eighteen years, except when policed by such other country; the answer would be that any government of South or Central America would be justified in using its forces to police and to preserve order in "New York" or "New Orleans." In other words, if the situation were reversed, as to both facts and responsibilities, and some South or Central American president, with his country in the same position of responsibility as that now of the United States, were welcoming United States delegates to that country, he would be justified in expressing the sentiments President Coolidge did, which are quoted further on in that editorial, to wit:

Toward the governments of countries which we have recognized this side of the Panama Canal, we feel a moral responsibility that does not attach to other nations.

If any such Latin-American country were so involved in conditions at a place like the Isthmian Highway but called New York or New Orleans, it would be very surprising if such republic did not feel a "moral responsibility" for that place "which does not attach to other nations." "Where your treasure is there will your heart be also."

President Coolidge or any other citizen of the United States, sitting as a delegate to such a conference, could not justly take offence at such a statement, by the president of such a country, acting similarly as host and spokesman for the occasion.

As we have seen, the necessity for a convenient transit across the Isthmus was realized several centuries before any of the republics, holding the Caribbean, came into existence. It was a necessity of which the Old World was itself conscious at a time when the New World, as we know it today, had scarcely come to the birth.

As early as May 30th, 1865, the United States had concluded a treaty with Honduras in which the above principle of eminent domain is implied. A contract had been signed between the republic and the Honduras Inter-Oceanic Railway Company. By this contract, the company was empowered to build a railway from coast to coast. By Article V, Section 6, of the contract, it is laid down that

the Government of Honduras with the view to secure the route herein contemplated from all interruption and disturbance from any cause, or under any circumstances engages to open negotiations with the various governments with which it may have relations, for their separate recognition of the perpetual neutrality, and for the protection of the aforesaid route;

The Government of Honduras agrees that the right of way or transit over such route or road, or any other that may be constructed within its territories, from sea to sea, shall be at all times open and free to the Government and citizens of the United States, for all lawful purposes whatever.

In other words, Honduras engaged herself to secure neutrality for the railway, and in order to "carry out the obligations thus incurred," she entered into an undertaking to the United States which is stated in Article XIV of the Treaty.

The railway across Honduras is defined specifically as a "right of way." It was not a mere permission, granted as a favour but a facility to which the public were entitled as a matter of claim. Trusteeship of such a right of way implies a responsibility to construct, maintain, protect and operate the method of transport involved in the use of the route in question. In effect, Honduras became responsible to mankind as a common carrier of commerce. She held her territory as a nation. But that ownership was subject to an eminent domain in which all nations were legitimately interested.

The Republic of Colombia, like the Republic of Honduras, was subject to the principle of eminent domain. By admitting the French engineers to the Isthmus of Panama, the republic conceded the proposition that she was a trustee for an international communication as defined later in the Covenant of the League of Nations. The failure of the French to construct the Canal obviously meant a failure on the part of Colombia also to fulfil her trust, and it was only after this failure had become absolute that, in 1903, there was negotiated the Hay-Herrán Treaty between Colombia and the United States, which would have enabled this country to proceed with the Canal.

On August 12th, 1903, that Treaty was rejected at Bogota by the Colombian Senate. Whatever may have been the motives of the 24 Senators who voted against it, whether patriotic or otherwise, one thing at least is certain. The defeat of the Treaty was a repudiation of the right of eminent domain, asserted in the Covenant of the League of Nations. The only question was by what agency that right was to be vindicated.

The trusteeship devolved inevitably to the most capable and willing world-power, selected in closest proximity to the Highway, and therefore the best able to complete the Canal, to operate it and adequately to defend it. Indeed, by the very implications of the Monroe Doctrine, the United States had no choice but to proceed. Had she declined to fulfil the trust, she would have had to consent to some other Power, either Britain or Germany, taking her place.

Indeed, we will press the argument further. As a trustee, responsible for the execution of her trust, the United States is not at liberty, equitably and in accordance with well recognized principles of law, to withdraw from the responsibilities to mankind which she has assumed. Such withdrawal would involve mankind in grave inconvenience and loss, to say nothing of the danger of war.

If, moreover, the United States were to fail in the fulfilment of her trust and were to abandon the task which she has assumed, it would be open to another power to take her place, and that power—suppose for the sake of argument it were Mexico—would be faced by precisely the same problems of law and order and health and finance which the United States has had to solve. A transference of the Canal to another power at a valuation based upon the cost of construction, equipment and improvements would not in any way eliminate the essential trusteeship for a public utility, the nature of which we are examining. It would be merely a change in the identity of the nation charged with the trust.

When the Hay-Herrán Treaty with Colombia failed of ratification, President Roosevelt was in office. During the controversy over the Tolls, he was quoted in the press as stating his position thus:

For four hundred years there had been conversation about the need of the Panama Canal. The time for further conversation had passed, the time to translate words into deeds had come.

It is only because the then (my) administration acted precisely as it did that we now have the Panama Canal.

The interests of the civilized people of the world demanded the construction of the canal. Events had shown that it could not be built by a private concern. We as a nation would not permit it to be built by a foreign Government. Therefore, we were in honor bound to build it ourselves.

Panama declared her independence, her citizens acting with absolute unanimity. We promptly acknowledged her independence. She forthwith concluded with us a treaty substantially like that we had negotiated with Colombia for the same sum of money. We then immediately took the Canal Zone and began the construction of the canal.

The case demanded immediate and decisive action. I took this action. Taking the action meant taking the Canal Zone and building the canal. Failure to take the action would have meant that the Canal Zone would not have been taken and that the canal would not have been built.

The title of the United States to the Isthmian Highway was thus made good, at the critical moment, by force.

In justice to the United States, it should be added that Panama conquered her independence from Spain by her own efforts and joined the federal republic of Colombia as a sovereign state. Confronted by what she considered to be a curtailment of her sovereign rights, Panama withdrew from the association on repeated occasions, for instance, 1830, 1831, 1841, 1860 and 1861. She returned to Colombia on the understanding that her autonomy would be assured yet was subjected to military repression in the year 1885.

It has to be remembered, moreover, that, apart altogether from any revolution in Panama, the United States enjoyed certain rights under the treaty of 1846 with New Granada or Colombia. President Roosevelt was advised by John Bassett Moore, the distinguished judge on the international court at The Hague that he had an unquestionable case for bringing pressure to bear on an obstructive Colombia and it was this course that he was actually considering when the revolution broke out. The clause is as follows:

The Government of New Granada guarantees to the Government of the United States that the right of transit across the Isthmus of Panama upon any modes of communication that now exist or that may be hereafer constructed shall be open and free to the Government of the United States. . . .

It is possible to argue that the use of all force is wrong. That is the Pacifist contention and, according to it, the

VISCOUNT GREY

action of President Roosevelt, as described by himself, would have to be condemned. But for those who are not Pacifists, the question is whether the particular use of force which opened up a route for the Panama Canal, was or was not defensible on the merits.

Our own view is not that President Roosevelt's action was unjustified, but that its only and sufficient justification will be based upon the principle of eminent domain. That justification means that the United States assumed a responsibility to act not alone in her own interest but as trustee for the world. It was—we emphasize—only as a trustee for interests larger than her own that she had an equitable right to act as she did act.

The chief legal advisers of the United States have recognized our peculiar position in Panama. In 1909 Attorney General Bonaparte said the Canal Zone was not a "territory" of the United States, "but a place held by us for a very special and peculiar purpose." Later in the same year, Acting Attorney General Wade Ellis said:

The Canal Zone is not one of the possessions of the United States within the meaning of the Tariff Act of 1909, but rather a place subject to the use, occupation and control of the United States for the purpose of constructing and maintaining a ship canal connecting the waters of the Atlantic and Pacific Oceans.

For half a century the relations between Colombia and the province of Panama had been disturbed. In the year 1903, Panama, with the approval—some would add, at the instigation—of the United States, declared her independence.

That the loss of her historic province was a severe blow to Colombia is not to be denied. Hard words were used against the United States and Hymns of Hate were sung. On April 17th, 1927, a Colombian, addressing his fellow citizens, wrote thus in the *Herald-Tribune:*

I invite the author of this proposition, and all who participate in his brand of "patriotism," to study the results of actuation by the United States in Spanish-America; and, putting aside all such misconceived notions of patriotism, to ask themselves the following:

1. Whether or not it is true that in all the Latin countries where American intervention has occurred such action has been justified by the savagery of our intestine struggles, for the protection of rights legitimately acquired by natives and foreigners alike, whose lives and properties were constantly in peril from groups of bandits who, under the pretext of "civil" warfare, gave themselves to indiscriminate plundering and murder in all the revolutions of Central America and the Antillas—*e.g.,* Haiti, Santo Domingo and Nicaragua.

2. Whether those countries where the United States has intervened, effectively applying American scientific methods, are not today more civilized and prosperous than those other nations which have sought that other alliance with Spain, where even their independence is still considered fictitious, and in which prevail absolute ignorance of the masses, poor means of communication, filth, ignorance of the rudiments of hygiene and an obvious degeneration of the race.

3. Whether it is not true that, had not the Monroe Doctrine prevailed, the European powers, always thirsting for conquest, would not, long ago, have competed to conquer and absorb a rich continent, sparsely peopled by a race without culture, and that did not present the obstacles of remoteness nor effective resistance, like that opposed, for example, by the Boers of South Africa or the natives of Australasia? And does the author of that proposition imagine that the ferrule of Great Britain, Germany or France would have been less heavy and hard to bear than the tutelage of America as demonstrated in Cuba or Panama, where Yankee influence is shown principally in advancing prosperity, and where the rare complaint heard of *"wounded independence"* comes only from those who, for their own ends, yearn to see their country again rotting in retrograding inertia or torn by petty tyrants and civil strife, rather than under the protection and guidance of that nation which, despite its invidious detractors who envy and malign her, marches in the van of civilization through perfection of her institutions, education and enlightenment of her people and the virility of her race.

Let the Señor Londoño consider these points and endeavor to divest himself of that false and vain "patriotism" which leads to nothing practical. Let us civilize ourselves; let us educate a population of illiterates; let us establish means of communication and schools; let us clean up the moral and material filth in which our people and our cities wallow. At least let us put ourselves on a level with Chile and Argentina, and we shall have nothing to fear from any *"Colossus of the North"*—which, however, is not likely to be scared away from our shores by our demonstrations of "anti-imperialism" nor by official anathemas printed on the back of telegraph blanks.

It is to be regretted that compensation was not paid to Colombia with greater promptitude by the United States. The course of events, as narrated in the *Encyclopedia Americana,* was as follows:

On 4 November 1913 the Congress at Bogota adopted a resolution affirming Colombia's isthmian rights, 10 years having passed since the severe loss had been sustained. Don José Vicente Concha (clerical-conservative) became President in 1914. During that year there was "no little satisfaction at the prospect of receiving under a pending treaty, $25,000,000 (from the United States) and of acquiring special privileges in respect to the Panama Canal. Taking advantage of the presumably more favorable spirit which the treaty had created in Colombia, an American "scientific mission" was sent to spend eight years and $400,000 exploring the country. But in 1915, when the proposed treaty was under consideration by the Senate of the United States, its provision for the payment just named, coupled with apology for the methods employed in securing the Canal Zone privileges and obligations, made favorable action by that body entirely impossible. However, the following year (18 February 1916) the Senate of the United States, by a vote of 55 to 18, ratified a plan to pay Colombia $15,000,000 in return for her acknowledgment of the American government's right to the Canal Zone.

The difficulty on the side of the United States lay not in the payment of the money but in the admission that the action, taken by President Roosevelt, constituted an offence for which apology and reparation must be made. This country did not agree and will never be argued into agreeing that so considerable service to mankind as the inauguration of the Panama Canal was an achievement of which she has reason to be ashamed.

In 1921 there was a final settlement with Colombia for $25,000,000 to be paid in four yearly instalments of $5,000,000 apiece.

XV

THE STATUS OF PANAMA

WE have now to consider the relations between the United States and the Republic of Panama. On the one hand, we have the richest and potentially the most powerful country in the world. On the other hand, we have a population outside the Canal Zone of roughly 450,000 divided as follows:

Whites	52,069
Negroes	85,970
Indians	33,425
Orientals	3,061
Mestizos	267,961

On November 18th, 1903, the United States and Panama signed what has come to be known as the Hay-Bunau-Varilla Treaty, determining their mutual relations.

In an Appendix, we print this Treaty in full, but we may here present a brief outline of its provisions.

By Article I "the United States guarantees and will maintain the independence of the Republic of Panama." On this Article, we need only remark that the obligation is limited to the United States and in this form is shared by no other Power.

Articles II to IV confer on the United States in perpetuity the full right to use what is known as the territorial "zone"—five miles on each side of the Canal—for all purposes connected with the enterprise. The zone includes the high seas within "three marine miles from mean low water

225

mark," with islands situated therein and the "small islands in the Bay of Panama named Perico, Naos, Culebra and Flamenco," which lie outside of the three mile limit. Other land which may be "necessary and convenient" for the use of the Canal is also "granted" and the concession guarantees the right to use available water for power, sanitation or other purposes.

It will thus be seen that the leasehold from Panama is not precisely defined in terms of exact boundaries. The ten mile zone and the three mile limit at the seaboards are subject to extension if there should arise a necessity affecting the Canal itself. The size of the controlled area must be governed by the presence in the neighbourhood of the Canal of disease and disorder which might menace the Canal and its approaches. The United States as a trustee is thus entitled to make use of whatever facilities may be essential in Panama to the due fulfilment of her trust.

By Article V, the United States receives the right to construct and maintain the Canal as "a monopoly," the full significance of which word should be appreciated. It is not only that. Along the Panama Route itself, there cannot be, in the nature of things, any competition with the Canal by a rival enterprise of the same character. The monopoly extends to alternative routes.

Across the Isthmus, there appear to be three, and only three available opportunities for constructing a possible canal, namely, Panama, Atrato and Nicaragua. It is today an axiom that none of those routes would be developed except with the consent of and indeed through the initiative of the United States. The monopoly on Panama is thus absolute, not only in the present but for the future. The status of the Canal is thus similar to that of a Public Service Corporation as defined by Wyman:

It is common knowledge that there are certain businesses which are so affected with a public interest that those who undertake them must serve the public properly. It is thus the character of the business which makes it public, and this character it takes from the conditions surrounding the business. This is most clear in the case of those businesses which have by reason of physical limitation a natural monopoly. In such circumstances the ordinary laws of competition either practically fail to operate, or act but feebly.

The Canal is thus wholly distinct in its character from a manufacturing plant which is subject to the Sherman Anti-Trust Laws. Of the canal or canals across the Isthmus, there must be unified management by one unchallenged authority.

By Article VI, the owners of private property, required for the use of the enterprise, are secured of compensation. No unsettled claim by a private person shall be allowed, however, to delay the progress of the undertaking. It is agreed, moreover, that roads crossing the Canal shall be open to public use.

Article VII awards to the United States the right to purchase property in the cities of Panama and Colon under "the right of eminent domain," and among the responsibilities of the United States is to be the due sanitation of those cities.

Under Article VIII, the Republic of Panama transfers to the United States the property of the New Panama Canal Company (that is, the Canal as left by the French) and of the Panama Railroad Company.

By Article IX, the United States as the responsible trustee of the Canal is entitled to use the ports of Colon and Panama without charge for customs or other dues. On the other hand, Panama may levy customs on goods entering her territory for the use of "other portions of Panama" and may "prevent contraband trade."

Article X relieves the Canal of taxation and Article XI secures to the Republic of Panama the use of telegraphs and telephones, owned by the Canal, "at rates not higher than those required from officials in the service of the United States."

By Articles XII and XIII, the United States receives the right to import "employees and workmen of whatever nationality" for the purposes of the Canal, who shall be "free and exempt from the military service of the Republic of Panama." Also, there is to be free import of materials necessary to the Canal—this on the understanding that "if any such articles are disposed of for use outside of the zone and auxiliary lands granted to the United States," they shall be subject to whatever duty is leviable on goods of like character.

Under Article XIV, the United States pays to the Republic of Panama a sum of $10,000,000 and an annual payment of $250,000 "during the life of this Convention," as "the price or compensation" due on the Canal. It is obvious that the acceptance of this money by the Republic of Panama is in the nature of a further ratification of the contract.

Article XV appoints a joint commission by the United States and Panama for the settlement of differences arising out of the Concession; Article XVI provides for the enforcement of order and punishment of crime; and Article XVII throws the Canal open to vessels in distress.

There follow a series of provisions to which particular attention should be drawn. Article XVIII reads:

The Canal, when constructed, and the entrances thereto shall be neutral in perpetuity, and shall be opened upon the terms provided for by Section 1 of Article III of, and in conformity with all the stipulations of, the treaty entered into by the Governments of the United States and Great Britain on November 18, 1901.

This means that the Treaty with Panama expressly carries forward the undertakings included in the Hay-Pauncefote Treaty with Great Britain. The two Treaties, though concluded with single powers—Great Britain in the one case and Panama in the other—are thus international in their real character.

By Article XIX, the Republic of Panama is entitled without charge to use the Canal and its facilities for the movement of its troops and munitions.

By Article XX, the Republic of Panama agrees to "cancel or modify" any previous treaty with a third power which may affect the Isthmus and so conflict with the position of the United States as now defined. In other words, the prior commitments of Colombia, whatever they may have been, insofar as they were inherited by Panama, are annulled; and by Article XXI the principle underlying this provision is extended to "all anterior debts, liens, trusts, or liabilities, or concessions or privileges to other governments, corporations, syndicates or individuals"—a safeguard amplified by Article XXII, which deals with the legal transference of the properties involved in the Canal.

The succeeding articles should be quoted in full:

ARTICLE XXIII

If it should become necessary at any time to employ armed forces for the safety or protection of the Canal, or of the ships that make use of the same, or the railways and auxiliary works, the United States shall have the right, at all times and in its discretion, to use its police and its land and naval forces or to establish fortifications for these purposes.

ARTICLE XXIV

No change either in the Government or in the laws and treaties of the Republic of Panama shall, without the consent of the United States, affect any right of the United States under the present convention, or under any treaty stipulation between the two countries that now exists or may hereafter exist touching the subject matter of this convention. If the Republic of Panama shall hereafter enter as a constituent into any other Government or into any union or confederation of States, so as to merge her sovereignty or independence in such Government, union or confederation, the rights of the United States under this convention shall not be in any respect lessened or impaired.

Article xxv

For the better performance of the engagements of this convention and to the end of the efficient protection of the canal and the preservation of its neutrality, the Government of the Republic of Panama will sell or lease to the United States lands adequate and necessary for naval or coaling stations on the Pacific coast and on the Western Caribbean coast of the Republic at certain points to be agreed upon with the President of the United States.

It was, then, to the United States that the Republic of Panama, like the Republic of Cuba, owed the inauguration of her sovereignty. It is a sovereignty which owes its stability to the guarantee of the United States.

The interpretation of the Treaty with Panama has not been free, however, from difficulty. One embarrassment arose over the boundary separating Panama and Costa Rica. In the year, 1900, the French President had given an arbitral award adjusting this frontier, then of course held by Colombia. But as often happens in such cases, the award itself had to be interpreted and it was not until the year 1914, that a decision by Chief Justice White settled the line on the Pacific side. Not only did Panama refuse to give up the territory that had been assigned to Costa Rica, but she even seized an additional area. It is enough to add that in 1921, the United States insisted that awards be complied with, a verdict which but for the United States would have been resisted by Panama into which country arms were being imported.

As early as the year 1904, Panama made certain com-

plaints, namely, first, that the United States had opened the
Canal Zone to the commerce of friendly nations, secondly,
that she had established rates of customs duties for importations of merchandise into the Zone, and thirdly, that she
had established post offices in the Zone.

The argument of Panama was that, in all these matters,
the United States should have been guided by that "indispensable antecedent," the Hay-Herrán Treaty with Colombia, which, if ratified by Colombia, would have determined
the status of the Canal Zone.   The Hay-Herrán Treaty,
Article IV, reads as follows:

> The Government of the United States . . . disclaims any inten-
> tion . . . to increase its own territory at the expense of Colombia
> or of any of the sister republics of Central and South America; it
> desires, on the contrary, to strengthen the power of the republics on
> this continent, and to promote, develop, and preserve their prosperity
> and independence.

In a despatch dated October 24th, 1904, Mr. Hay insisted that the Hay-Herrán Treaty, having been rejected by
Colombia, was no longer relevant.   He added that the policy
by which the United States refrains from seizing territory,
did not originate with that Treaty but is traditional to the
United States.   He wrote:

> It is the long-established policy of the United States, constantly
> adhered to; but said policy does not include the denial of the right
> of transfer of territory and sovereignty from one republic to another
> of the western hemisphere upon terms amicably arranged and
> mutually satisfactory, when such transfer promotes the peace of
> nations and the welfare of the world. That the United States may
> acquire territory and sovereignty in this way and for this purpose
> from its sister republics in this hemisphere is so manifest as to pre-
> clude discussion.

On the other hand, Secretary Hay insisted that by the
Treaty with Panama, the United States was entitled to exer-

cise within the Zone, "all the rights, powers and authority" which it would "exercise if it were the sovereign of the territory." Hence, he argued,

If it could or should be admitted that the titular sovereign of the Canal Zone is the Republic of Panama, such sovereign is mediatized by its own acts, solemnly declared and publicly proclaimed by treaty stipulations, induced by a desire to make possible the completion of a great work which will confer inestimable benefit upon the people of the Isthmus and the nations of the world. It is difficult to believe that a member of the family of nations seriously contemplates abandoning so high and honorable a position in order to engage in an endeavor to secure what at best is a "barren scepter."

Panama had acquiesced in "entire exclusion" as sovereign from the Canal Zone and had accepted payment in compensation, namely, $10,000,000 in gold.

Into the detailed argument, we need not enter. It is possible to contend—as many have contended—that the Treaty with Panama was a diplomatic paraphrase for annexation of the Canal Zone. But there cannot be a serious doubt as to the significance of the absolute rights which, in fact, the United States acquired under the Hay-Bunau-Varilla Treaty. That authority, as of a sovereign, includes beyond question the right to import goods, levy customs and establish a postal service.

In December, 1904, Mr. Taft, then Secretary for War, visited Panama. He negotiated an agreement with Panama, adjusting certain imports. It is a fact that, by this agreement, the United States limited the exercise of certain of its sovereign rights in the Canal. But in the words of an official communication from the State Department, dated October 1st, 1927 "it was expressly stipulated that this agreement was only temporary and was not to be considered as an interpretation of the Treaty of 1903 or as relinquishing any of the sovereign rights that the United States enjoyed in the Canal Zone."

WILLIAM HOWARD TAFT

Over the technical question of sovereignty, it cannot be suggested seriously that Panama has any grievance. In the year 1907, the Republic was affected seriously by the general unrest which was troubling Central America as a whole, and as an election was pending in which—judging by previous contests—fraud would play a part, the United States was requested to appoint a commission under which a contest might be held under fair conditions. Secretary Taft again visited Panama and arranged that the election should take place under American observation. To the political parties it was made plain that, in the event of riot or disturbance, the United States would intervene to preserve order. A list of actual voters in each precinct was drawn up.

The effect of these measures was remarkable. The fear had been that Ricardo Arias, the Foreign Secretary of Panama, would hold a dummy election and declare himself President. What happened was that he withdrew his candidature and José Obaldia was elected almost without opposition.

If, then, there is discontent in Panama, it is due wholly to other causes than questions of sovereignty. Of these causes, a lucid account has been given (October, 1927) in the New York *Times* by Mr. Drew Pearson.

Before the Canal had been completed, Panama merchants invested heavily in goods which they expected to sell to ships passing through the Canal and to the employés and police of the Canal Zone.

The War Department, however, set up its own warehouses and commissaries which sold in competition with the Panama merchants. The right of the War Department under the Treaty can scarcely be disputed. The United States has been granted the authority which it "would possess if it were the sovereign of the territory, to the entire exclusion of the exercise by the Republic of Panama of any such sovereign rights, power or authority." In addition,

the War Department has maintained that it has every right
to furnish the necessities of life to its own employés, a contention which Panama does not challenge.

But it is urged that the commissaries do not confine their
activities to this purpose. They sell, not only necessities,
but jewelry and luxuries, like Chinese silks, South African
diamonds and French perfumes which are advertised outside as well as inside the Zone. Moreover, the very fact
that there is no customs barrier between the Zone and the
rest of Panama means that goods, purchased from the commissaries, can be carried without difficulty to any point
within the territory of the Republic. This applies to tobacco
which is a government monopoly and an important source of
revenue to the Republic. The competition, so developed by
the commissaries, is the more serious for the Panama merchants because it affects trade with passing ships.

The merchants have to pay customs duty and internal
taxes. The commissaries are immune from both. The merchants, moreover, are charged standard rates on their
goods by the railways. The commissaries enjoy the advantage of a very low rate on all such merchandise. Hence, it
is no matter of surprise that Panama merchants have suffered a good deal of disappointment over the prospects of
their trade and that not a few of them have been driven
into bankruptcy.

It is, we submit, manifest that the United States holds no
specific franchise to carry on trade and commerce as such in
the Canal Zone. The only question is how the United
States is to supply legitimate goods within the Canal Zone
to her own people without developing a general commerce
that would be unfair to Panaman enterprise.

In 1926, the United States and Panama signed a new
treaty which, however, has still to be ratified. By Clause IV
of this Treaty, it is laid down as follows:

"With the exception of sales to ships which the United States will continue to make as heretofore, the sale of goods imported into the Canal Zone by the Government of the United States shall be limited by it to the officers, employes, workmen and laborers in the service or employ of the United States or of the Panama Railroad Company and the families of all such persons and other persons who may be permitted to dwell in the Canal Zone."

It will be noted that this clause still permits the United States to carry on the direct trade with ships using the Canal.

It would scarcely have been supposed that this dispute over the sale of tobacco and trinkets would assume a world-wide significance. But it must not be forgotten that Panama belongs to the League of Nations. Indeed, Latin-America as a whole, with the single important exception of Mexico, has joined the League, from actual membership of which the United States has stood aloof.

The question of the jurisdiction of the League within the Americas is thus of grave significance. The United States does not admit this jurisdiction. It was not at Geneva, or even at The Hague, that the quarrel between Chili and Peru over Tacna and Arica was discussed, but at Washington. When, therefore, Dr. E. Morales proposed that the League should adjudicate upon questions of Sovereignty in Panama, the Administration at Washington—to use an expressive phrase—put its foot down.

"I believe the League of Nations finds itself busy trying to keep peace in Europe without coming into this hemisphere," was the comment of Senator Borah of Idaho, chairman of the Senate Foreign Relations Committee.

"The United States possesses absolute sovereignty over the Canal Zone and does not propose to surrender that sovereignty to any nation or to submit any disputes over it to any tribunal," said Senator Swanson.

Over the *de facto* sovereignty of the United States in the

Panama Canal Zone, the spokesmen of the Republican and Democratic Parties are thus agreed.

We do not demur in any way to the exclusion of the League of Nations from the settlement of differences which arise between the United States and Panama. In the similar case of Egypt, which, like Panama, is a member of the League, Great Britain assumed an attitude similar to our own. It was agreed by Britain that Egypt is a sovereign independent power. But to this sovereignty, there are irreducible reservations of which the world has been warned. On February 21st, 1922, Lord Curzon issued the following statement:

"The following matters are absolutely reserved to the discretion of His Majesty's Government until such time as it may be possible by free discussion and friendly accommodation on both sides to conclude agreements in regard thereto between His Majesty's Government and the Government of Egypt:

(a) The security of the communications of the British Empire in Egypt.

(b) The defense of Egypt against all foreign aggression or interference, direct or indirect.

(c) The protection of foreign interests in Egypt and the protection of minorities.

(d) The Sudan. Pending the conclusion of such agreements the *status quo* in all these matters shall remain intact.

The reservations to Egyptian sovereignty may appear to be provisional and subject to discussion. But the discussion is confined to Great Britain and Egypt alone and the last word in the discussion obviously rests with Great Britain.

That this is the British view, has been affirmed by Britain in terms of unmistakable candor. In 1924, it was feared that Egypt would sign the Protocol, elaborated by the League, with a view to disarmament. On December 4th, Great Britain sent a note to Geneva recalling the fact that, between Britain and Egypt, "certain questions were abso-

lutely reserved," insisting upon "the special relations between Egypt and itself long recognized by other countries,"
and resenting "any attempt at interference in the affairs of
Egypt."

During the year 1928, there developed an affair which
illustrated the various aspects of this problem. A serious
dispute arose between Bolivia and Paraguay, both of them
members of the League. There were appeals to Geneva
and the League on its side claimed a diplomatic jurisdiction
in the New World. It was demonstrated, however, that
the New World had the will and the machinery to settle its
own difficulties without such European assistance.

It is thus a fact not to be gainsaid that in Egypt as in
Panama, the intervention of the League of Nations is not
welcomed. But we submit that this fact does not exhaust
the situation. The very fact that the paramount power acts
in these cases as a sole trustee lays upon that power the
greater obligation to respect the worldwide opinions and interests of which the League is an organized expression.

The defence of the Panama Canal is a problem of strategy, distinct in itself. It is obviously for the responsible
trustee and no other authority to decide what measures
must be taken to guarantee an adequate security.

Of all the administrations recorded in the history of the
United States, none is less respected than that of President
Buchanan. It is agreed that he allowed the nation to drift
into civil war. It is also agreed that he failed to take many
precautions, for instance, the removal of national property
from the South, which, in the event of civil war, would have
limited its duration. A provisional government was set up
in the South and it was then too late to remove the stores
and munitions which were used later against the forces of
the Union.

In the case of President Buchanan, it has been asserted

that in text books at West Point and Annapolis it was taught
and he believed in, the right of the South to secede. That is
no answer to the charge against him, but at least it suggests
an explanation.

If there be a failure adequately to defend the Isthmian
Highway, the only conceivable explanation would be a similarly mistaken sympathy with the ultrapatriotic susceptibilities of the smaller Latin-American republics. It is enough
to reply that adequate defense would not injure—rather it
would establish—their true prosperity and well being. No
Latin-American interested is here wounded except in a pride,
essentially provincial in its inspiration, which ignores wholly
the broader interests of the world as a whole. In those
world-wide interests, there are included the best interests of
Latin-Americans themselves.

It has to be borne in mind that the Panama Canal, with its
vast locks, and complicated equipment, is essentially vulner-
able. In the *Herald Tribune* of April 10th, 1927, Edward
Van Zile, after a visit to the Caribbean, described the Canal
as "our heel of Achilles" and declared that "a single explo-
sive bomb could put the Canal out of commission in ten minutes." That may be a picturesque way of putting it. But
there is no doubt that, before the days of aircraft, the management of the Suez Canal had to be on guard against mis-
haps. The scuttling of a ship might block the waterway. A ship, loaded with explosives, might injure the
Canal itself.

According to the *World's Work* for March, 1927, there
were 5197 ships using the Panama Canal in the year 1926.
Of this tonnage, 53 per cent belonged to the United States
and 47 per cent to the rest of the world. This country thus
shared with mankind a supreme concern for the uninter-
rupted use of the Isthmian Highway as a channel of commerce. As the Canal grows in importance, so will it be

regarded with the greater emphasis as a strategic link in the communications across this planet.

In the year 1926, a new Treaty was negotiated between the United States and Panama. It was this Treaty that included the commercial provision quoted in the last chapter. But its main purpose is defense.

By the old treaty, as we have seen, the Republic of Panama authorized the United States to establish fortifications on the Canal and to send armed forces to defend it. But the Republic of Panama itself remains uncommitted by these measures to any course of action.

By the new treaty, there is set up a hard and fast defensive alliance between the powers. If, for any reason, the United States finds herself at war, the Republic of Panama agrees that, automatically, she will enter the war on the side of the United States.

Also, the United States acquires the right to use any part of the territory of Panama for military operations and, during peace as well as war, will exercise control over aircraft and wireless communications, including the grant of licenses and installations. Also, the United States takes over the Island of Manzanello at the Atlantic terminus of the Canal.

There is no doubt that this treaty led to a world-wide discussion. As a member of the League of Nations, the Republic of Panama is a party to Article XII of the Covenant. This Article is as follows:

The members of the League agree that if there should arise between them any dispute likely to lead to a rupture, they will submit the matter either to arbitration or to inquiry by the Council, and they agree in no case to resort to war until three months after the award by the arbitrators or the report by the Council.

In any case under this Article the award of the arbitrators shall be made within a reasonable time, and the report of the Council shall be made within six months after the submission of the dispute.

But by Article II of her Treaty, Panama finds herself at war at the instant when the United States finds herself at war. There are no preliminaries. There is no "cooling off period" of three months.

In a technical sense, as the London *Times* has pointed out, there is here an apparent contradiction. It could be resolved, of course, by the withdrawal of Panama from the League.

In the comment of the Chicago *Tribune,* there was a touch of wit. Discussing the proposed treaty, its view was:

"The little republic will not suffer morally because the blame will be pinned on the United States, which can afford to stand it. If charged with contributing to the delinquency of a ward of Geneva, the United States should blame the League for beguiling a minor."

For does Panama stand alone? Let us suppose that Great Britain herself were to be in a state of war. Would it be a fact that her Dominions and India, all of them separate members of the League, would continue at peace? If they did so continue at peace, would it not mean that the British Empire, as a sovereignty of commonwealths, had been reduced to a memory?

Again, are there not treaties in Europe, signed by members of the League, the force of which, whatever be the precise wording, is not different from that of the new Treaty with Panama? What precisely are the relations between France and Belgium and between Italy and Albania, to give two instances alone? Also, what is the full significance of the undisclosed agreements between Italy and Spain?

The reply of the *New York Times*, early in January 1927, seems to us to set out the case for the new Treaty with simple lucidity. It is merely the form of the Treaty that embarrasses. The facts of the case are not modified.

If the United States were to be engaged in war, it is obvious that, even under the old treaty, she would be under the necessity of defending the whole of the Republic of Panama. All that the United States is now doing may be described as putting down in black and white what this obligation really means.

The idea that the United States would be guilty of rushing Panama into a world war, is unthinkable. Faced by such a crisis, her deliberation would be at least as cautious as any procedure embodied in the Covenant of the League of Nations. Indeed, at Geneva itself, it is an obvious fact that the issues of peace and war, though they affect the small nations, are decided by the big ones, and the supposition that such issues could be changed one way or the other by the action of a Republic like Panama is—if we may speak plainly—as fantastic as to suppose that the balance of power in the Mediterranean is determined by the armies and navies of Monaco.

Concessions within the territory of the Republic of Panama may involve delicate issues. In 1927, the Tonosi Fruit Company, a subsidiary of the United Fruit Company obtained such a concession to construct a railroad across the Isthmus. A note was sent to Panama by the United States whose consent had not been asked, in which objections were waived, but only on the understanding that no benefits enjoyed by this Government under the Panama Railroad Concession of 1867 were relinquished. Rights granted more than sixty years before were thus involved.

The Panama Corporation, Ltd., is a British organization which holds a mining concession, reported to cover one-sixth of the total area of the Republic of Panama. These rights are limited in point of time and in other ways but the concession was denounced by Senator Borah as a danger to the Canal. However, investigation did not disclose any peril.

In April 1928, Mr. D. Elliott Alves, Chairman of the Panama Corporation, Ltd., announced that he had concluded negotiations with Panama for making surveys for a road across the Isthmus. President Chiari's comment was "my Government is ready to hear proposals from Mr. Alves as well as other companies because it is apparent that this new road would benefit the economic development of the country." It was denied that any actual concession at that date had been granted.

Here undoubtedly there arises a serious question of principle. The roads both of the Canal Zone and of Panama itself are necessary to the protection of the Canal. For this reason, they are constructed of a military dimension. While the United States as trustee would not obstruct the economic development of Panama, she must control inter-oceanic highways across the Isthmus. Under the treaty of 1903, associated with the original concession to the Panama Railroad, the United States claims the exclusive right to construct and maintain railroads, canals and carriage roads across the Isthmus in the territory through which the road in question would pass—that is through the territory west of Cape Tiburon on the Atlantic and Point Garachine on the Pacific.

The question is thus whether such a road should be built by the United States or by a private and foreign corporation. Apparently financial considerations are involved. By the new treaty with Panama which failed to pass the National Assembly of that Republic, provision was made for a new road by way of the Alajuela Dam, connecting the present canal roads and providing a highway between Panama and Colon, also a branch to Porto Bello. Except for a contribution of $1,250,00C, the cost of this undertaking was to fall on Panama. The opponents of the Treaty protested that in view of the military value of the road, the United States should bear more of the expense and that Panama could not afford to pay the amount required of her. Hence the Panama National Assembly of 1928 passed a law authorizing the Government to grant a concession for the construction of a highway connecting Panama Colon and Porto Bello, the concessionaire to pay all costs, to be permitted to charge tolls and to receive 500 hectares of Government land for each mile of road, built and put into use.

It is such a concession that has come under debate. We will only suggest that these strategic roads, irrespective of expense, should be subject to the absolute control of the trustee power—a control exercised under similar circumstances by Britain over the Suez Canal.

XVI

NICARAGUA

WHEN the United States entered into special relations with the Republic of Panama, there were observers of her policy, admirers and critics who declared that the South Western frontier of this country had been moved from the Rio Grande to the northern boundary of Colombia. The whole of Mexico and the six Central American republics— so it was suggested—had been annexed, if not in form, then in fact, by the Colossus of the North. The expansion of the United States—so it was said—was following the precedent which Sir John Seeley in a famous book called *The Expansion of England.*

That the influence of the United States has grown, cannot be, and need not be, denied. But how has that influence been used? "Politicos," who play the part of Demosthenes, should note that in South America, at any rate, the United States has not only excluded Europe from all chance of aggressive penetration, but has herself refrained, for more than a century, from acquiring control over or ownership of a foot of territory.

Nor has there been any attempt by the United States to enforce on any part of Latin America, whether "South" or "Central" or Mexico, her own English-expressed culture. Neither with language, thought, art or religion, has the United States shown the slightest inclination to interfere.

Early in 1927, the *Manufacturers' Record* thus defined the special circumstances which affect the Isthmian Highway:

Central America has been another Balkans. Every country there boasts men of high education, men of great refinement, families of distinction. Contests for power have chiefly been between great families. The peoples themselves have been mere pawns in the game. To a peculiar degree, Central America has been the habitat of soldiers of fortune, of adventurers in Government, of palace revolutions. Governmentally, it has been a disease stricken region. We cannot ignore that fact any more than we can ignore an epidemic of yellow fever in that part of the world.

That description is entirely just. It means that Central America has offered an inviting field for international intrigue.

What then has been the record of the United States in this troubled region? In their assertion of independence of Europe, the republics were supported wholeheartedly by the United States to which support they owed their liberties. When, moreover, the five Central American states, Guatemala, Salvador, Costa Rica, Honduras and Nicaragua, federated in 1823, the United States recognized the Federation and extended to it a wholehearted good will.

After the dissolution of the Central American sovereignty in 1847, the United States, though regretting the severance, recognized each of the five separated republics, all of which to this day retain their independence and integrity.

From the year 1874 till the end of the nineteenth century, there were many unsuccessful attempts to achieve or to restore Central American union, to which movement in the direction of stability, the United States was favourable; and, in the year 1906 President Roosevelt acted as a mediator in a dispute between Guatemala on the one side and Salvador and Honduras on the other. A treaty of peace, to which all the Central American republics except Nicaragua, agreed, expressly recognized the obligation of the United States to intervene as mediator in Central American affairs, and it was such mediation that, in August 1907, averted war between

Nicaragua and Salvador. The aim of the United States, once more, was to enable Central American democracy to attain to an orderly and secure civilization.

In 1907, the five republics, encouraged by President Roosevelt, held a conference at Washington, the object of which was to find a basis of friendlier relations—political, commercial and financial. Among the results was the establishment of a Central American International Bureau on the lines of the Pan American Union. There was founded, moreover, a Central American Court of Justice, sitting in Costa Rica, and it was agreed to hold, every year, a Central American Conference.

The mere recital of these events, we submit, disposes of the charge that, in dealing with these republics, the United States was animated by aggressive aims. Obviously and on the face of the record, she desired to see, south of her own territory, a sister federation, comparable with herself in order, in developing resources and in a progressive well being.

It is this desire that is still the motive of the United States. Indeed, her interest in the Isthmian Highway has stimulated her hope that the Central American republics will justify their free sovereignty by maintaining the essentials of order and the public peace.

To these republics the United States applies no principles which she does not also apply to herself. When Grover Cleveland was President there were riots in Chicago which held up the federal mail. The government intervened, and against this intervention, Governor John P. Altgeld of Illinois, pleading state rights, made a protest. President Cleveland replied, "Time for discussion is past. The marines are on the way." A domestic upheaval was not permitted to menace the communications which are necessary to the organized life of the continent.

It is this principle which has been applied by President Coolidge to Central America. During the year 1927, he said:

The stability, prosperity and independence of all Central America can never be a matter of indifference to us.

He also said this:

Toward the governments of countries which we have recognized this side of the Panama Canal, we feel a moral responsibility that does not attach to other nations.

President Coolidge, following President Taft, thus declared that the United States has a "special interest" in the Central American republics. Senator Borah also refers to the "countries that are near at hand and where we have large and peculiar interests."

It is a declaration that has arisen out of no threat by the Old World against the New. The Old World is not challenging the Monroe Doctrine. It is the inherent instabilities of the New World itself that have to be steadied. Just as the riots in Chicago touched interests that extended far beyond the State of Illinois, so the troubles of Central America affect a great public utility in which the whole world is legitimately concerned.

The argument does not end there. Let us imagine the highly improbable situation in which, for some reason, say a revolution in this country, the Canal had passed into other hands than our own. In that case, a new trustee would be responsible for its maintenance as a Highway. That trustee would be bound to ensure, as the present trustee is bound to ensure, that no power, not even the United States herself, interferes with orderly traffic through the Isthmian Highway. The argument applied by the United States to Central America would be applicable, in those circumstances, to the

United States herself. The United States does not hold the Canal because she is the United States. She holds it because, after long delay, it was shown by experience that she alone could exercise this function.

President Coolidge limits the special concern of the United States to "countries which we have recognized this side of the Panama Canal." This territory consists of Mexico, the six Central American republics, British Honduras, and the islands of the Caribbean, whatever flag they fly.

It is to be noted that no question has arisen in respect of any territory held by Great Britain. It is undeniable that Jamaica, Trinidad and even the Bermudas might be regarded as of great strategic significance; so with British Honduras and British Guiana. But it has been enough for the United States to know that these possessions are in peaceful occupation and that no problem of disorder is allowed there to arise. With regard to the Latin American sovereignties, peace and order are the sole requisites to a complete harmony with the United States.

The Canal Zone itself, roughly defined, is a ten mile strip of territory. But it is obvious that, in these days of aircraft, of submarines, and of radio, the security of the Canal depends upon the tranquillity of a much wider area than that. The Isthmian Highway cannot be regarded as secure if there are adjacent settlements dominated by influences, near and distant, which are jealous of the United States and inclined to be hostile to her guardianship of a great utility. The naval bases at Key West, Guantanamo, Samana Bay, More St. Nicholas, in Porto Rico, in the Virgin Islands, in the Corn Islands of Nicaragua and in Fonseco Bay on the Pacific side, are indications of the wide areas on land and sea which are now involved in the defence of the Isthmian Highway.

The Isthmus, which we call Central America, extends for more than a thousand miles. The Highway across that Isthmus—Canal, River, Road and Railway—is not a single track but complex, and as traffic increases, the complexity of the Highway cannot but be elaborated. The carrying capacity of the Panama Canal itself is not unlimited. It is estimated to be about 60,000,000 tons of shipping annually and the tonnage accommodated is steadily increasing. When the traffic reaches the point of congestion, there will arise the same reason for a second canal that led to the construction of the first. It will not be the United States alone that will require the additional facilities. Every commercial nation, whose ships are delayed at Panama, will incur loss thereby and will desire a remedy.

Before the United States undertook the completion of the Panama Canal, there had been an animated debate between the advocates of that route and the advocates of the alternative route through Nicaragua which had been under discussion since the days of President Van Buren. Preference was awarded ultimately to Panama, but the alternative route has always been regarded as not less possible. It is this alternative which is now of an immediate importance. A second canal through Nicaragua not alternative but supplemental to Panama is within the range of commercial and naval policy. In March, 1928, Senator McKellar of Tennessee, proposed the construction of such a waterway at a cost of $200,000,000.

On August 5th, 1914, there was concluded a convention between the United States and Nicaragua. Owing to delays on the part of the Senate at Washington, that Convention was only ratified on June 22nd, 1916. By the Convention, the United States obtained the exclusive proprietary rights for the construction and operation of an interoceanic canal by a Nicaraguan route, the lease of certain islands for 99 years, with an option to renew the lease for a second such period, and the right to establish a naval base on the Gulf of Fonseca. A payment of $3,000,000 was to be made to Nicaragua "for the purposes contemplated by this Convention and for the purpose of reducing the present indebtedness of Nicaragua." The original treaty was signed by William Jennings Bryan and, on behalf of Nicaragua, by Emiliano Chamorro.

It will not be suggested that Mr. Bryan, as Secretary of State, was an imperialist. But he foresaw that a canal through Nicaragua would be useless unless it was safe. He wished, therefore, to introduce into his treaty, a clause by which there would be conceded to the United States the right to intervene in Nicaraguan affairs "when necessary to preserve her independence or to protect life and property in her domain."

While we do not accept without reservation President Coolidge's plea for unity at the "water's edge," our view is that, in many matters, the decision of the State Department, with its record of continuous experience and tradition, is usually justified by events.

Washington himself submitted an arbitration treaty to the Senate, only to have it rejected. In 1838, the Committee on Foreign Affairs of the House of Representatives refused to endorse a movement for arbitration. In 1839 and 1846, they took the same negative action. In 1850 a resolution favouring arbitration was reported to the Senate by the Committee on Foreign Relations. Senator Clemens of Alabama moved to "let it lie over" and it still does. An able report favouring arbitration got to the Senate in 1853, though the Committee on Foreign Relations really opposed it. It was never even debated in the Senate. In 1897, Secretary of State Olney negotiated a notable arbitration treaty with Great Britain. President Cleveland earnestly recommended it to the Senate, but after prolonged delays, the Senate so amended the treaty that President McKinley, then in office, had to abandon it. Secretary Hay, under President Roosevelt, returned to the attack and the President personally pleaded the cause with leading senators. But again the opposition of senators caused the destruction of the treaty by impossible amendments. President Taft had the same experience and after he ceased to be President he said of the Senate: "that august body truncated them (the treaties) and amended them and qualified them in such a way that their own father could not recognize them."

Finally we may recall that the Senate defeated the attempts of Presidents Harding and Coolidge and Secretaries Hughes and Kellogg to have the United States join the Permanent Court of International Justice. Though both the Democratic and Republican parties approved our entrance with the reservation suggested by the Administration, the Senate thought it knew better. It thought it knew better than Elihu Root who helped draw up the plan of the Court; better than Secretary of State Hughes and eminent Republicans and Democrats.

It was this "defeatism" in foreign policy that the Senate applied to Mr. Bryan's provisions, designed to secure law and order in Nicaragua. The "protector plan" was eliminated.

That the Bryan-Chamorro Convention aroused Latin-American sentiment is undeniable. Protests against the Convention were advanced by Costa Rica, Salvador and Honduras to which the Senate replied by a "proviso" stating "that nothing in said Convention is intended to affect any existing right of any of the said named states." But, as events have proved, no self-denying ordinance could eliminate the facts of the case. Treaty or no treaty, there has had to be intervention in Nicaragua.

For a wider question is involved. The proposed canal through Nicaragua will lie about 250 miles north of the present Highway. This means that its security will depend on the stable equilibrium not only of Nicaragua itself but of Costa Rica, Guatemala, Honduras and Salvador. A distance of 250 miles north of Panama means a distance of 250 miles nearer to Mexico.

In international as in national politics, there is no gratitude. The fact that the United States, by her insistence on the Monroe Doctrine for more than a century, has preserved the smaller Latin-American States from European intrigue and aggression, does not govern the sentiments of these weak nations towards a strong neighbour. Inevitably there is a danger lest some such country, uncertain in its politics, allow itself to be used, in a phrase familiar to students of our diplomacy as "a springboard" from which base of propaganda and other activities a distant and a stronger power or group of powers might influence the future of the Isthmian Highway.

Into the merits of our discussions with Mexico which affect oil lands and titles to property of every kind, we do not propose to enter. Still less is it relevant to our purpose to comment upon the religious issue which has arisen in that country. What concerns us and all that concerns us is the place of any Latin-American country—Mexico included—in that strategic scheme of things which encircles the Isthmian Highway.

As the world has long been aware, Mexico has been disturbed for many years by a succession of disorders ranging in gravity from brigandage to civil war. These disturbances, insofar as they are confined to Mexico, do not affect, save indirectly, the security of the Isthmian Highway. All that has here to be said is that, despite many losses to her citizens, the United States, though constantly accused of

WILLIAM JENNINGS BRYAN

aggression, has kept her hands off Mexico and, save for the incident at Vera Cruz in 1915, has refrained from intervention.

But a different situation arises when Mexico, not content with this immunity from interference by the United States, proceeds herself to interfere with her smaller neighbours to the South.

In the *Saturday Evening Post* of April 16th, 1927, Mr. Isaac Marcosson describes two organizations in Mexico which, in his opinion, are hostile to the influence of the United States:

The first is the Anti-Imperialistic League of America. Its object is to spread radical propaganda in all the Latin-American countries and to aid the Soviet Government in its campaign against us. Branches have been set up in most of the Latin-American republics, but the headquarters are at the Mexican capital because of its geographical location.

The Anti-Imperialistic League of America was represented at a congress of so-called oppressed nations held in Brussels in February of this year. Its direct emissary was Julio A. Mella, the Cuban agitator. Aurelio Manrique went as delegate of the Mexican Agrarian League, composed of leaders in the Calles agricultural scheme which I have described in these columns.

At this convention resolutions were adopted demanding complete "independence of the Central and South American countries," neutrality of the Panama Canal, and denouncing the "imperialism of the United States."

The second instrumentality for the spread of radical propaganda in the Western world is the League of Latin-American Countries. The principal idea behind this organization is to place men of left tendencies in power in all Latin-American domains.

Its chief organizers and agitators are well-known Mexican radicals.

The period to which Mr. Marcosson refers was a period when the Third International of Mexico as the propagandist engine of Bolshevism, was at its highest activity. There was trouble, fomented by communism, in China, and owing to events in London, Great Britain broke off her diplomatic relations with the Soviet Republic.

That Russia was also fishing in the troubled waters of Mexico may be taken for granted.

Secretary Kellogg in the data he submitted to the Senate Committee on Foreign Relations, which now form part of the committee record, stated among other things:

The Bolshevik leaders have had very definite ideas with respect to the rôle which Mexico and Latin America are to play in their general program of world revolution. They have set up as one of their fundamental tasks the destruction of what they term American imperialism as a necessary prerequisite to the successful development of the international revolutionary movement in the New World.

The propagation of communist ideas and principles in the various countries of Latin America is considered secondary to the carrying on of propaganda against the aims and policies of the United States. Thus Latin America and Mexico are conceived as a base for activity against the United States. Communists in the United States have been repeatedly instructed to devote special attention to the struggle against "American Imperialism" in Latin America and to the organization of resistance to the United States.

Bolshevik aims in this respect were succinctly set forth in a resolution of the Third Congress of the Red Internationale of Trade Unions, July 8-22, 1924, as follows. It was resolved:

To unite the national struggle against American imperialism in individual countries in a movement on a scale of the whole American continent, embracing the workers of all countries of Latin America and the revolutionary forces of the United States. Mexico is a natural connecting link between the movement of the United States of North America and Latin America, therefore Mexico must be the center of the union.

To quote Mr. Marcosson:

When the Nicaraguan situation was at the sizzling point the Third Internationale proclaimed the necessity of war against the insolent and mighty capitalist régime and imperialism of the United States. In a manifesto issued on January thirtieth, and addressed to "the workers and peasants of the oppressed nations of the world," the communist organization invited "all anti-imperialistic forces to support the people of Nicaragua in their struggle against the base designs of American imperialism." Maintaining that the United States must resort to force in order to accomplish its fell purpose, the manifesto further stated:

This is why the mask has been thrown away and the country occupied under the pretense of protecting the lives and property of American citizens. From the Rio Grande to Tierra del Fuego the populations must organize a powerful movement against the exploitation and spoliation of the United States.

Broadly, we may say then that in Mexico, as in China, there has been an anti-foreign outburst directed against the most powerful foreigners to be seen, namely, British in the Far East, American in Latin-America, which outburst, not in itself communist in economic belief, has been exploited by the more extreme Bolshevists for their own purposes of attacking capitalist countries.

China has more recently discovered that Communism in any form is but a disappointing gospel, and in Mexico also the ambassadorship of Dwight W. Morrow with the more spectacular, but none the less valuable, diplomacy of Charles A. Lindbergh, has inaugurated, let us hope, a more encouraging era of good will. But the events of 1926 and 1927 are none the less significant of eventualities against the recurrence of which precautions must be taken.

The decisive fact that has to be faced is that Mexico, though she is in closer proximity than the United States to Nicaragua, is in no position financially to attempt the construction of a Nicaraguan or any other such canal, let alone its defence. Under the Taft Administration, the Army Engineers estimated that such a canal would cost 1,500,-000,000 dollars. Today, that cost would exceed 2,000,000,-000 dollars, a sum obviously exceeding the resources of Mexican credit. As a constructor of canals, Mexico is not in competition with the United States. If her influence were to be hostile, that hostility would be purely objective.

The recent history of Nicaragua exhibits a pitiful tale of human folly. In 1912, President Taft sent marines to the country and a force of 400 of these men remained there. The force was continued in the country by Presidents Wilson and Harding. President Coolidge, therefore, as he said on April 26th, 1927, found that "during this time, the people were peaceful, orderly and prosperous and their national debt was greatly reduced." With what we are bound to describe as undue caution, President Coolidge withdrew the marines, and as he puts it "almost at once . . . revolution was started." The marines, therefore, had to be sent back again, and—to quote President Coolidge, "Their presence has undoubtedly prevented the larger towns from being pillaged and confined the fighting for the most part to uninhabited areas."

There could not have been a more complete vindication by a Republican Administration of the Bryan-Chamorro provisions for order in Nicaragua which in 1914-16 the Senate refused to ratify.

After about five months of patient and *"watchful waiting"* for some improvement in the disorder and bloodshed in Nicaragua, President Coolidge finally sent former Secretary of War Henry L. Stimson as a personal emissary to that Republic in April 1927. On the causes of the trouble, Mr. Stimson reported:

My investigation has shown that this evil of Government domination of elections lies and always has lain at the root of the Nicaraguan problem.

Owing to the fact that a Government once in power habitually perpetuates itself, or its party, in such power by controlling the election, revolutions have become inevitable and chronic, for by revolution alone can a party once in control of the Government be dispossessed.

All persons of every party with whom I have talked admit the existence of this evil and its inevitable results, and all of them have expressed an earnest desire for the supervision of elections by the United States in an attempt to get rid of the evil forever.

The program for establishing peace and its continuance was included in the State Department comuniqué, as follows:

1. Complete disarmament of both sides.

2. An immediate general peace to permit planting for the new crop in June.

3. A general amnesty to all persons in rebellion or exile.

4. The return of all occupied or confiscated property to its owners.

5. Participation in the Diaz Cabinet by Liberals.

6. Organization of a Nicaraguan constabulary on a non-partisan basis, commanded by American officers.

7. American supervision of the 1928 election.

8. The continuance temporarily in the country of a sufficient force of American marines to guarantee order pending the organization of the constabulary.

In the interests of order in Nicaragua, several officers and a number of marines of the United States have lost their lives.

Reduced to simple terms, then, the intervention of the United States in Nicaragua has been, not for the purpose of depriving the people of their political or personal liberties but for the purpose of enabling them to exercise those liberties. The evidence on which this statement is based comes from both parties in Nicaragua. General Moncado as a Liberal is opposed to President Diaz but in the *New York Times* of Jan. 13th, 1928, he expressed confidence in the arrangement and said:

The presence of the marines in Nicaragua is for the guaranteeing of peace and liberty and for the defence of the citizens against an attempt of the government on the life and property of persons. . . . When the Nicaraguans are oppressed by the native authorities they always go to the marines for guarantee of liberty. They are the balance between the Conservatives and the Liberals. . . . The

Liberals have no hope of free election unless supervised by the marines.

Secretary Kellogg disclaimed in the strongest terms any desire by the United States to take sides in the election.

In the *New York Tribune* of March 8th, 1928, Mr. Horace G. Knowles, who has served as United States Minister in Nicaragua and other Latin American countries suggested that the marines had been "shooting high" thereby indicating their distaste for their task. The *Tribune* replied that this was shooting low and quoted the pronouncement made by Senator Borah on behalf of the Senate Committee on Foreign Affairs:

To remove our forces after all that has been said and done would justly subject us to bitter condemnation throughout all Central and South America, and particularly by the more liberal element as it would be the liberal element we would betray by our action, to say nothing of the discredit to ourselves and the turmoil and bloodshed which would be likely to follow. A withdrawal by the United States, pending the election, would have been a logical justification of the rebellion led by Sandino and the irreconcileables among the Liberals who on their side insisted that the ballot must be dominated by the bullet.

It is a matter of history that the chaos in Nicaragua was fomented by Mexico. This statement does not depend in any way on documents published by Mr. Hearst in his newspapers, which implicated Mexico in the Nicaraguan *embroglio*.

There exists, at the time of this writing, universal hope and confidence throughout the United States that the good diplomatic work of the Ambassador Mr. Dwight Morrow in conjunction with far seeing statesmen of the State Department of Mexico, in 1928, aided by the efforts and personal affability of President Calles, together with the visit of Col. Lindbergh, America's great unofficial "good

will" Ambassador, following the failure of the Sacasa upris-
ing or so called "revolution," will bring an end to the long
series of diplomatic misunderstandings and vexatious con-
tentions between the Mexican Government and the Government of the United States. In the light of that hope and
expectation we would have been glad to omit any reference
whatever to the connection of the Government of Mexico
with this 1927 and 1928 disturbance in Nicaragua which
menaced the Isthmian Highway and disturbed again the
peace and order of the Canal Littoral.

Mr. Hearst has admitted himself that certain of the published documents and particularly those which purported to
affect American statesmanship were forged. A Senate Committee has exonerated the Senators supposed to have been
involved in those documents. But on January 10th, 1927,
President Coolidge in a message to Congress, made the following definite disclosures:

"As a matter of fact I have the most conclusive evidence that arms
and munitions in large quantities have been, on several occasions
since August, 1926, shipped to the revolutionists in Nicaragua.
Boats carrying these munitions have been fitted out in Mexican
ports and some of the munitions bear evidence of having belonged
to the Mexican Government. It also appears the ships were fitted
out with the full knowledge of and in some cases with the encouragement of Mexican officials and were in one instance, at least, commanded by a Mexican naval reserve officer."

At a moment when the United States was limiting the
supply of arms to Nicaragua by an embargo, Mexico was
supplying this means of disorder. The attitude of the
"Liberal" opposition in Nicaragua was thus described by
President Coolidge on January 10th, 1927:

According to our reports, the Sacasa delegates on this occasion
stated freely that to accept any government other than one presided

over by Dr. Sacasa himself would be a breach of faith with their Mexican allies.

The action of Mexico in 1926-27 thus raised obviously an issue far more extensive than any question of property rights in that country. Indeed, it is not property rights in Nicaragua that have now to be considered. On April 26th, 1927, President Coolidge pointed out that there is no oil in Nicaragua and he poured ridicule on the cartoons which depict the country as covered with derricks. It is Nicaragua as a right of way for the human race that, in due course, will have to be opened up by engineering science. An indication of the prospects is to be found (September, 1928) in the agreement between the United States, Nicaragua, and Colombia, whereby the jurisdiction over certain islands and over the Mosquito Coast is defined. Into details, we need not enter but it is significant that, whereas Colombia retains her fishing rights, the United States obtains the right and accepts the duty of maintaining lighthouses and safeguarding navigation along the coast which would be an approach to the prospective canal.

Happily, there are evidences that, in Nicaragua herself, the motives of the United States are beginning to be understood and appreciated. On October 23, 1928, Adolfo Benard, the Conservative candidate, accepted a proposal by General José Maria Moncada, the Liberal candidate, that in 1932, as in 1928, the election should be supervised by this country. Such prospective supervision is thus requested by the leaders of both parties. In addition, Adolfo Benard proposed that both leaders should agree on a policy of financial reconstruction and the development of Nicaragua's resources. Senor Benard also suggests that steps be taken to strengthen the Guardia Nacional in order to insure the permanent peace of the country.

CALVIN COOLIDGE

The precise terms of General Moncada's proposal were, in part, as follows:

Now that we have seen the justice with which those in charge of the American supervision of the elections are proceeding, and the generous and laudable protection they give us, we who desire an era of peace and constructive work for Nicaragua should agree to accept the same supervision for future times.

For my part I offer that the Liberal Party will, if it is agreeable to the interests of the Conservative Party, accept willingly the intervention of the United States at the next Presidential election in the same form and manner as was established by the Stimson agreements.

Senor Benard replied, in part, as follows:

I entirely agree with your ideas. I understand that a stable and permanent peace based on the conciliation of the two historical parties would be the strongest and most efficient foundation for the prosperity of our homeland. That peace will necessarily arrive as the logical result of an honest and free election.

American supervision has made it possible for us to enjoy that electoral freedom which will doubtlessly bring good to all, either Liberal or Conservative. I think we should place without any reticence all our confidence on the American representatives who are going to secure a real and effective freedom of suffrage in the coming election.

I enthusiastically accept your praiseworthy idea of maintaining for another constitutional period the freedom of the suffrage under the friendly mediation of the United States.

It does not seem fit to close without making other proposals, equally necessary for the solidification of order and peace. Primarily, I refer to the economic outlook and I suggest we agree to amplify and perfect the financial plan now in force in a sense that will assure fair administration and honest use of the public funds.

If this inter-party agreement be carried out, it cannot fail to open a new era for Nicaragua.

XVII

PARITY ON THE OCEAN

IN the foregoing pages, the maritime traditions of the United States have been examined from various standpoints. We have seen how fundamental principles like the Freedom of the Seas and the Monroe Doctrine originated. We have also enunciated and applied a theory, at least as important as either of these. We hold that the control of the Suez Canal by Great Britain and of the Panama Canal by the United States are trusteeships. We also hold that influence of Great Britain, where she exercises influence, and of the United States, in like manner, are also trusteeships, whether in Egypt and Palestine, on the one hand, or in the Caribbean, on the other. As trustees, both these nations are equally responsible to mankind.

Hitherto, it has been the assumption that the sovereignty of the United States as a republic is essentially different from the sovereignty of Great Britain as a monarchy. The United States kept within her borders. Great Britain conquered beyond her borders and ruled where she had conquered. In the past, the distinction may have had a meaning. But today it is obsolescent. Both the United States and Great Britain are exercising power over other peoples. For both of them, it is a duty to exercise that power as a trust. The United States consists no longer of remote territories, peopled by pioneers. Even among the greatest of Powers, the United States is to be reckoned as a great Power, with world-wide contacts and an influence important and indeed essential to the maintenance of peace.

That the common task now confronting the English speaking nations, is one and the same may be demonstrated by the very difficulties encountered. The demand of the Philippines for independence is an echo of the demands of India and Egypt. The reasons why the demand cannot be granted are identical in all these cases. Moreover, the withdrawal of the United States from active administration in Cuba is in line with the withdrawal of Great Britain from participation in the domestic affairs of her Dominions. We will go further. The influence of Great Britain in the League of Nations is not wholly dissimilar from the influence of the United States in the Pan-American Union.

The maintenance of order is a thankless task. Porto Rico, the Philippines, India, Egypt, Syria—all such countries, governed by other countries, are inclined to be restive. Nor is any government perfect. All are open to criticism. Yet what would be the situation if, here and now, these governments were to be withdrawn? The world would be confronted by widespread chaos.

The fact that the trusteeship of the Panama Canal runs parallel with the trusteeship of the Suez Canal will come home in due course to the public opinion both of Great Britain and of the United States. A sentence from Henry J. Allen of Kansas, formerly Governor and proprietor of the Wichita *Beacon* puts the case thus:

When you hear an American talk in the Panama Canal Zone and an Englishman talk in Egypt you somehow get the idea there isn't much difference between the high quality of mission we are performing in the Panama Canal Zone and the mission the British are performing in the guardianship of the Suez Canal, and it is beautiful to hear both nations talk about it. But the British are doing it better than we are, because to them it has become a profound realisation of duty.

We take it to be undeniable that if Great Britain were to

obstruct the progress of commerce either through the Straits of Gibraltar or through the Suez Canal, the United States would not hesitate to enter a protest.

The evidence is, we suggest, overwhelming that the Monroe Doctrine has been used fairly as a shield and not as a sword. The Latin American Republics, commonly known as A.B.C., that is, the Argentine, Brazil and Chile, enjoy a stability of government which is wholly welcome to statesmanship at Washington. In their concerns, there is not, nor has there ever been, any imperialist interference. The utmost that can be alleged against the United States is that, during a dispute like that between Chile and Peru over Tacna and Arica, she has insistently urged that, in seeking a solution, resort shall not be had to war. The action of the United States in this matter has not differed in essentials from the action of the League of Nations when confronted by the rival claims of Poland and Lithuania to the city and province of Vilna.

At the Sixth Pan American Conference, held in Havana, Mr. Hughes insisted on the right of one country to intervene in the affairs of another country. His argument provoked a sensation. Yet it contained nothing new either to international law or to international practice. Unless it be Tibet, there is no country in the world today which does not admit the foreigner and foreign investment. Every nation has a right to be a nation, but no nation, having admitted foreigners and used their property, has a right to deny them the essentials of government. It is when government has broken down and only when government has broken down that the United States has intervened. In so far as government has been reëstablished, the United States has withdrawn her intervention.

The controversy over the League of Nations is not strictly germane to our subject. But the fact that we are still technically though only technically outside the League, makes it all the more important that our attitude towards the rest of the world should be carefully defined and adjusted. The United States has always stood for international law and equity. She has always repudiated the aggressive aims of traditional nationalism. She cannot abandon these rectitudes and adopt a selfish imperialism without surrendering the glory of her especial witness for justice and repeating the errors of autocracies, now humbled in the dust.

In certain quarters, it is suggested that the United States has drifted into imperialism. What is imperialism? It is the exercise of power and, in itself, the exercise of power is not wrong. The League of Nations itself claims the right to exercise power and delegates that right to its mandatories. The real question is whether a nation exercises its power for a legitimate or for an illegitimate purpose. There is all the difference conceivable between the imperialism that wages war and the imperialism that prevents the waging of war.

For all nations, the United States included, independence, pressed to the extreme of isolation, has become a delusion. It was, doubtless, as a separate community, that we won our early struggles against the suzerainty of Britain and the barriers of nature. But in our subsequent endeavours to build a more comfortable home in America for all our people, we have had to learn the lesson of collective effort. There has been social legislation, and social legislation leads us to the further step of adopting collective effort *with* others as well as among ourselves in order that the world as a whole may become a more comfortable home for mankind. Where a situation is cosmopolitan, it must be faced with a cosmopolitan mind.

We have described the sanitation, applied to Cuba and Panama, by which yellow fever was suppressed. That campaign against disease is only an illustration of the worldwide war against whatever weakens human life in which the United States is playing her part. The Rockefeller Foundation is but one of many agencies which has contributed to the health of the race. There are those who, not appreciating that this world moves on, still dream of wars for markets and raw materials. The real war that will bring prosperity is not a war waged by nation against nation, but a war waged by every nation against whatever depresses the vitality of any nation. The sick man is seldom a good customer. It is health that promotes trade. Heroes of hygiene like Walter Reed and Major Gorgas are men whose service and sacrifice, by conquering epidemics, create the field for productive and constructive commerce.

The argument in favour of a strictly scientific accountancy for the Panama Canal is also applicable to world-wide conditions. It is this accountancy that, since the war, American citizens have achieved, often under conditions of great delicacy. In Germany, Mr. S. Parker Gilbert is the responsible trustee for reparations. In Persia, Dr. Millspaugh, carrying forward the interrupted task of Morgan Shuster, reorganized for a time at any rate the national finances of that ancient country. With her abounding wealth, the United States has no need to indulge in profiteering, whether at home or abroad, and assuredly no profiteering should be attempted on the Isthmian Highway. A fidelity in the administration of public money and especially of public money derived from dues levied on mankind should be a matter of honour for a nation acknowledged to be the leader of the world along the path of material progress. Through the unselfish management of the Panama Canal, the United States has a golden opportunity of promoting world-wide good for all.

The interdependence of the modern world, expressed in commercial solidarity, is now apparent to all. With a compelling force, the European cataclysm has impressed on us the disastrous results of an armed conflict. The disturbance and destruction of established markets was and continues to be deplorable. The recurrence of the disaster can only be prevented by the creation of a proper world-wide tradition, which tradition will automatically become a social habit. As long as habit forms the greatest directive force in human life—we must take life as it is—it is important that the United States promote the habitual way of looking at things of world-wide import with an international mind, that is, a way of looking at things that will merge cosmopolitan and domestic interest into a harmonious whole.

It is the preservation of peace, then, that should be the absorbing aim of diplomacy. Such a stable peace must be dependent upon relations between powerful countries and, as is obvious from the map itself, upon the relations especially between the United States and Great Britain. If those relations are strained, peace everywhere is uncertain. If those relations are satisfactory, peace everywhere is as nearly guaranteed as can be any blessing on this imperfect planet.

There was no more high-spirited American than Grover Cleveland, yet as President, he replied to a petition signed by 232 members of the House of Commons in Great Britain and by 1,300,000 persons in terms which support our point of view:

I am reminded that in the administration of government difficulty often arises in the attempt to carefully apply ideas which in themselves challenge unqualified approval. Thus it may be that the friends of international arbitration will not be able at once to secure the adoption, in its whole extent, of their humane and beneficent scheme. But surely great progress should be made by a sincere and hearty effort. I promise you a faithful and careful consideration of the matter; and I believe I may speak for the American people in giving the assurance that they wish to see the killing of men for the accomplishment of national ambition abolished, and that they will gladly hail the advent of peaceful methods in the settlement of national disputes, so far as this is consistent with the defense and protection of our country's territory, and with the maintenance of our national honor.

For a century, the four thousand-mile-frontier between the United States and Canada has been immune under the Rush-Bagot Agreement from fortifications and warships on the Great Lakes. That has been a triumph of common sense often extolled in oratory.

But the mere absence of preparations for war has not been enough. Between the two countries, there have been developed many links, domestic, financial, and cultural, and these ties were symbolized in 1927 by the opening of the international bridge at Buffalo, dedicated by the United States and Great Britain to perpetual peace. At the dedication of the bridge, Vice President Dawes used these words:

What has been said of the relations of the English-speaking peoples and what I am to say is but the verbal acknowledgment of a common feeling, shared equally and alike by the Englishmen, Canadians and Americans who are gathered here. We speak the same language, we cherish the same ideals of citizenship, we hold to a common principle in government of individual liberty under law.

The foundation of this great peace structure which we dedicate today rests upon the firm bed-rock of the Niagara, and the peace of the English-speaking peoples is as firmly based upon common instincts and ideals. The instinct of self-preservation—the most deep-seated of mankind—binds us together, and in that unbroken tie is the ultimate guarantee of the safety and progress of western civilization. The bond will never break.

At times temporary misunderstandings may annoy us, but they are only eddies in the great current of fixed public opinion. Differences of opinion in smaller matters will always be exploited by the few, and at times the press will be filled with foreboding. But when any differences among themselves assume real importance in the minds of the English-speaking peoples, there will come from their heart and conscience—inarticulate upon trivial things—a universal cry for peaceful and reasonable adjustment.

On the British side, the Prince of Wales, addressing the American Legion in London on October 6th, 1927, said:

We of the British Legion never have and never will forget the links which those hard days of war forged between our brethren from the United States and ourselves.

It is the duty of the two great English-speaking nations of the world to see to it that these links do not become a mere sentimental association, to see that they remain and continue always as strong, practical ties to unite us in the big task of maintaining peace in a world which is realizing that continued peace is absolutely necessary for its very existence.

Into tradition we need not enter at any length. "Current disputes," so we read in the *New York Sun* of October 22nd, 1927, "over whether text books on the history of the Revolutionary War are pro-British or anti-British will leave most scholarly Americans unmoved except for a feeling of amusement." We agree, and as it seems to us the verdict on this matter is expressed by the newspaper in terms in which it would not be easy to suggest an improvement:

The Colonies were legitimate heirs of English law, language and history, of Runnymede and Magna Carta and the Revolution of 1688. For an American historian to assume that all knowledge and power and virtue developed on this side of the Atlantic, or that all Colonials were wise and just and virtuous, and all others stupid and tyrannical, would be to assume a lie. America does not base its glorious records of achievements upon a lie.

What the American schoolboy chiefly needs to be told is that here on this continent, thanks to its remoteness from effective European interference, liberty-loving men were able to rebuild the political structure of civilized society; that they borrowed whatever was best and noblest from the past, added contributions from the abundance of their own particular genius and built a structure that has defied the ravages of time. It is a structure which is not yet finished, but must go on building for an incalculable future. Its foundations are laid deep in the imperishable stone of history—not the history of our land alone but that of all other lands which have witnessed the age-old unfoldings of human liberty and human progress.

We have recalled the fact that the Monroe Doctrine was suggested by George Canning, a British statesman. By that doctrine, we mean that North and South America shall be immune forever from military and naval aggression by the nations of other continents, whether of Europe or of Asia, and from colonization or other forms of penetration calculated to lead to political embarrassments. The Monroe Doctrine is today firmly established and accepted by the world. It is a doctrine which Great Britain herself, by her reservations to the Kellogg Treaty has recently adapted to her own spheres of influence. The only question in regard to it is how far it extends and to what matters it applies.

It is as a cosmopolitan principle that we should insist on the freedom of the seas. With every year that passes, doubtless, the principle becomes of a more vital significance to the United States. Under stress of a blockade, this country could doubtless feed itself. But it has ceased to be, if ever it was, a self-contained world of production and consumption. We export; we import; and our exports and imports are rapidly increasing. Let us suppose that Mr. Henry Ford develops a vast plantation of rubber in Brazil. Such a plantation may enable us to be independent of British supply at British prices, but, none the less, the rubber will have to be carried over sea. Brazil is Brazil and not the United States.

By the freedom of the seas, we mean the right to use the seas as an international highway. We are wholly unable to see why this right should be regarded as a claim made by the United States on her own behalf alone. For our own shipping, we ask nothing that we do not concede in full and

FRANK B. KELLOGG

equal measure to the shipping of every other nation.   The
freedom of the seas is and always has been an international
charter of commerce.

A charter, thus absolute and world-wide, cannot be fully
applied in peace and war without encountering whatever
traditions there may be of a less universal character.   The
unselfish in diplomacy has always been to combat the selfish
and here have arisen our discussions with Great Britain in
which, as we think, there has been misunderstanding on both
sides.

Assuming a perpetual peace, we must agree that the British have not only accepted freedom of the seas but applied
it with a rectitude fully equal to our own.   For there can be
no freedom of the seas except as a phrase unless there be an
equal right for all nations to use ports and waterways and
straits.   In her trusteeship of seaports and the Suez Canal,
in her liberation of the Dardanelles, and in the hospitalities
of her own coastline, Great Britain has developed rules of
equity which could scarcely have been more honourable.

The Panama Canal is conducted today on the same principle of equity.   We submit that, to any other canal constructed across the Isthmus, no other principles should be applicable.   Any inequality of toll would subject the United
States to international criticism, would invite reprisals,
would undermine the recognized rules of the ocean and
would be a blow at the freedom of the seas itself.

That Great Britain demurred to the freedom of the seas,
when it was asserted by President Wilson in his Fourteen
Points, is true.   But the meaning of the demurrer should be
appreciated.   There was no proposal by Great Britain to
interfere in time of peace with those principles of equal use
of the ocean and of seaports and canals on which depends
the growing commerce of the United States.   On the contrary, the very fact that this commerce is largely carried by

British shipping, however regrettable it may be from an-other point of view, indicates that no nation has a greater interest in asserting the freedom of the seas than has Great Britain.

The British demurrer was and is limited to the single eventuality of war—an important and, it may be, a decisive eventuality but happily an eventuality only to be regarded as occasional. Rightly or wrongly, the British Navy exer-cised a right of search and seizure of shipping during the late war which exceeded the usual interpretation of a close blockade. Cargoes consigned to neutral countries, like Hol-land, were held on the ground that their ultimate destina-tion was not a neutral but a belligerent like Germany. Against this search and seizure President Wilson protested and, as we think, protested with justification.

Yet there remains the fact that, when the United States entered the war, she did not hesitate to pursue the methods of bringing pressure to bear upon a powerful enemy which as a neutral she had condemned. In the extended blockade, if we may use the term, she acted as a partner of Great Britain and France, and with a decision, at least as emphatic as theirs.

In settling their differences over prospective blockade, the United States and Great Britain might, with advantage, adopt as a basis of discussion the Declaration of Paris, negotiated in 1856. Summarised, this famous diplomatic instrument laid it down that

(1) privateering be abolished;

(2) the neutral flag covers enemy's goods, except contraband of war, which goods, unless contraband, are immune from capture;

(3) blockades, if binding, must be effectively maintained. The mere declaration of a blockade does not create the blockade.

The United States has to recognise that she herself may be so placed as to welcome the pressure of the British Navy on an aggressive belligerent. On the other hand, Great Britain must understand that a claim to defend herself from starvation by means of her navy, is by no means the same as a further claim to impose starvation on others. Such a measure involves the world as a whole and should only be undertaken with international approval. To such a general admission of necessity, the United States, as a matter of course, would have to be an acquiescent party.

The United States has, undoubtedly, stood for the rights of neutral shipping. But her record is, by no means, free from inconsistency. As the *New York Times* said on January 11, 1929:

That position maintained by our delegates in the International Conference of 1856, led them to refuse to sign for this nation the Declaration of Paris, though it abolished privateering and took some other useful steps.

Cynical foreigners did not fail to observe that the United States, five years later, when civil war broke out in America, abandoned its own doctrine of neutral rights in the blockade of the Confederate ports. At that time, too, the courts of the United States developed the doctrine of "continuous voyage," which in the hands of the British returned to plague our government during the early years of the war with Germany. Our State Department made vigorous protests, but no sooner had we joined the Allies in 1917 than our own ships of war vied with the British in disregarding the rights of neutral commerce on the ocean. In spite of these breaches of our own professions, there is no doubt that the United States has a continuing and substantial interest in the question of defining and defending neutral rights at sea, which this country would surely be pleased to get embodied not only in treaties but in international law.

The truth is that, during a war, every great principle of equity is apt to be held in abeyance. To quote Cicero, *silent enim leges inter arma*. If land and sea are thrown by statesmen into chaos, the usual guarantees of good faith become mere postscripts to the demands of necessity. It is war itself, then, that negatives the freedom of the seas, and this freedom depends, therefore, not on rules of war but on the perpetuation of peace.

We have to allow for the Constitution of the United States herself. Whatever the future may have in store, there is no serious proposal at the moment to amend the fundamental provisions of that great document. By the Constitution, the President as Executive and Congress as legislature, are separately elected authorities, situated at a distance measured by the historic Pennsylvania Avenue. The arrangement has been criticized by historians. It has its inconvenience as well as its value. But the point here is that to alter the Constitution in this respect is not practical politics. We must assume its continuance.

But there is something that can be and ought to be altered; and this is the temperamental hostility which too often throws the Capitol into an unreasonable opposition to the White House. It is an opposition often independent of party. Republican Senators will embarrass a Republican President; so with Democrats.

It should be borne in mind that, in the Senate, a majority of two-thirds is necessary to the ratification of a treaty. Such a majority far exceeds the usual inequality of parties and, according to John Hay, when he was Secretary of State, it had become unlikely that any important treaty would receive assent in years to come. His forecast has not been wholly fulfilled. Treaties like the Four Power Agreement over the Pacific and the Limitation of Naval Armaments have been ratified despite the two thirds rule. But the warning of John Hay deserves attention. The powers of the Senate were intended to be used as a safeguard, not as a *non possumus* and, in the working of every constitution, especially of a written constitution, there ought to be coöperation of all authorities in the public interest. The United States cannot now avoid continuous negotiations with other Powers, and the time has come when she ought to be able to approach other Powers, and to be approached by them, with the reasonable assurance that the word of her responsible statesmen will be her bond.

These discussions are not merely academic. They are of an immediate and urgent importance to the prospects of a stable peace. By invitation of the United States, the nations of the world which control the progress of civilization, have entered into a solemn treaty renouncing war as an instrument of policy. In logic, that treaty should be followed by a large measure of disarmament, on land, at sea and in the air. Yet we are faced by the fact that Great Britain and the United States, the two great English-speaking sovereignties discussed a naval agreement and failed to come to terms.

A question and a very grave question is thus whether the power of the United States and the power of Great Britain, both of them growing in range and effectiveness, are to be regarded as competitors or as coöperative. It is a question that was brought to a sharp issue at the Geneva Conference in 1927, called by President Coolidge for the purpose of extending the Naval Agreement of 1921 from battleships to cruisers and auxiliary vessels. The Conference failed and the comment of Prime Minister Baldwin included a speech to the American Legion:

Our peoples are friendly enough and great enough to thresh the subject out, and, if they cannot agree, differ like friends and gentlemen. It is far better to say to the world that we have examined this question and for the moment it has baffled us—for the moment.

The United States asked for parity between the fleets and obviously, she could not submit to a pledge of inferiority. Into what should be meant by parity in a technical sense, we do not enter. The arguments over tonnage, over calibres of guns, over coaling stations, were obviously well founded on both sides. But only on one assumption—that the respective navies might have to fight one another. If that assumption be unthinkable, the dialectics are reduced to irrelevance.

Into the intricacies of naval schedules, it would be useless for us here to enter. There is an obvious reason why the United States, with few coaling stations, should desire large cruisers. Equally obvious is the reason why Great Britain, with many coaling stations, should desire small cruisers. But the fallacy of setting the small cruisers of Great Britain to fight at least a diplomatic contest with the large cruisers of the United States should be more obvious by far than this logic on either side.

Great Britain and the United States talk, each with emphasis, about protecting commerce. It is vital that commerce should be protected. But what has happened in London? Aerial manoeuvres have proved that, in the event of war, no great city can be defended from attack, except by sheer distance. The talk about defending cities has been reduced to nonsense. So with commerce. The British argument itself, based on the damage effected by no more than two German cruisers, shows that there is no safeguard for commerce except peace. Certainly, there would be no safeguard for commerce, if peace were not preserved between the United States and Great Britain. Whatever else be the truth about these great countries, they have, each of them, the ability to inflict, if they wish, a terrible loss on the other and on mankind as a whole.

It is impossible for the United States—it is impossible for Great Britain to avoid the conclusion, the very grave conclusion that destiny has imposed on them not merely a trusteeship, but a joint trusteeship for the freedom of the seas. If the United States and Great Britain approach this problem as partners, that security on the ocean is achieved. If they approach this problem as rivals, that security is, *ipso facto,* destroyed. No one, who has crossed the Atlantic and seen successions of liners and freight steamers passing continually between American and European shores, can be in any doubt, if he thinks about realities, that a further misunderstanding between Washington and London over the rights and duties of the ocean would be an obstinate betrayal of both nations involved.

At the Washington Conference in 1921, the principle of parity on the ocean was applied to the battleships and aircraft carriers of the United States and British navies. This principle was enunciated by the United States Government on November 12, 1928, as follows:

To create, maintain and operate a navy second to none, in conformity with the ratios for capital ships established by the Washington treaty limiting naval armament.

On Armistice Day, 1928, President Coolidge explained the naval requirements of the United States in these terms:

We have not only a long coast line, distant outlying possessions, a foreign commerce unsurpassed in importance, and foreign investments unsurpassed in amount, the number of our people and value of our treasure to be protected, but we are also bound by international treaty to defend the Panama Canal. Having a few fueling stations, we require ships of large tonnage, and having scarcely any merchant vessels capable of mounting five or six inch guns, it is obvious that, based on needs, we are entitled to a larger number of warships than a nation having these advantages.

Failing an agreement on the ocean between the United States and Great Britain, that is the position.

On July 9th, 1927, Viscount Grey, speaking on the British attitude with a diplomatic authority, recognized as unchallengeable, thus stated the position:

I can go back as far as the naval relations with the United States before the war, and the policy of the Liberal Government then.

We had to meet a very severe naval competition, but we built a fleet against a European standard and it was common ground with some of us, and it was certainly my strong opinion, that in laying down the strength of the British Navy we should leave the United States out of account and not regard it as a rival, partly because a war between Britain and the United States would be such an offence to humanity, such a setback to human progress, and so opposed to the interests of this country that it must be the policy of the British Government to make that contingency impossible. But that was not the only reason. There was more statesmanship in our view than that. Statesmanship consists largely in recognising facts and in devoting efforts to what is practicable. It was obvious to us before the war that if the United States—the richest, the most powerful and most selfcontained country in the world—desired to build the biggest navy they could do it. If that was true before the war, it is at least as true now. With Europe exhausted by the Great War the United States is the most prosperous country in the world.

I would therefore say this. That if the principle of parity has been laid down, and equality between the United States and the British Navies is to lead to illfeeling and the measuring of strength between the two, I would rather go back to the old plan and say to the United States: "We must build a navy of a certain size to protect British interests and British trade routes and especially trade routes between the Cape and Australia which the United States does not for a moment threaten, and if you choose to build a larger navy and think it necessary for your interests we are not going to enter into competition.

What does this mean? It is a plain confession that the United States Navy, whatever be its size, is no menace to the British Empire. Nor is Viscount Grey the only witness. On August 2nd, 1927, Mr. Lloyd George attending the Liberal Summer School at Cambridge was questioned in specific terms on this aspect of the maritime situation:

Mr. J. M. Keynes asked: Would you agree that the more ships the United States builds the safer we are?
Mr. Lloyd George: I would not like to put it in that form. I

agree that so far from the building of ships by America being a reasonable course of apprehension, it is something we can look to as a means of support if we are attacked unjustly by any other countries.

A hostility between Great Britain and the United States would be, then, not only a suicidal wrong inflicted by each sovereignty on the other. It would be a deliberate and unforgivable crime, perpetrated by both nations against mankind as a whole. Such a crime would result in no victory worth having for either offender. It would mean that a disillusioned humanity would have to reconstruct out of shattered hopes and achievements a civilization in which the Anglo-Saxon tradition would have been reduced from its present prestige to an evil memory.

We have thus two approaches to the principle of parity. On the one hand, there is a desire that the principle be expressed in definitive formulæ, schedules of tonnage and so on. On the other hand, Lord Grey insists that, if such formulæ cannot be arrived at, no competition between the United States and the British Navy should be permitted. On November 5, 1928, he said:

The Government should make it quite clear that we do not take the United States into calculation in our naval building. I cannot help suspecting that there is a feeling among British naval experts and American naval experts that there is real rivalry about the fleets. What we want to be sure of is that the Government has instructed the Admiralty that in drawing up its program of British naval requirements it should not take the United States fleet into account. Previous British governments have never done it.

It is accepted throughout the world that the day is over when "Britannia ruled the waves," as sole trustee for the maritime interests of mankind. That responsibility to act as the international fire brigade is shared by the United States.

Between the two sovereignties, no diplomatic alliance is needed or would be advisable. Even in the relation between Great Britain and France before the war, there was no alliance or treaty. But on July 31st, 1914, Sir Eyre Crowe, Under Secretary at the British Foreign Office addressed a long memorandum to Sir Edward Grey in which we read:

The argument that there is no written bond binding us to France is strictly correct. There is no contractual obligation. But the Entente has been made.

The Entente between the United States and Great Britain does not need to be "made." Anything other than such an assumption is unthinkable.

It is no part of this argument to emphasize the errors of Germany when she was under the direction of a military autocracy which has now disappeared. But according to Mr. Poultney Bigelow, the fact that this earlier Germany "has persistently ridiculed our pretensions to the so-called Monroe Doctrine," and that "England threw neutrality to the winds in 1898 when our Admiral Dewey in the Far East was menaced by a German Fleet of superior force" are well-known to the historian. Lord Salisbury, asked to join in a naval demonstration in favor of Spain in Caribbean waters, is reported to have answered, "Yes, I have been thinking of this but in connection with the American fleet."

The United States on her side declined during the South African War to be drawn into an attitude of hostility to Great Britain. Recently, there has been published a letter by Secretary John Hay, written on Jan. 4th, 1900, which reads thus:

My Dear Ambassador,
I have conversed with the President in regard to the matter mentioned between us this morning. As I anticipated he feels that

we are precluded by all our traditions from joining in any representations such as were suggested.

We are greatly gratified by such evidence of his Imperial Majesty's
confidence and I need not say the matter will not be mentioned to
any of my colleagues in the Government.

Yours Faithfully,

JOHN HAY.

The identity of the Imperial Majesty is not disclosed but
at the time Secretary Hay was in frequent contact with the
German Ambassador.

Asked by an American journalist in 1927 what he considered to be significant in the relations between the United
States and Canada, Mr. Mackenzie King, the Prime Minister of the Dominion, said:

One hundred years of international peace over the greater part of
an entire continent! Is not this an achievement of which the world
should be made aware? Europe has not known it; Asia has not
known it; other continents have not known it. What might it not
mean to the future of the world if Europe could utter such a boast?
What may it not mean to mankind if we, through time, can hold
in unbroken continuity this evidence of international good will.

Our own hope is that Canada may see her way to join
the Pan-American Union, so exercising helpful influence in
the New World and supporting the international trusteeship
of the Panama Canal.

The word parity should be applied not to sea power alone
but to national responsibility. The reason why the United
States supervises elections in Nicaragua is essentially the
reason why Great Britain supervises elections in Egypt.
The Isthmian Highway is to the New World what the Suez
Canal is to the Old World. The administration of the
Philippines is no different in its principles from the administration of India. The United States and Great Britain
are engaged on what is and must be a common task, and

neither can fulfil the task in hostility to the other. That task is the maintenance of order, the perpetuation of peace, the development of constitutional liberty and the promotion of health and increased prosperity throughout the world.

In the Clayton-Bulwer Treaty of 1850, Great Britain and the United States subscribed to certain "general principles" of equitable conduct. They recognised that, like the British Constitution and the Monroe Doctrine themselves, diplomacy may be unwritten as well as written.

The foregoing pages have illustrated abundantly the importance of such "general principles" when applied to specific problems like the Panama Tolls. We have seen that, in accordance with "general principles," the United States, as an international trustee, amended a law, favorable to herself, which she had every power to maintain—this, in face of honest difference of opinion.

Another "general principle" of wider range has now been adopted. It is the Pact of Peace, associated with the name of Secretary Kellogg. To this "general principle," Great Britain and the United States, leading the rest of the world, have signified their adherence.

What is the Pact of Peace? It means that war as an instrument of policy is declared unlawful and that all disputes must be settled by other means. The glory that has surrounded war is thus abated, and the world passes out of the military into the commercial, the scientific and the cooperative era in which not good alone but ideas and ideals are interchanged.

We are satisfied that the Pact of Peace, without reservations, leaves the Monroe Doctrine undisturbed. On January 5, 1929, Senator Swanson, senior Democratic member of the Committee on Foreign Affairs, put the case thus:

HERBERT HOOVER

Those who favor the Monroe Doctrine being maintained as a shield of protection to all Latin-America from foreign aggression and not as an excuse for interference in their domestic affairs, and the extension of the power and influence of the United States by force and war, can approve this treaty, since it proclaims sentiments of peace and good-will, and its declarations condemnatory of war, if adhered to, would prevent a recurrence of deplorable transactions which have recently occurred in Central America.

Senator Swanson pointed out that Sir Austen Chamberlain, in an interpretive note to Secretary Kellogg, had appealed to the Monroe Doctrine and had himself applied such a Doctrine "to certain regions where she (Britain) claims a vital interest," in which note, Secretary Kellogg had acquiesced by an omission to reply. Hence argued Senator Swanson:

Great Britain would not, under this treaty, be prohibited from waging war in those regions of the world where she considers she has a vital interest. As Great Britain has interests in all parts of the world, this treaty would hardly apply to her in any conceivable case.

It is left to her decision and judgment under this understanding to determine what these interests are and where located. If this right belongs to Great Britain where she has special interests, it belongs equally to other nations. If Great Britain is unfettered and unrestrained by this treaty to wage war in China, Egypt, the Soudan, India, and Afghanistan, Italy is equally unrestrained in the Adriatic, and Italy and France are unrestrained in the Mediterranean and Africa, where they have special interests and possessions.

These reservations of Great Britain are of little value and importance, since they are all included in the right of self-defense, which under the treaty is reserved to each nation, and each nation determined the necessity for means to be used.

Whether or not this be a way of putting it in which all will agree, one thing is clear. There is no doubt that the British contention is based upon and, indeed, arises out of a wholehearted acceptance of the Monroe Doctrine.

On November 9, 1928, Stanley Baldwin, speaking as Prime Minister of Great Britain, said at the Mansion House:

Believe me, the alternative before Europe is very simple and the choice should be easy. We either keep faith with the spirit of the pact we signed or in time we will go down the steep places together and perish eternally.

Prime Minister Baldwin added:

I should say that I believe the time may come when in the histories of this period there will be no greater act credited to the United States than that in this year she had the highest honor of voicing the aspirations of mankind in presenting that pact for signature. . . . It is so tremendous a thing that few of us realize it.

Not only Europe but America must keep faith; and faith means the curtailment of armaments, whether on land, on sea or in the air.

Viscount Grey of Fallodon, speaking in London on November 5, 1928, said:

We shall never secure our position against the United States by armaments. The principle on which the Canadian boundary is secure is the only method on which Anglo-American security can be maintained. If you stick to that principle in practice, as the Canadian Government sticks to it in its own sphere, there will never be any risk of the British commonwealth of nations being interfered with by the United States.

We have quoted the statements of Lord Grey, Mr. Lloyd George and Mr. Stanley Baldwin. We have also quoted numerous declarations by statesmen in the United States. All of these pronouncements point to an Anglo-Saxondom, united in the maintenance of peace. President Hoover enters on his term of office also as an "internationally minded" man of affairs. These leaders on both sides of the

Atlantic enunciate what is essentially the same principle of policy.

On December 13, 1928, Prime Minister Baldwin hailed Lincoln "as one of the greatest Americans and one of the greatest Anglo-Saxons." Said Mr. Baldwin:

Sixty-five years ago this Christmas, when America was not the great power she is today, when she was not a world power, when the Union was split, it appeared, beyond the hope of redemption, and when the workingmen of Lancashire were starving and cotton was not coming in because of the war in America and the Union blockade of the Confederate States, these Lancashire men, to their eternal credit, wrote to Abraham Lincoln and said, "Carry on."

And Lincoln wrote to them, sixty-five years ago this coming New Year, finishing his letter with these words:

"I hail this interchange of sentiments as a happy augury that, whatever else may happen, whatever misfortune may befall your country or my own, the peace and friendship which now exists between the two nations will be, as it is my desire to make them, perpetual."

APPENDICES

APPENDIX I

CLAYTON-BULWER TREATY OF APRIL, 1850

The United States of America and Her Britannic Majesty, being desirous of consolidating the relations of amity which so happily subsist between them, by setting forth and fixing in a convention their views and intentions with reference to any means of communication by ship-canal which may be constructed between the Atlantic and Pacific Oceans by the way of the river San Juan de Nicaragua and either or both of the lakes of Nicaragua or Managua, to any port or place on the Pacific Ocean, the President of the United States has conferred full powers on John M. Clayton, Secretary of State of the United States, and Her Britannic Majesty on the Right Honorable Sir Henry Lytton Bulwer, a member of Her Majesty's most honorable privy council, knight commander of the most honorable Order of the Bath, and envoy extraordinary and minister plenipotentiary of Her Britannic Majesty to the United States, for the aforesaid purpose; and the said plenipotentiaries having exchanged their full powers, which were found to be in proper form, have agreed to the following articles:

ARTICLE I

The Governments of the United States and Great Britain hereby declare that neither the one nor the other will ever obtain or maintain for itself any exclusive control over the said ship canal; agreeing that neither will ever erect or maintain any fortifications commanding the same, or in the vicinity thereof, or occupy, or fortify, or colonize, or assume, or exercise any dominion over Nicaragua, Costa Rica, the Mosquito coast, or any part of Central America; nor will either make use of any protection which either affords or may afford, or any alliance which either has or may have to or with any state or people, for the purpose of erecting or maintaining any such fortifications, or of occupying, fortifying, or colonizing Nicaragua, Costa Rica, the Mosquito coast, or any part of Central America, or of assuming or exercising dominion over the same; nor will the United States or Great Britain take advantage of any intimacy, or use any alliance, connection or influence that either may possess with any State or Government through whose territory the said canal may pass, for the purpose of acquiring or holding, directly or indirectly, for the citizens or subjects of the one, any rights or advantages in regard to commerce or navigation through the said canal which shall not be offered on the same terms to the citizens or subjects of the other.

ARTICLE II

Vessels of the United States or Great Britain traversing the said canal shall, in case of war between the contracting parties, be exempted from blockade, detention or capture by either of the belligerents; and this provision shall extend to such a distance from the two ends of the said canal as may hereafter be found expedient to establish.

ARTICLE III

In order to secure the construction of the said canal, the contracting parties engage that if any such canal shall be undertaken upon fair and equitable terms by any parties having the authority of the local Government or Governments through whose territory the same may pass, then the persons employed in making the said canal, and their property used, or to be used, for that object, shall be protected, from the commencement of the said canal to its completion, by the Governments of the United States and Great Britain, from unjust detention, confiscation, seizure or any violence whatsoever.

ARTICLE IV

The contracting parties will use whatever influence they respectively exercise with any State, States or Governments possessing or claiming to possess any jurisdiction or right over the territory which the said canal shall traverse, or which shall be near the waters applicable thereto, in order to induce such States or Governments to facilitate the construction of the said canal by every means in their power. And furthermore, the United States and Great Britain agree to use their good offices, wherever or however it may be most expedient, in order to procure the establishment of two free ports, one at each end of the said canal.

ARTICLE V

The contracting parties further engage, that when the said canal shall have been completed, they will protect it from interruption, seizure or unjust confiscation, and that they will guarantee the neutrality thereof, so that the said canal may forever be open and free, and the capital invested therein secure. Nevertheless, the Governments of the United States and Great Britain, in according their protection to the construction of the said canal, and guaranteeing its neutrality and security when completed, always understand that this protection and guarantee are granted conditionally, and may be withdrawn by both Governments, or either Government, if both Governments, or either Government, should deem that the persons or company undertaking or managing the same adopt or establish such regulations concerning the traffic thereupon as are contrary to the spirit and intention of this convention, either by making unfair discriminations in favor of the commerce of one of the contracting parties over the commerce of the other, or by imposing oppressive exactions or unreasonable tolls upon the passengers, vessels, goods, wares, merchandise or other articles. Neither party, however, shall withdraw the aforesaid protection and guarantee without first giving six months' notice to the other.

ARTICLE VI

The contracting parties in this convention engage to invite every State with which both or either have friendly intercourse to enter into stipulations with them similar to those which they have entered into with each other, to the end that all other States may share in the honor and advantage of having contributed to a work of such general interest and importance as the canal herein contemplated. And the contracting parties likewise agree that each shall enter into treaty stipulations with such of the Central American States as they may deem advisable, for the purpose of more effectually carrying out the great design of this convention, namely, that of constructing and maintaining the said canal as a ship communication between the two oceans for the benefit of mankind, on equal terms to all, and of protecting the same; and they also agree that the good offices of either shall be employed, when requested by the other, in aiding and assisting the negotiation of such treaty stipulations; and should any differences arise as to right or property over the territory through which the said canal shall pass between the States or Governments of Central America, and such differences should in any way impede or obstruct the execution of the said canal, the Governments of the United States and Great Britain will use their good offices to settle such differences in the manner best suited to promote the interests of the said canal, and to strengthen the bonds of friendship and alliance which exist between the contracting parties.

Article VII

It being desirable that no time should be unnecessarily lost in commencing and constructing the said canal, the Governments of the United States and Great Britain determine to give their support and encouragement to such persons or company as may first offer to commence the same, with the necessary capital, the consent of the local authorities, and on such principles as accord with the spirit and intention of this convention; and if any persons or company should already have, with any State through which the proposed ship canal may pass, a contract for the construction of such a canal as that specified in this convention, to the stipulations of which contract neither of the contracting parties in this convention have any just cause to object, and the said persons or company shall moreover have made preparations and expended time, money and trouble on the faith of such contract, it is hereby agreed that such persons or company shall have a priority of claim over every other person, persons or company to the protection of the Governments of the United States and Great Britain, and be allowed a year from the date of the exchange of the ratifications of this convention for concluding their arrangements, and presenting evidence of sufficient capital subscribed to accomplish the contemplated undertaking; it being understood that if, at the expiration of the aforesaid period, such persons or company be not able to commence and carry out the proposed enterprise, then the Governments of the United States and Great Britain shall be free to afford their protection to any other persons or company that shall be prepared to commence and proceed with the construction of the canal in question.

Article VIII

The Governments of the United States and Great Britain having not only desired, in entering into this convention, to accomplish a particular object, but also to establish a general principle, they hereby agree to extend their protection, by treaty stipulations, to any other practicable communications, whether by canal or railway, across the isthmus which connects North and South America, and especially to the interoceanic communications, should the same prove to be practicable, whether by canal or railway, which are now proposed to be established by the way of Tehuantepec or Panama. In granting, however, their joint protection to any such canals or railways as are by this article specified, it is always understood by the United States and Great Britain that the parties constructing or owning the same shall impose no other charges or conditions of traffic thereupon than the aforesaid Governments shall approve of as just and equitable; and that the same canals or railways, being open to the citizens and subjects of the United States and Great Britain on equal terms, shall also be open on like terms to the citizens and subjects of every other State which is willing to grant thereto such protection as the United States and Great Britain engage to afford.

ARTICLE IX

The ratifications of this convention shall be exchanged at Washington within six months from this day, or sooner if possible.

In faith whereof we, the respective plenipotentiaries, have signed this convention and have hereunto affixed our seals.

Done at Washington the nineteenth day of April, anno Domini one thousand eight hundred and fifty.

JOHN M. CLAYTON. (L. S.)

HENRY LYTTON BULWER. (L. S.)

APPENDIX II

THE SUEZ CANAL TREATY OF MARCH, 1863

ARTICLE I

The Suez Maritime Canal shall always be free and open, in time of war as in time of peace, to every vessel of commerce or of war, without distinction of flag.

Consequently, the High Contracting Parties agree not in any way to interfere with the free use of the canal, in time of war as in time of peace.

The canal shall never be subjected to the exercise of the right of blockade.

ARTICLE II

The High Contracting Parties, recognizing that the fresh-water canal is indispensable to the maritime canal, take note of the engagements of His Highness the Khedive towards the Universal Suez Canal Company as regards the fresh-water canal; which engagements are stipulated in a convention bearing date the eighteenth of March, 1863, containing an *expose* and four articles.

They undertake not to interfere in any way with the security of that canal and its branches, the working of which shall not be exposed to any attempt at obstruction.

ARTICLE III

The High Contracting Parties likewise undertake to respect the plant, establishments, buildings and works of the maritime canal and the fresh-water canal.

ARTICLE IV

The maritime canal remaining open in time of war as a free passage, even to the ships of war of belligerents, according to the terms of Article I of the present treaty, the High Contracting Parties agree that no right of war, no act of hostility, nor any act having for its object to obstruct the free navigation of the canal, shall be committed in the canal and its ports of access, as well as within a radius of three marine miles from these ports, even though the Ottoman Empire should be one of the belligerent powers.

Vessels of war of belligerents shall not revictual or take in stores in the canal and its ports of access, except in so far as may be strictly necessary. The transit of the aforesaid vessels through the canal shall be effected with the least possible delay, in accordance with the regulations in force, and without any other intermission than that resulting from the necessities of the service.

Their stay at Port Said and in the roadstead of Suez shall not exceed twenty-four hours, except in case of distress. In such case they shall be bound to leave as soon as possible. An interval of twenty-four hours shall always elapse between the sailing of a belligerent ship from one of the ports of access and the departure of a ship belonging to the hostile power.

Article V

In time of war belligerent powers shall not disembark nor embark within the canal and its ports of access either troops, munitions or materials of war. But in case of an accidental hindrance in the canal, men may be embarked or disembarked at the ports of access by detachments not exceeding one thousand men, with a corresponding amount of war material.

Article VI

Prizes shall be subjected, in all respects, to the same rules as the vessels of belligerents.

Article VII

The powers shall not keep any vessel of war in the waters of the canal (including Lake Timsah and the Bitter Lakes).

Nevertheless, they may station vessels of war in the parts of access of Port Said and Suez, the number of which shall not exceed two for each power.

This right shall not be exercised by belligerents.

Article VIII

The agents in Egypt of the Signatory Powers of the present treaty shall be charged to watch over its execution. In case of any event threatening the security or the free passage of the canal, they shall meet on the summons of three of their number under the presidency of their Doyen, in order to proceed to the necessary verifications. They shall inform the Khedival Government of the danger of which they may have perceived, in order that that Government may take proper steps to insure the protection and the free use of the canal. Under any circumstances, they shall meet once a year to take note of the due execution of the treaty.

The last-mentioned meetings shall take place under the presidency of a Special Commissioner nominated for that purpose by the Imperial Ottoman Government. A Commissioner of the Khedive may also take part in the meeting, and may preside over it in case of the absence of the Ottoman Commissioner.

They shall especially demand the suppression of any work or the dispersion of any assemblage on either bank of the canal, the object or effect of which might be to interfere with the liberty and the entire security of the navigation.

ARTICLE IX

The Egyptian Government shall, within the limits of its powers resulting from the Firmans, and under the conditions provided for in the present treaty, take the necessary measures for insuring the execution of the said treaty.

In case the Egyptian Government should not have sufficient means at its disposal, it shall call upon the Imperial Ottoman Government, which shall take the necessary measures to respond to such appeal; shall give notice thereof to the Signatory Powers of the Declaration of London of the seventeenth of March, 1885; and shall, if necessary, concert with them on the subject.

The provisions of Articles IV, V, VII and VIII shall not interfere with the measures which shall be taken in virtue of the present article.

ARTICLE X

Similarly, the provisions of Articles IV, V, VII and VIII shall not interfere with the measures which His Majesty the Sultan and His Highness the Khedive, in the name of His Imperial Majesty, and within the limits of the Firmans granted, might find it necessary to take for securing by their own forces the defence of Egypt and the maintenance of public order.

In case His Imperial Majesty the Sultan, or His Highness the Khedive, should find it necessary to avail themselves of the exceptions for which this article provides, the Signatory Powers of the Declaration of London shall be notified thereof by the Imperial Ottoman Government.

It is likewise understood that the provisions of the four articles aforesaid shall in no case occasion any obstacle to the measures which the Imperial Ottoman Government may think it necessary to take in order to insure by its own forces the defence of its other possessions situated on the eastern coast of the Red Sea.

ARTICLE XI

The measures which shall be taken in the cases provided for by Articles IX and X of the present treaty shall not interfere with the free use of the canal. In the same cases, the erection of permanent fortifications contrary to the provisions of Article VIII is prohibited.

ARTICLE XII

The High Contracting Parties, by application of the principle of equality as regards the free use of the canal, a principle which forms one of the bases of the present treaty, agree that none of them shall endeavour to obtain with respect to the canal territorial or commercial advantages or privileges in any international arrangements which may be concluded. Moreover, the rights of Turkey as the territorial power are reserved.

ARTICLE XIII

With the exception of the obligations expressly provided by the clauses of the present treaty, the sovereign rights of His Imperial Majesty the Sultan, and the rights and immunities of His Highness the Khedive, resulting from the Firmans, are in no way affected.

ARTICLE XIV

The High Contracting Parties agree that the engagements resulting from the present treaty shall not be limited by the duration of the Acts of Concession of the Universal Suez Canal Company.

ARTICLE XV

The stipulations of the present treaty shall not interfere with the sanitary measures in force in Egypt.

Article XVI

The High Contracting Parties undertake to bring the present treaty to the knowledge of the States which have not signed it, inviting them to accede to it.

Article XVII

The present treaty shall be ratified, and the ratifications shall be exchanged at Constantinople within the space of one month, or sooner, if possible.

APPENDIX III

THE HAY-PAUNCEFOTE TREATY OF 1900

Showing the original treaty and the treaty as amended in one as follows:

(1) Amendments by the United States Senate are printed in italics.

(2) Article III, stricken out by the United States Senate, is printed in brackets.

The United States of America and Her Majesty the Queen of the United Kingdom of Great Britain and Ireland, Empress of India, being desirous to facilitate the construction of a ship canal to connect the Atlantic and Pacific Oceans, and to that end to remove any objection which may arise out of the convention of April 19, 1850, commonly called the Clayton-Bulwer treaty, to the construction of such canal under the auspices of the Government of the United States, without impairing the "general principle" of neutralization established in Article VIII of that convention, have for that purpose appointed as their plenipotentiaries:

The President of the United States, John Hay, Secretary of State, of the United States of America;

And Her Majesty the Queen of Great Britain and Ireland, Empress of India, The Right Honorable Lord Pauncefote, G. C. B., G. C. M. G., Her Majesty's Ambassador Extraordinary and Plenipotentiary to the United States;

Who, having communicated to each other their full powers, which were found to be in due and proper form, have agreed upon the following articles:

Article I

It is agreed that the canal may be constructed under the auspices of the Government of the United States, either directly at its own cost or by gift or loan of money to individuals or corporations or through subscription to or purchase of stock or shares, and that, subject to the provisions of the present convention, the said Government shall have and enjoy all the rights incident to such construction, as well as the exclusive right of providing for the regulation and management of the canal.

ARTICLE II

The High Contracting Parties, desiring to preserve and maintain the "general principle" of neutralization established in Article VIII of the Clayton-Bulwer convention, *which convention is hereby superseded,* adopt, as the basis of such neutralization, the following rules, substantially as embodied in the convention between Great Britain and certain other powers, signed at Constantinople October 29, 1888, for the Free Navigation of the Suez Maritime Canal, that is to say:

1. The canal shall be free and open, in time of war as in time of peace, to the vessels of commerce and of war of all nations, on terms of entire equality, so that there shall be no discrimination against any nation or its citizens or subjects in respect of the conditions or charges of traffic, or otherwise.

2. The canal shall never be blockaded, nor shall any right of war be exercised nor any act of hostility be committed within it.

3. Vessels of war of a belligerent shall not revictual nor take any stores in the canal except so far as may be strictly necessary; and the transit of such vessels through the canal shall be effected with the least possible delay, in accordance with the regulations in force, and with only such intermission as may result from the necessities of the service.

Prizes shall be in all respects subject to the same rules as vessels of war of the belligerents.

4. No belligerent shall embark or disembark troops, munitions of war or warlike materials in the canal except in case of accidental hindrance of the transit, and in such case the transit shall be resumed with all possible despatch.

5. The provisions of this article shall apply to waters adjacent to the canal, within three marine miles of either end. Vessels of war of a belligerent shall not remain in such waters longer than twenty-four hours at any one time except in case of distress, and in such case shall depart as soon as possible; but a vessel of war of one belligerent shall not depart within twenty-four hours from the departure of a vessel of war of the other belligerent.

It is agreed, however, that none of the immediately foregoing conditions and stipulations in sections numbered one, two, three, four and five of this article shall apply to measures which the United States may find it necessary to take for securing by its own forces the defense of the United States and the maintenance of public order.

6. The plant, establishments, buildings and all works necessary to the construction, maintenance and operation of the canal shall be deemed to be part thereof, for the purposes of this convention, and in time of war as in time of peace shall enjoy complete immunity from attack or injury by belligerents and from acts calculated to impair their usefulness as part of the canal.

7. No fortifications shall be erected commanding the canal or the waters adjacent. The United States, however, shall be at liberty to maintain such military police along the canal as may be necessary to protect it against lawlessness and disorder.

[ARTICLE III]

[The High Contracting Parties will, immediately upon the exchange of the ratifications of this convention, bring it to the notice of the other powers and invite them to adhere to it.]

ARTICLE IV

The present convention shall be ratified by the President of the United States, by and with the advice and consent of the Senate thereof, and by Her Britannic Majesty; and the ratifications shall be exchanged at Washington or at London within six months from the date hereof, or earlier if possible.

In faith whereof the respective plenipotentiaries have signed this convention and thereunto affixed their seals.

Done in duplicate at Washington the fifth day of February in the year of our Lord one thousand nine hundred.

JOHN HAY.
PAUNCEFOTE.

APPENDIX IV

THE HAY-PAUNCEFOTE TREATY OF NOVEMBER, 1901

The United States of America and His Majesty Edward the Seventh, of the United Kingdom of Great Britain and Ireland, and of the British Dominions beyond the Seas, King, and Emperor of India, being desirous to facilitate the construction of a ship canal to connect the Atlantic and Pacific Oceans, by whatever route may be considered expedient, and to that end to remove any objection which may arise out of the convention of the nineteenth of April, 1850, commonly called the Clayton-Bulwer treaty, to the construction of such canal under the auspices of the Government of the United States, without impairing the "general principle" of neutralization established in Article VIII of that convention, have for that purpose appointed as their plenipotentiaries:

The President of the United States, John Hay, Secretary of State of the United States of America;

And His Majesty Edward the Seventh, of the United Kingdom of Great Britain and Ireland, and of the British Dominions beyond the Seas, King, and Emperor of India, the Right Honourable Lord Pauncefote, G. C. B., G. C. M. G., His Majesty's Ambassador Extraordinary and Plenipotentiary to the United States;

Who, having communicated to each other their full powers, which were found to be in due and proper form, have agreed upon the following articles:

ARTICLE I

The High Contracting Parties agree that the present treaty shall supersede the afore-mentioned convention of the nineteenth of April, 1850.

ARTICLE II

It is agreed that the canal may be constructed under the auspices of the Government of the United States either directly at its own cost, or by gift or loan of money to individuals or corporations, or through subscription to or purchase of stock or shares, and that, subject to the provisions of the present treaty, the said Government shall have and enjoy all the rights incident to such construction, as well as the exclusive right of providing for the regulation and management of the canal.

ARTICLE III

The United States adopts, as the basis of the neutralization of such ship canal, the following rules, substantially as embodied in the convention of Constantinople signed the twenty-eighth of October, 1888, for the free navigation of the Suez Canal, that is to say:

1. The canal shall be free and open to the vessels of commerce and of war of all nations observing these rules, on terms of entire equality, so that there shall be no discrimination against any such nation, or its citizens or subjects, in respect of the conditions or charges of traffic or otherwise. Such conditions and charges of traffic shall be just and equitable.

2. The canal shall never be blockaded, nor shall any right of war be exercised nor any act of hostility be committed within it. The United States, however, shall be at liberty to maintain such military police along the canal as may be necessary to protect it against lawlessness and disorder.

3. Vessels of war of a belligerent shall not revictual nor take any stores in the canal except so far as may be strictly necessary; and the transit of such vessels through the canal shall be effected with the least possible delay in accordance with the regulations in force, and with only such intermission as may result from the necessities of the service.

Prizes shall be in all respects subject to the same rules as vessels of war of the belligerents.

4. No belligerent shall embark or disembark troops, munitions of war, or warlike materials in the canal, except in case of accidental hindrance of the transit, and in such case the transit shall be resumed with all possible dispatch.

5. The provisions of this article shall apply to waters adjacent to the canal, within three marine miles of either end. Vessels of war of a belligerent shall not remain in such waters longer than twenty-four hours at any one time, except in case of distress, and in such case shall depart as soon as possible; but a vessel of war of one

belligerent shall not depart within twenty-four hours from the departure of a vessel of war of the other belligerent.

6. The plant, establishments, buildings and all works necessary to the construction, maintenance and operation of the canal shall be deemed to be part thereof, for the purposes of this treaty, and in time of war, as in time of peace, shall enjoy complete immunity from attack or injury by belligerents, and from acts calculated to impair their usefulness as part of the canal.

Article IV

It is agreed that no change of territorial sovereignty or of international relations of the country or counties traversed by the before-mentioned canal shall affect the general principle of neutralization or the obligation of the High Contracting Parties under the present treaty.

Article V

The present treaty shall be ratified by the President of the United States, by and with the advice and consent of the Senate thereof, and by His Britannic Majesty; and the ratifications shall be exchanged at Washington or at London at the earliest possible time within six months from the date hereof.

In faith whereof the respective plenipotentiaries have signed this treaty and hereunto affixed their seals.

Done in duplicate at Washington, the eighteenth day of November, in the year of our Lord one thousand nine hundred and one.

JOHN HAY.   (SEAL.)
PAUNCEFOTE.   (SEAL.)

APPENDIX V

TREATY WITH PANAMA OF NOVEMBER, 1903

The United States of America and the Republic of Panama being desirous to insure the construction of a ship canal across the Isthmus of Panama to connect the Atlantic and Pacific Oceans, and the Congress of the United States of America having passed an act approved June 28, 1902, in furtherance of that object, by which the President of the United States is authorized to acquire within a reasonable time the control of the necessary territory of the Republic of Colombia, and the sovereignty of such territory being actually vested in the Republic of Panama, the High Contracting Parties have resolved for that purpose to conclude a Convention and have accordingly appointed as their plenipotentiaries,—

The President of the United States of America, John Hay, Secretary of State, and

The Government of the Republic of Panama, Philippe Bunau-Varilla, Envoy Extraordinary and Minister Plenipotentiary of the Republic of Panama, thereunto specially empowered by said Government, who after communicating with each other their respective full powers, found to be in good and due form, have agreed upon and concluded the following articles:

Article I

The United States guarantees and will maintain the independence of the Republic of Panama.

Article II

The Republic of Panama grants to the United States in perpetuity the use, occupation and control of a zone of land and land under water for the construction, maintenance, operation, sanitation and protection of said canal of the width of ten miles extending to the distance of five miles on each side of the center line of the route of the canal to be constructed; the said zone beginning in the Caribbean Sea, three marine miles from mean low water mark, and extending to and across the Isthmus of Panama into the Pacific Ocean to a distance of three marine miles from mean low water mark, with the proviso that the cities of Panama and Colon and the harbors adjacent to said cities, which are included within the boundaries of the zone above described, shall not be included within this grant. The Republic of Panama further grants to the United States in perpetuity the use, occupation and control of any other lands and waters outside of the zone above described which may be necessary and convenient for the construction, maintenance, operation, sanitation and protection of the said canal or of any auxiliary canals or other works necessary and convenient for the construction, maintenance, operation, sanitation and protection of the said enterprise.

The Republic of Panama further grants in like manner to the United States in perpetuity all islands within the limits of the zone above described and in addition thereto the group of small islands in the Bay of Panama, named Perico, Naos, Culebra and Flamenco.

ARTICLE III

The Republic of Panama grants to the United States all the rights, power and authority within the zone mentioned and described in Article II of this agreement and within the limits of all auxiliary lands and waters mentioned and described in said Article II which the United States would possess and exercise if it were the sovereign of the territory within which said lands and waters are located to the entire exclusion of the exercise by the Republic of Panama of any such sovereign rights, power or authority.

ARTICLE IV

As rights subsidiary to the above grants the Republic of Panama grants in perpetuity to the United States the right to use the rivers, streams, lakes and other bodies of water within its limits for navigation, the supply of water or water-power or other purposes, so far as the use of said rivers, streams, lakes and bodies of water and the waters thereof may be necessary and convenient for the construction, maintenance, operation, sanitation and protection of the said canal.

ARTICLE V

The Republic of Panama grants to the United States in perpetuity a monopoly for the construction, maintenance and operation of any system of communication by means of canal or railroad across its territory between the Caribbean Sea and the Pacific Ocean.

ARTICLE VI

The grants herein contained shall in no manner invalidate the titles or rights of private land holders or owners of private property in the said zone or in or to any of the lands or waters granted to the United States by the provisions of any article of this treaty, nor shall they interfere with the rights of way over the public roads passing through the said zone or over any of the said lands or waters unless said rights of way or private rights shall conflict with rights herein granted to the United States in which case the rights of the United States shall be superior. All damages caused to the owners of private lands or private property of any kind by reason of the grants contained in this treaty or by reason of the operations of the United States, its agents or employees, or by reason of the construction, maintenance, operation, sanitation and protection of the said canal or of the works of sanitation and protection herein provided for, shall be appraised and settled by a joint commission appointed by the Governments of the United States and of the Republic of Panama, whose decisions as to such damages shall be final and whose awards as to such damages shall be paid solely by the United States. No part of the work on said canal or the Panama railroad or on any auxiliary works relating thereto and authorized by the terms of this treaty shall be prevented, delayed or impeded by or pending such proceedings to ascertain such damages. The appraisal of said private lands and private property and the assessment of damages to them shall be based upon their value before the date of this convention.

ARTICLE VII

The Republic of Panama grants to the United States within the limits of the cities of Panama and Colon and their adjacent harbors and within the territory adjacent thereto the right to acquire by purchase or by the exercise of the right of eminent domain, any lands, buildings, water rights or other properties necessary and convenient for the construction, maintenance, operation and protection of the canal and of any works of sanitation, such as the collection and disposition of sewage and the distribution of water in the said cities of Panama and Colon, which, in the discretion of the United States may be necessary and convenient for the construction, maintenance, operation, sanitation and protection of the said canal and railroad. All such works of sanitation, collection and disposition of sewage and distribution of water in the cities of Panama and Colon shall be made at the expense of the United States, and the Government of the United States, its agents or nominees shall be authorized to impose and collect water rates and sewerage rates which shall be sufficient to provide for the payment of interest and the amortization of the principal of the cost of said works within a period of fifty years and upon the expiration of said term of fifty years the system of sewers and water works shall revert to and become the properties of the cities of Panama and Colon respectively, and the use of the water shall be free to the inhabitants of Panama and Colon, except to the extent that water rates may be necessary for the operation and maintenance of said system of sewers and waters.

The Republic of Panama agrees that the cities of Panama and Colon shall comply in perpetuity with the sanitary ordinances whether of a preventive or curative character prescribed by the United States and in case the Government of Panama is unable or fails in its duty to enforce this compliance by the cities of Panama and Colon with the sanitary ordinances of the United States the Republic of Panama grants to the United States the right and authority to enforce the same.

The same right and authority are granted to the United States for the maintenance of public order in the cities of Panama and Colon and the territories and harbors adjacent thereto in case the Republic of Panama should not be, in the judgment of the United States, able to maintain such order.

Article VIII

The Republic of Panama grants to the United States all rights which it now has or hereafter may acquire to the property of the New Panama Canal Company and the Panama Railroad Company as a result of the transfer of sovereignty from the Republic of Colombia to the Republic of Panama over the Isthmus of Panama and authorizes the New Panama Canal Company to sell and transfer to the United States its rights, privileges, properties and concessions as well as the Panama Railroad and all the shares or part of the shares of that company; but the public lands situated outside of the zone described in Article II of this treaty now included in the concessions to both said enterprises and not required in the construction or operation of the canal shall revert to the Republic of Panama except any property now owned by or in the possession of said companies within Panama or Colon or the ports or terminals thereof.

ARTICLE IX

The United States agrees that the ports at either entrance of the canal and the waters thereof and the Republic of Panama agrees that the towns of Panama and Colon shall be free for all time so that there shall not be imposed or collected custom house tolls, tonnage, anchorage, lighthouse, wharf, pilot or quarantine dues or any other charges or taxes of any kind upon any vessel using or passing through the canal or belonging to or employed by the United States, directly or indirectly, in connection with the construction, maintenance, operation, sanitation and protection of the main canal, or auxiliary works, or upon the cargo, officers, crew or passengers of any such vessels, except such tolls and charges as may be imposed by the United States for the use of the canal and other works, and except tolls and charges imposed by the Republic of Panama upon merchandise destined to be introduced for the consumption of the rest of the Republic of Panama, and upon vessels touching at the ports of Colon and Panama and which do not cross the canal.

The Government of the Republic of Panama shall have the right to establish in such ports and in the towns of Panama and Colon such houses and guards as it may deem necessary to collect duties on importations destined to other portions of Panama and to prevent contraband trade. The United States shall have the right to make use of the towns and harbors of Panama and Colon as places of anchorage, and for making repairs, for loading, unloading, depositing or trans-shipping cargoes either in transit or destined for the service of the canal and for other works pertaining to the canal.

ARTICLE X

The Republic of Panama agrees that there shall not be imposed any taxes, national, municipal, departmental or of any other class upon the canal, the railways and auxiliary works, tugs and other vessels employed in the service of the canal, storehouse, workshops, offices, quarters for laborers, factories of all kinds, warehouses, wharves, machinery and other works, property, and effects appertaining to the canal or railroad and auxiliary works, or their officers or employees, situated within the cities of Panama and Colon, and that there shall not be imposed contributions or charges of a personal character of any kind upon officers, employees, laborers and other individuals in the service of the canal and railroad and auxiliary works.

ARTICLE XI

The United States agrees that the official dispatches of the Government of the Republic of Panama shall be transmitted over any telegraph and telephone lines established for canal purposes and used for public and private business at rates not higher than those required from officials in the service of the United States.

ARTICLE XII

The Government of the Republic of Panama shall permit the immigration and free access to the lands and workshops of the canal and its auxiliary works of all employees and workmen of whatever nationality under contract to work upon or seeking employment upon or in any wise connected with the said canal and its auxiliary works, with their respective families and all such persons shall be free and exempt from the military service of the Republic of Panama.

ARTICLE XIII

The United States may import at any time into the said zone and auxiliary lands, free of custom duties, imposts, taxes or other charges, and without any restrictions, any and all vessels, dredges, engines, cars, machinery, tools, explosives, materials, supplies and other articles necessary and convenient in the construction, maintenance, operation, sanitation and protection of the canal and auxiliary works, and all provisions, medicines, clothing, supplies and other things necessary and convenient for the officers, employees, workmen and laborers in the service and employ of the United States and for their families. If any such articles are disposed of for use outside of the zone and auxiliary lands granted to the United States and within the territory of the Republic; they shall be subject to the same import or other duties as like articles imported under the laws of the Republic of Panama.

ARTICLE XIV

As the price or compensation for the rights, powers and privileges granted in this convention by the Republic of Panama to the United States, the Government of the United States agrees to pay to the

Republic of Panama the sum of ten million dollars ($10,000,000) in gold coin of the United States on the exchange of the ratification of this convention and also an annual payment during the life of this convention of two hundred and fifty thousand dollars ($250,000) in like gold coin, beginning nine years after the date aforesaid.

The provisions of this article shall be in addition to all other benefits assured to the Republic of Panama under this convention.

But no delay or difference of opinion under this article or any other provisions of this treaty shall affect or interrupt the full operation and effect of this convention in all other respects.

Article XV

The joint commission referred to in Article VI shall be established as follows:

The President of the United States shall nominate two persons and the President of the Republic of Panama shall nominate two persons and they shall proceed to a decision; but in case of disagreement of the commission (by reason of their being equally divided in conclusion) an umpire shall be appointed by the two Governments, who shall render the decision. In the event of the death, absence or incapacity of a commissioner or umpire, or of his omitting, declining or ceasing to act, his place shall be filled by the appointment of another person in the manner above indicated. All decisions by a majority of the commission or by the umpire shall be final.

Article XVI

The two Governments shall make adequate provision by future agreement for the pursuit, capture, imprisonment, detention and delivery within said zone and auxiliary lands to the authorities of the Republic of Panama of persons charged with the commitment of crimes, felonies or misdemeanors without said zone and for the pursuit, capture, imprisonment, detention and delivery without said zone to the authorities of the United States of persons charged with the commitment of crimes, felonies and misdemeanors within said zone and auxiliary lands.

Article XVII

The Republic of Panama grants to the United States the use of all the ports of the Republic open to commerce as places of refuge for any vessels employed in the canal enterprise, and for all vessels passing or bound to pass through the canal which may be in distress and be driven to seek refuge in said ports. Such vessels shall be exempt from anchorage and tonnage dues on the part of the Republic of Panama.

Article XVIII

The canal, when constructed, and the entrances thereto shall be neutral in perpetuity, and shall be opened upon the terms provided for by Section 1 of Article III of, and in conformity with all the stipulations of, the treaty entered into by the Governments of the United States and Great Britain on November 18, 1901.

Article XIX

The Government of the Republic of Panama shall have the right to transport over the canal its vessels and its troops and munitions of war in such vessels at all times without paying charges of any kind. The exemption is to be extended to the auxiliary railway for the transportation of persons in the service of the Republic of Panama, or of the police force charged with the preservation of public order outside of said zone, as well as to their baggage, munitions of war and supplies.

Article XX

If by virtue of any existing treaty in relation to the territory of the Isthmus of Panama, whereof the obligations shall descend or be assumed by the Republic of Panama, there may be any privilege or concession in favor of the Government or the citizens and subjects of a third power relative to an interoceanic means of communication which in any of its terms may be incompatible with the terms of the present convention, the Republic of Panama agrees to cancel or modi y such treaty in due form, for which purpose it shall give to the s id third power the requisite notification within the term of four months from the date of the present convention, and in case the existing treaty contains no clause permitting its modifications or annulment, the Republic of Panama agrees to procure its modifications or annulment in such form that there shall not exist any conflict with the stipulations of the present convention.

Article XXI

The rights and privileges granted by the Republic of Panama to the United States in the preceding articles are understood to be free of all anterior debts, liens, trusts or liabilities, or concessions or privileges to other Governments, corporations, syndicates or individuals, and consequently, if there should arise any claims on account of the present concessions and privileges or otherwise, the claimants shall resort to the Government of the Republic of Panama and not to the United States for any indemnity or compromise which may be required.

Article XXII

The Republic of Panama renounces and grants to the United States the participation to which it might be entitled in the future earnings of the canal under Article XV of the concessionary contract with Lucien N. B. Wyse, now owned by the New Panama Canal Company, and any and all other rights or claims of a pecuniary nature arising under or relating to said concession, or arising under or relating to the concessions to the Panama Railroad Company or any extension or modification thereof; and it likewise renounces, confirms and grants to the United States, now and hereafter, all the rights and property reserved in the said concessions which otherwise would belong to Panama at or before the expiration of the terms of ninety-nine years of the concessions granted to or held by the above-mentioned party and companies, and all right, title and interest which it now has or may hereafter have, in and to the lands, canal, works, property and rights held by the said companies under said concessions or otherwise, and acquired or to be acquired by the United States from or through the New Panama Canal Company, including any property and rights which might or may in the future either by lapse of time, forfeiture or otherwise, revert to the Republic of Panama under any contracts or concessions, with said Wyse, the Universal Panama Canal Company, the Panama Railroad Company and the New Panama Canal Company.

The aforesaid rights and property shall be and are free and released from any present or reversionary interest in or claims of Panama and the title of the United States thereto upon consummation of the contemplated purchase by the United States from the New Panama Canal Company, shall be absolute, so far as concerns the Republic of Panama, excepting always the rights of the Republic specifically secured under this treaty.

Article XXIII

If it should become necessary at any time to employ armed forces for the safety or protection of the canal, or of the ships that make use of the same, or the railways and auxiliary works, the United

States shall have the right, at all times and in its discretion, to use its police and its land and naval forces or to establish fortifications for these purposes.

Article XXIV

No change either in the Government or in the laws and treaties of the Republic of Panama shall, without the consent of the United States, affect any right of the United States under the present convention, or under any treaty stipulation between the two countries that now exists or may hereafter exist touching the subject matter of this convention.

If the Republic of Panama shall hereafter enter as a constituent into any other Government or into any union or confederation of States, so as to merge her sovereignty or independence in such Government, union or confederation, the rights of the United States under this convention shall not be in any respect lessened or impaired.

Article XXV

For the better performance of the engagements of this convention and to the end of the efficient protection of the canal and the preservation of its neutrality, the Government of the Republic of Panama will sell or lease to the United States lands adequate and necessary for naval or coaling stations on the Pacific coast and on the western Caribbean coast of the Republic at certain points to be agreed upon with the President of the United States.

Article XXVI

This convention when signed by the plenipotentiaries of the contracting parties shall be ratified by the respective Governments and the ratifications shall be exchanged at Washington at the earliest date possible.

In faith whereof the respective plenipotentiaries have signed the present convention in duplicate and have hereunto affixed their respective seals.

Done at the city of Washington the eighteenth day of November, in the year of our Lord nineteen hundred and three.

John Hay.   (seal.)
Bunau-Varilla.   (seal.)

APPENDIX VI

NICARAGUA CONVENTION OF AUGUST, 1914

A PROCLAMATION

WHEREAS a Convention between the United States of America and the Republic of Nicaragua granting to the United States the exclusive proprietary rights for the construction and operation of an interoceanic canal by a Nicaraguan route, the lease of certain islands, and the right to establish a naval base on the Gulf of Fonseca, was concluded and signed by their respective Plenipotentiaries at Washington, on the fifth day of August, one thousand nine hundred and fourteen, the original of which Convention, being in the English and Spanish languages is, as amended by the Senate of the United States, word for word as follows:

The Government of the United States of America and the Government of Nicaragua being animated by the desire to strengthen their ancient and cordial friendship by the most sincere cooperation for all purposes of their mutual advantage and interest and to provide for the possible future construction of an interoceanic ship canal by way of the San Juan River and the great Lake of Nicaragua, or by any route over Nicaraguan territory, whenever the construction of such canal shall be deemed by the Government of the United States conducive to the interests of both countries, and the Government of Nicaragua wishing to facilitate in every way possible the successful maintenance and operation of the Panama Canal, the two Governments have resolved to conclude a Convention to these ends, and have accordingly appointed as their plenipotentiaries:

The President of the United States, the Honorable William Jennings Bryan, Secretary of State; and

The President of Nicaragua, Señor General Don Emiliano Chamorro, Envoy Extraordinary and Minister Plenipotentiary of Nicaragua to the United States;

Who, having exhibited to each other their respective full powers, found to be in good and due form, have agreed upon and concluded the following articles:

315

Article I

The Government of Nicaragua grants in perpetuity to the Government of the United States, forever free from all taxation or other public charge, the exclusive proprietary rights necessary and convenient for the construction, operation and maintenance of an interoceanic canal by way of the San Juan River and the great Lake of Nicaragua or by way of any route over Nicaraguan territory, the details of the terms upon which such canal shall be constructed, operated and maintained to be agreed to by the two governments whenever the Government of the United States shall notify the Government of Nicaragua of its desire or intention to construct such canal.

Article II

To enable the Government of the United States to protect the Panama Canal and the proprietary rights granted to the Government of the United States by the foregoing article, and also to enable the Government of the United States to take any measure necessary to the ends contemplated herein, the Government of Nicaragua hereby leases for a term of ninety-nine years to the Government of the United States the islands in the Caribbean Sea known as Great Corn Island and Little Corn Island; and the Government of Nicaragua further grants to the Government of the United States for a like period of ninety-nine years the right to establish, operate and maintain a naval base at such place on the territory of Nicaragua bordering upon the Gulf of Fonseca as the Government of the United States may select. The Government of the United States shall have the option of renewing for a further term of ninety-nine years the above leases and grants upon the expiration of their respective terms, it being expressly agreed that the territory hereby leased and the naval base which may be maintained under the grant aforesaid shall be subject exclusively to the laws and sovereign authority of the United States during the terms of such lease and grant and of any renewal or renewals thereof.

Article III

In consideration of the foregoing stipulations and for the purposes contemplated by this Convention and for the purpose of reducing the present indebtedness of Nicaragua, the Government of the United States shall, upon the date of the exchange of ratification of this Convention, pay for the benefit of the Republic of Nicaragua the sum of three million dollars United States gold coin, of the present weight and fineness, to be deposited to the order of the Government of Nicaragua in such bank or banks or with such banking corporation as the Government of the United States may determine, to be applied by Nicaragua upon its indebtedness or other public purposes for the advancement of the welfare of Nicaragua in a manner to be determined by the two High Contracting Parties, all such disbursements to be made by orders drawn by the Minister of Finance of the Republic of Nicaragua and approved by the Secretary of State of the United States or by such person as he may designate.

This Convention shall be ratified by the High Contracting Parties in accordance with their respective laws, and the ratifications thereof shall be exchanged at Washington as soon as possible.

In witness whereof the respective plenipotentiaries have signed the present treaty and have affixed thereunto their seals.

Done at Washington, in duplicate, in the English and Spanish languages, on the 5th day of August, in the year nineteen hundred and fourteen.

WILLIAM JENNINGS BRYAN. (SEAL.)
EMILIANO CHAMORRO. (SEAL.)

And whereas, the advice and consent of the Senate of the United States to the ratification of the said Convention was given with the following proviso: "*Provided,* That, whereas, Costa Rica, Salvador and Honduras have protested against the ratification of the said Convention in the fear or belief that said Convention might in some respect impair existing rights of said States; therefore, it is declared by the Senate that in advising and consenting to the ratification of the said Convention as amended such advice and consent are given with the understanding, to be expressed as a part of the instrument of ratification, that nothing in said Convention is intended to affect any existing right of any of the said named States;"

And whereas, the said understanding has been accepted by the Government of Nicaragua;

And whereas, the said Convention, as amended by the Senate of the United States, has been duly ratified on both parts, and the ratifications of the two governments were exchanged in the City of

Washington, on the twenty-second day of June, one thousand nine hundred and sixteen;

Now, therefore, be it known that I, Woodrow Wilson, President of the United States of America, have caused the said Convention, as amended, and the said understanding to be made public, to the end that the same and every article and clause thereof may be observed and fulfilled with good faith by the United States and the citizens thereof.

In testimony whereof, I have hereunto set my hand and caused the seal of the United States to be affixed.

Done at the City of Washington this twenty-fourth of June in the year of our Lord one thousand nine hundred and six-
[SEAL.]   teen, and of the Independence of the United States of America the one hundred and fortieth.

WOODROW WILSON.

By the President:
ROBERT LANSING,
        Secretary of State.

INDEX

319